OCCUPATIONAL STRESS IN A CARING PROFESSION

To my Mother

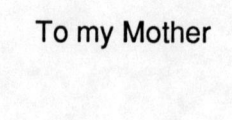

Occupational Stress in a Caring Profession

The Social Context of Psychiatric Nursing

JOCELYN HANDY
Department of Behaviour in Organisations
University of Lancaster

Avebury

Aldershot · Brookfield USA · Hong Kong · Singapore · Sydney

© J. Handy, 1990

All rights reserved. No part of this publication may be
reproduced, stored in a retrieval system, or transmitted in
any form or by any means, electronic, mechanical, photocopying,
recording, or otherwise without the prior permission of
Gower Publishing Company Limited.

Published by

Avebury

Gower Publishing Company Limited,
Gower House, Croft Road, Aldershot,
Hants. GU11 3HR, England

Gower Publishing Company,
Old Post Road, Brookfield, Vermont 05036
USA

British Library Cataloguing in Publication Data
Handy, Jocelyn, 1953-
  Occupational stress in a caring profession: the social
context of psychiatric nursing.
  1. Medical personnel. Stress
  I. Title
  610.69'01'9

ISBN 0-566-07047-2

RC
440
.H336
1990

Printed and Bound in Great Britain by
Athenaeum Press Ltd., Newcastle upon Tyne.

Contents

PART I	THEORY AND METHODOLOGY	1
1	Introduction	3
2	Rethinking Stress and Burnout	13
3	Psychology and Social Context	27
4	Critical Psychiatry	43
5	Methodology	55
PART II	THE ADMISSION WARD	73
6	Structure and Routine on 'F' Ward	75
7	Life on 'F' Ward	89
8	Reflections on Ward Life	123
PART III	COMMUNITY PSYCHIATRIC NURSING	135
9	Structure and Routine on the Community Unit	137
10	Life On the Community Unit	155
11	Reflections on the Community Unit	183

PART IV	**CONCLUSION**	**195**
12	Conclusion	197
APPENDICES		**215**
A	Activity Schedule/Diary	217
B	Interview Schedule	221
REFERENCES		**229**

Acknowledgements

I would like to extend my thanks to Gibson Burrell and Colin Brown, my Ph.D. supervisors at the University of Lancaster, for their patience and help throughout this research. I am also grateful to the other members of the Department of Behaviour in Organisations for providing a stimulating and challenging intellectual climate in which to work.

I also wish to acknowledge the financial support of the E.S.R.C. during the first three years of this project.

Finally, but by no means least, I should like to thank Dick for financial, emotional and intellectual support throughout this project.

PART I
THEORY AND METHODOLOGY

1 Introduction

This book sets out to examine the effects of the psychiatric system on the lives of those who work within it. In so doing, it complements and extends the insights provided by several earlier studies of psychiatry which have sought to illustrate the problems which the psychiatric system creates for those who enter it as patients. Valuable and disturbing as these critiques are, they only address one half of the problem, for they generally fail to acknowledge that the negative effects of our current psychiatric structures and ideologies can be as distressing for those who work within the system as those who are treated by it. The dynamics of the psychiatric system are not those of 'oppressors and oppressed' but of an institution manifestly failing to meet the human needs of both those it exists to help and those who labour within it. As this book will try and show, the feelings and actions of staff and patients exert reciprocal pressures whose form is shaped by, and helps recreate, the structural and ideological constraints of psychiatry. The problems of staff are therefore inextricably linked to the experiences of patients and, in consequence, the occupational stresses which they face cannot be fully understood without interpreting the various ways in which the psychiatric system structures the lives of all who participate within it.

In recent years, the occupational problems besetting the various caring professions have become a prominent concern within the burgeoning literature on occupational stress and burnout. Unfortunately, these literatures tend to concentrate on the perspective of staff without interpreting either the inter-relationship between the experiences of care-givers and recipients, or the ways in which the social context of care influences all participants' interpretations of their situation. As a result, these literatures tend to underestimate the complexity of people's relationship to their environment and oversimplify the problems which they face. In contrast to traditional stress research, this book argues that the occupational dilemmas of the caring professions cannot be fully understood without interpreting the ambivalent role of welfare institutions within our society. In the case of psychiatry, this necessitates addressing two central problems and examining firstly, the reasons why an institution which purports to heal those troubled individuals who have difficulty coping in our society is so often accused of contributing to their problems, and secondly, the relationship between this paradox and the actions and experiences of staff. Such a task cannot be undertaken without first locating the problem of occupational stress amongst psychiatric professionals within a wider analysis of the deeply sedimented contradictions and ambiguities which characterize the psychiatric sector's troubled relationships with both the individuals within it and the wider society of which it forms a part.

The conceptual differences between the individualistic and psychologically oriented framework which underpins most research into occupational stress and the more sociologically oriented perspective which informs this study have ensured that this book has developed beyond its original purpose. At one level, it remains true to my original intention of linking the empirical investigation of stress amongst psychiatric professionals to the theoretical analysis of psychiatry's equivocal role within modern society. From a slightly different perspective, the book can be interpreted as a case study of both the problems of care within psychiatric institutions and the effects of deinstitutionalization upon psychiatric practices. At a more general level, the book is relevant to the problems of occupational stress in a variety of caring professions, for the contradictions of the psychiatric sector are also prevalent within the other caring professions of modern society, albeit in a slightly different superficial form. Finally, this book can be interpreted as a plea for stress researchers to develop a more sophisticated awareness of the relationship between subjective experience and social context and a greater sensitivity towards the implicit theoretical assumptions governing their research. As recent writers in the philosophy of social science have pointed out, the theoretical framework within which research is conceived exerts a definitive influence upon the types of question which can be asked, the kinds of information which can be collected and the species of explanation which can be proffered. A greater willingness to admit these issues openly and to question the tacit premises on which our research endeavours are based can only enhance our progress towards a genuine social science and increase our ability to understand the perspectives and experiences of others.

Since the research described here adopts a rather different theoretical perspective to conventional stress research it may be useful to give a slightly more detailed outline of the considerations which eventually led me to reject the more traditional approaches. I started this project believing that the orthodox conceptualization of the person as a psychological entity distinct from the social milieu, though influenced by it, seriously underestimates the intimacy of the relationship between the psyche and the pervasive socio-historical context surrounding it. This viewpoint is endorsed by a growing body of social scientists who argue that human subjectivity and action are so inextricably interwoven with the social context which people inhabit that a theoretical separation between the individual and society is conceptually inadequate. Unfortunately, this position is still incompatible with the dominant paradigm within academic psychology, which remains wedded to an essentially asocial, transhistorical model of the individual. The social and applied branches of the discipline do, it is true, pay lipservice to the importance of the environment upon the individual. However, the social context they describe remains a shadowy backdrop against which distinctively psychological processes occur, rather than becoming an integral aspect of the total picture. As a result, the psychological literature seldom transmits a clear image of either the effects which people's social circumstances have on their experiences and actions or the ways in which humans recreate and alter their social world.

The occupational stress and burnout literatures generally adopt the positivist theoretical paradigm which permeates the rest of psychology. As a consequence, they tend to describe people's relationship with their work environment in atomized and mechanistic terms and to neglect more holistic interpretations of organizational life. Most empirical research concentrates on the statistical relationship between discrete characteristics of individual jobs and questionnaire measures of stress. Whilst this approach can provide some insights into specific stress producing job characteristics it remains highly limited, providing few insights into either the experiential world of those it studies or the wider organizational and societal context in which individual jobs are located. Since I wanted to communicate the subjective experiences of participants within the psychiatric system in terms which conveyed their full richness and complexity to the reader, and to provide a theoretical account which located these experiences within the structural and ideological context of psychiatry, I felt obliged to turn away from the traditional stress literature, and seek an alternative theoretical framework.

Recent theorizing within the area of sociological social psychology seemed to offer a more promising paradigm in which to locate this research. In contrast to most psychological writing, this strand of the literature is explicitly concerned with interpreting the often enigmatic and convoluted relationship between individual subjectivity and the social domain and it is open to the theoretical insights which the related discipline of sociology can contribute to this task. One of the dominant themes within this literature centres on the idea that people's relationship with their social environment is essentially recursive. Human society therefore has to be interpreted as being simultaneously the product of knowledgeable and purposive human activity and the medium through which those actions and understandings are produced and interpreted. If we wish to develop a comprehensive understanding of social phenomena such as occupational stress we have to grapple with the full complexity of this relationship. This involves acknowledging and interpreting not only the conscious, but also the unconscious, motives which people bring to their actions and assessing both the intended and the unintended consequences of their acts. Society may be created and sustained by intentional human activity but unfortunately this does not prevent it from developing in unexpected, contradictory and highly problematic directions. These unintended social patterns are often a core element in the continued reproduction of our social environment and are frequently perpetuated by repetitive human activity designed to achieve quite different goals. For many social theorists, the key task of social science is therefore that of elucidating the intimate relationship between the contradictions of our social system and people's fragmentary and ambivalent knowledge of their social world. Such knowledge is an essential first step in the task of helping people understand and transform problematic social institutions such as the psychiatric system into more humane structures.

Whilst the theoretical writings of the more sociologically oriented social psychologists provide a suitable framework for interpreting the relationship between the contradictions of our social system and the confusions of the human psyche, such writings generally remain too abstract to furnish precise insights into the specific contradictions of individual social institutions. Since this study was concerned with the particular contradictions of psychiatry it became important to discover a set of mediating concepts which would help illuminate the precise ways in which the paradoxes of this system influenced the knowledge and actions of those employed within it. Recent theorizing within the critical psychiatry literature provided a useful conceptual model for tackling this task. Theorists within this area have paid relatively little attention to the occupational problems of psychiatric professionals and have tended to be highly critical of staff whenever they have considered their actions. However, these critics have analysed the functions and structures of the psychiatric sector in some depth and their writings therefore provide a valuable basis for understanding the contradictory role of the psychiatric sector within our society and the possible effects of this on nursing staff and patients.

Such writings usually identify three key interlinked structural contradictions in the relationship between the psychiatric sector and society. The first, and most important, contradiction which they point to is that psychiatry is simultaneously part of the ideological and regulatory superstructure of our society and an institution which aims to alleviate the personal distress which this form of social organization sometimes creates. The institution thus has a dual mandate to help troubled individuals and to control them for their own good or that of society. A second, and related, contradiction centres on the equivocal implications which cultural concepts of mental illness have for individual responsibility. On the one hand, cultural norms concerning mental illness highlight the concepts of unintelligibility and lack of responsibility, whilst on the other hand, norms concerning appropriate sick role behaviour give patients a clear duty to comply with medical treatment. This ambiguity can allow patients to behave in a socially unacceptable manner and then deny responsibility for their actions, whilst simultaneously giving staff a mandate to deny the validity of the patient's perspective whenever it conflicts with their own goals. The final contradiction identified within the literature centres on the realization that psychiatry is not only committed to the alleviation of mental illness but also to expanding its own sphere of influence by identifying increasingly subtle behavioural deviations and personal distress as the legitimate province of psychiatric intervention. The existence of an institution designed to decrease mental illness thus has the unintended effect of transforming many personal and social problems into issues requiring the expertise of qualified mental health professionals. In the view of its more radical critics most of the difficulties faced by psychiatry are linked to these central contradictions, for it is these tensions which make it possible for the psychiatric system to become implicated in the oppression of the very people whom those working within it genuinely intend to help.

The empirical sections of this book set out to trace the various ways in which the three key contradictions of the psychiatric system influence the daily lives of psychiatric professionals and their patients. The actual occupational group concentrated upon is psychiatric nursing. This occupation is still under-researched in both the stress and burnout literatures and the critical psychiatry literature, all of which reveal a propensity for focussing on the higher status profession of medicine. Whilst the structural position of psychiatrists undoubtedly gives them a privileged power base within the mental health system, and the activities and problems of their profession clearly merit continued scrutiny, they remain a single element within the psychiatric nexus. An excessive concentration upon this professional group may therefore inadvertently serve to obscure other, equally important, aspects of daily life within the psychiatric system. As many writers have observed, nurses are not only the largest occupational group within the health care system they are also the group in closest daily contact with patients. A detailed examination of the strategies which psychiatric nurses use to manage the stresses of both hospital based and community work can therefore enhance our knowledge of both the occupational problems of psychiatric professionals and the social context of psychiatric care.

As the ensuing chapters of this book will reveal, the structural contradictions of the psychiatric system were reflected in the equivocal motives and understandings which the various participants habitually brought to their everyday interactions. As a result of these ambiguities, the activities of all parties tended to take place within various unacknowledged conditions and to have a range of unintended and paradoxical consequences. These could be highly distressing for all involved and often reflected the emotionally charged and personally significant nature of psychiatry's subject matter. Unfortunately, the structural contradictions which created the initial conditions for these unintended outcomes often ensured that the coping strategies which the various participants employed also rebounded upon them and had the unforseen consequence of intensifying the initial tensions within the system. Thus, the conflicting strategies which the different participants employed to help them tackle the stresses facing them frequently interacted to help re-create many of the more pernicious aspects of organizational life and exacerbate the very feelings which their perpetrators were struggling to avoid.

Within this study, nurses working within the hospital setting often tried to cope with the personal insecurities aroused by their inability to predict and control the course of events on their ward by adopting increasingly routinized patterns of interactions with their patients. Unfortunately, control-oriented activities of this type were frequently incompatible with strategies which might have helped patients understand, alter or come to terms with, the personal circumstances of their lives and also with the nurses' self-image as professional carers. One result of this was that the nurses often experienced doubts concerning both their therapeutic competence and the meaning of their daily activities and frequently sought to justify their actions by blaming patients for forcing them to act in a coercive manner. The conceptual framework which the nurses used to interpret the actions of problem patients illustrates this process clearly. Such patients were generally seen as either 'bad' or 'mad'. The first group were then regarded as abusers of the system who were not only undeserving of help but who also prevented other patients from receiving the help they deserved. The second group tended to be conceptualized as lacking control as a result of their illness, which enabled control oriented activities such as the administration of tranquillizing medication to disruptive patients to be re-interpreted as therapeutic activities. This interpretation neatly integrated the social control and treatment concerns of staff in a manner which helped maintain the psychiatric ideology of uncoercive care, but which often had the unintended consequence of heightening the patients' hostility towards the nurses and increasing the necessity for further control-oriented activities. This could aggravate the nurses' feelings of insecurity and lead to further defensive reactions in which they blamed patients for being unmotivated to change and adopted still more instrumental and routine oriented attitudes towards work. The initial potential for change which was often inherent in the nurses' dissatisfaction with their working conditions and dislike of a control oriented ward regime thus tended to become channelled into the maintenance of existing patterns and ultimately to facilitate the re-creation of the very system many nurses found unsatisfactory and stress-producing.

The community psychiatric nurses who took part in this study also tended to tackle the personal anxieties which their work aroused by developing highly routinized relationships with their patients. However, the structural differences between hospital and community based nursing ensured that the form which these relationships took was superficially very different. In contrast to the ward-based nurses, who had communal responsibility for their patients, the community nurses generally worked alone and carried personal caseloads of patients whom they saw on an individual basis. This structural change facilitated the development of closer emotional bonds between nurses and patients and heightened the nurses' desire to help their patients to resolve the problems within their lives. Unfortunately, it could also trigger feelings of intense insecurity when crises arose or patients failed to respond positively to the nurses' therapeutic ministrations. One strategy which the nurses used to master such feelings involved attempting to increase the predictability of their environment by frequent visiting and by maintaining contact with preferred patients for as long as possible. Whilst this strategy often helped to alleviate the nurses' anxieties by increasing their familiarity with their patients, it could also have the two unintended consequences of exacerbating the patients' tendency to abnegate responsibility for their problems and of reinforcing their dependence of the nurses. In response, the nurses tended either to blame the patients for lacking a genuine desire to alter their life circumstances or to redouble their efforts to direct their patients' activities. This often had the inadvertent effect of further augmenting the various tensions in nurse-patient relationships. Thus, the community nurses' tactics for alleviating the stresses of their work often had a similar outcome to the strategies of the hospital based nurses and once again helped to perpetuate the structural contradictions of the psychiatric system.

The marked similarity between the dilemmas of the ward-based and community nurses in this study suggests that the same fundamental contradictions permeate all manifestations of the psychiatric system. Critiques which define the problems of psychiatry in terms of a simple dichotomy between the oppressive characteristics of an organic and institutionally oriented system and a life-enhancing psychotherapeutic alternative located within the community clearly oversimplify the social and political implications of psychiatry's equivocal role within modern society. It is these contradictions which structure the experiences of staff and patients, and it is these issues which must be addressed if the problems of occupational stress within the psychiatric professions are to be adequately interpreted. If the expanding field of occupational stress research is to make a richer contribution to our understanding of these issues researchers who work within this area must strive to develop more sophisticated conceptual frameworks which recognize the true complexity of the relationship between the structural contradictions of modern organizations and the employee's subjective experience of personal distress.

Before finishing this introduction it seems important to make it clear that whilst the empirical research described here is based upon a detailed study of one hospital during the two year period between the summer of 1984 and the middle of 1986 it was never intended as a critique of either a specific hospital or the individuals within it. Generally speaking, the nurses who took part in this research expressed deep concern for the well-being of their patients and were frequently upset and disappointed if their therapeutic endeavours failed. The hospital in this study functioned better than several I became acquainted with during my career as an N.H.S. clinical psychologist, and it is my belief that it provided more humane care than many psychiatric institutions. The situations described in this research are intended to exemplify general problems within psychiatry rather than specific problems within one hospital, and it is for this reason that the hospital in question has been left unnamed throughout this book and the individuals studied given pseudonyms and slightly altered identities.

It may also be useful to set this research within its personal context by acknowledging that my own work experiences within the psychiatric sector provided the initial impetus for this study. As a newly qualified clinical psychologist I was somewhat perturbed to discover that the profession I had struggled long and hard to enter provided few satisfactions and many frustrations; the people I sought to help were often awkward, bad tempered, and ungrateful; my confidence in my own ability to help them was limited; inter-disciplinary relations were fraught with hidden agendas and thinly disguised power struggles and the dead hand of bureaucracy eventually stifled my modest attempts to create a working environment in which the culture of therapeutic individualism and professional expertise was replaced by a more egalitarian and community oriented approach. In discussing these disappointments with friends and colleagues in the psychiatric sector I became aware that my feelings were not unique and that the problems faced by other psychiatric professionals were as invidious as my own. This realization, coupled with an appreciation of the key role which nurses play within the psychiatric system, contributed to my decision to research this particular occupational group. Although the precise form of the situations described in this research often reflects the specific organizational role of psychiatric nurses the issues raised are, at a deeper level, common to most professions working within both the psychiatric sector and the other caring institutions of modern society.

Finally, it may be worth clarifying the relationship between the organization of this book and the research process itself. I have tried to structure this book as clearly as possible and have found that the conventional ordering of theory, methodology and empirical evidence seems to facilitate the most coherent presentation of this research. The actual development of my ideas was rather less orderly than this and involved a far more interactive relationship between theorizing and data gathering. When I started this research my conceptual scheme was somewhat hazy and was really little more than a conviction that the conventional approach to occupational stress research distorts the complexity and richness of our social world. The theoretical framework I am presenting here emerged during the course of the research as I struggled to understand my empirical data and to make sense of the fact that time and time again the data seemed highly contradictory and confusing. It was only when I stopped trying to explain away the apparent anomalies in my data and started looking for a theoretical framework which allowed me to acknowledge their validity that I turned to the critical psychiatry literature. Whilst an awareness of this literature had been part of my intellectual knowledge before I started the research it only became integrated with the concept of occupational stress under the relentless pressure of the empirical data. In the final analysis, it was the concrete expression of the contradictions of psychiatry within the daily routines and subjective experiences of psychiatric nurses and their patients which dictated the theoretical framework that is presented here.

2 Rethinking stress and burnout

INTRODUCTION

As this book utilizes a rather different theoretical perspective to that of most stress research it seems important to start by discussing the considerations which eventually led to the rejection of the more traditional approaches. The main aim of this chapter is therefore to examine the implicit theoretical assumptions underlying current research into occupational stress and burnout and to show how the conceptual straitjacket of conventional approaches limits our understanding of the problems which people experience within their work environment.

The orthodox psychological literature on occupational stress has split into two distinct categories during the past decade. One the one hand, there is the well established tradition of occupational stress research which historically concentrated on industry and neglected the human service sector. On the other hand, there is the burnout literature which emerged in the mid-seventies and originally focussed on the caring professions whilst disregarding industry. Initially, there was little cross-fertilization between the two areas, even though their theoretical assumptions, models and research techniques seem to be very similar, however, the two fields have overlapped increasingly in recent years. Researchers within the stress literature have focussed more closely on the caring professions (e.g. Marshall, 1980; Fineman, 1985; Leatt and Schneck, 1985; Payne and Firth, 1987; Dewe, 1988; Wallis and de Wolff, 1988). Conversely, the concept of burnout is now being applied to very many occupational groups, and researchers in this specialism are drawing increasingly on the occupational stress literature (e.g. Maslach and Jackson, 1981; Golembiewski, Munzenrider and Phelan-Carter, 1983; Cahoon and Rowney, 1984; Burke, 1987; Seltzer and Numerof, 1988). These developments have led Payne (1984) to conclude that the burnout literature is simply an inferior and sensationalist version of the stress literature which is rediscovering the same concepts and perpetuating poorly designed empirical research.

Systematic attempts to compare the two fields are rare, even though many theoretical and empirical problems are common to both. Previous reviews of each field have tended to concentrate on intra-paradigmatic issues such as definitions, variations between models, validity of measures and relationships between variables (e.g. Beehr and Newman, 1978; Fletcher and Payne, 1980; Sharit and Salvendy, 1982; Glowinkowski and Cooper, 1985; Cooper and Kasl, 1987; Eulberg, Weekley and Bhagat, 1988; Newton, 1989;/ Perlman and Hartman, 1982; Farber, 1983; Golembiewski, Munzenrider and Stevenson, 1986).† Whilst these reviews help refine the two fields they seldom examine the fundamental assumptions upon which both fields are based. In contrast to such previous reviews this chapter argues that the fundamental problems within both traditions are similar and centre on their interpretation of the inter-relationship between individual experience and the social order. It suggests that researchers need to pay equal attention to both the psychology of individuals and to the functions and structures of organizations and society which constrain them to think and act in particular ways, and goes on to argue that previous research into occupational stress and burnout has tended to over-emphasise the psychological level of analysis. This does not mean that previous research is without merit. Individual differences in stress tolerance and coping skills obviously exist and are worth investigating. Similarly, individually or interpersonally based treatment programmes will clearly be more sensitive to personal issues and more appropriate where inter or intra-personal characteristics are the main precipitants of stress.

---

† This chapter will adopt the convention of citing references to stress first and separating them from the burnout literature with a slash notation (/).

These types of solution may also be the simplest to implement as they do not disrupt organisational functioning or challenge organization power holders. However, if individually focussed analyses are given undue emphasis they may have the major disadvantage of diverting attention away from organizational disfunctions and towards individual faults.

The rest of this chapter is divided into three sections. The first section argues that psychologically based models of stress and burnout need to be augmented with analyses which pay more attention to the effects of organizational and societal functions and structures on individual experience. The second section argues that both literatures are based on an implicit systems model of organizations which pays insufficient attention to the problems both of individual action and of power structures within organizations. The final section assesses the way recent developments in empirical research within the mainstream stress and burnout literatures have dealt with these particular issues.

DEFINITIONS AND MODELS

The psycho-social literature on occupational stress usually defines stress as an individually based, affect-ladened experience caused by subjectively perceived stressors. McGrath's (1970) definition of job stress as

> "a (perceived) substantial imbalance between demand and response capability under conditions where failure to meet demand has important (perceived) consequences" (p.20)

is widely accepted and emphasizes the inter-relationship between the immediate environment and personal characteristics. In contrast, the most influential definition of burnout defines it as

> "a syndrome of physical and emotional exhaustion involving the development of negative self concept, negative job attitudes and loss of concern and feeling for clients"

(Pines and Maslach, 1978, p233). This definition is clearly more extreme and illustrates the somewhat sensationalist character of much of the burnout research. Unlike the earlier definition it is response-based and concentrates on mental health and work outcomes without indicating a putative causal mechanism.

Although the two definitions differ, they are similar in that both are tied to a predominantly psychological level of analysis. This pattern is repeated in the various models within the two literatures. A few psychoanalytically oriented theorists writing within the burnout literature have proposed intrapsychic theories which repudiate the role of environmental stressors (e.g. Fischer, 1983). However, the majority of researchers in both fields have advanced transactional models (e.g. Van Harrison, 1978; Fletcher and Payne, 1980; Cox and Mackay, 1981; Cooper, 1986; / Cherniss, 1980a; Perlman and Hartman, 1982; Golembiewski, Munzenrider and Stevenson, 1986). Whilst the various models differ in complexity and in the explicitness with which individual and environmental variables are differentiated they all centre on the stressed individual and then either work backwards to analyse the causes of stress or forwards to investigate the individual's response to stress.

Two basic themes emerge from the various definitions and models currently in use. Firstly, stress and burnout are generally conceptualized as the product of a complex transaction between individual needs and resources and the various demands, constraints and facilitators within the individual's immediate environment. Secondly, both are conceptualized as highly subjective phenomena in which perceived stressors are more important than actual environmental conditions (e.g. Cox, 1978; Caplan, 1983; / Maslach, 1982; Golembiewski, Munzenrider and Stevenson, 1986). Superficially, individual perception seems the logical, and perhaps the only, starting place for models of stress or burnout as both are undeniably a subjective psychological experience. Unfortunately, the root causes of both stress and burnout are often far removed from the individual person or job and may be more appropriately conceptualized in societal or organizational terms. For example, the working lives of many people may be detrimentally affected by problems within the world economy without their having much understanding of these issues. It is hardly tenable to argue that these factors are irrelevant to individual experience simply because people are unable to perceive their effects. Admittedly, people tend to identify stressors in terms of lower order constructs with a tangible effect on their own lives. However, this does not mean that the explanations offered by social scientists should remain at a similar level. The task of social science is to explicate social problems more clearly and to provide accounts which explain and complement the respondents' perspectives. This may involve developing conceptual analyses which interpret and locate the accounts offered by respondents within higher order explanations of structural and societal influences on individual experience.

The strengths and limitations of transactional models of occupational stress and burnout may be illustrated by examining the similarity between this approach and the traditional position adopted by medicine in relation to illness. Conventional models of medicine concentrate on individual pathology and generally operate through individually focussed methods of prevention and treatment. Whilst this approach has resulted in some spectacular achievements, critics of the traditional model point out that the major improvements in health standards are due to improvements in social conditions (Illich, 1976; Doyal, 1980; Navarro, 1986). They also note that many of the epidemics of Western society (e.g. coronary heart disease) are mainly attributable to social and economic factors and that medicine may help perpetuate these problems by deflecting scrutiny away from society and towards the individual. This criticism also applies to preventative medicine as the responsibility for leading a healthy life is predominantly placed on the individual whilst less pressure is applied to large economic power groups who may set up structural conditions making it difficult for people to do so.

The limitations resulting from the stress and burnout literatures' neglect of the relationship between higher order organizational and societal issues and the subjective experiences of employees could, perhaps, be overcome by augmenting psychologically based models with salient concepts from the sociological literature. In contrast to psychological models, which tend to assume that organizational and societal issues are unproblematic, sociological theories generally emphasise their multifaceted and complex nature. Two of the more useful conceptual tools which the sociological literature provides for understanding the complexity of organizations and society are those of manifest versus latent functions and surface versus deep structures. The meaning of these concepts may be clarified by an example from the educational system. The manifest function of state schools is to offer all children equal educational opportunities. However, one of their latent functions is to help socialize children into a class society and prepare them to take their place in work organizations. This function frequently contradicts the educational system's stated aims since it involves facilitating the reproduction of specific forms of social inequality and, in consequence, it may not be fully recognized by either staff or pupils. Whilst the manifest function of schools is apparent in the surface structure, and can be investigated by analysing the curriculum and exam results, the latent function of schools is less explicit and forms part of the deep structure of the educational system. As Willis (1977) showed, the socialization process within and across schools is not uniform and is heavily influenced by the oppositional group culture which informs the response of many working class males to school authority. Whilst this opposition to school goals stems from the children's partial appreciation of the limited work opportunities for their social class, their rebelliousness also has the paradoxical effect of trapping them within the unskilled labour market. The children's ostensibly rational reasons for developing a counter-culture which opposes the manifest goals of the school thus have the unintended outcome of helping the educational system to fulfill its latent function within the wider economic structure. The full complexity of this process cannot be deduced simply by examining the children's explanations for rejecting the educational system's manifest goals for, as Willis showed, their subjective experience is directly shaped by various unperceived features of the wider social context.

IMPLICIT ASSUMPTIONS

Although both the occupational stress and burnout literatures are based on psychological models which neglect the explicit analysis of higher order social structures they do contain an implicit model of organizations and society. In essence, writers within both fields tend to assume that organizations are specialised subsystems of the wider social system which have specific structural forms geared to the rational achievement of various socially agreed goals. In consequence, both occupational stress and burnout are frequently linked with decreases in organizational efficiency and moves to reduce them are seen as simultaneously beneficial to staff, employers and clients (e.g. Corlett and Richardson, 1981; Jackson, 1983a; Cooper, 1986; Quick et al., 1987; / Pines and Maslach, 1978; Golembiewski, 1984; Golembiewski, Hilles and Daly, 1987).

This perspective resembles a convetional systems approach and has similarities with the more sophisticated systems models developed within organisation theory (e.g. Aldrich, 1979; Hall, 1982; Robbins, 1983). The use of systems models within organization theory has been increasingly criticised over the last fifteen years (e.g. Silverman, 1970; Elger, 1975; Burrell and Morgan, 1979; Heydebrand, 1983; Reed, 1985). The two sets of criticisms which have been raised are, in fact, equally apposite to the stress and burnout literatures although they have not yet been directly applied to them.

The two alternative perspectives from which systems theories have been criticised concur in seeing conventional systems models as normative accounts which reinforce the status quo. The first set of criticisms have been advanced by 'social action' theorists and centre on problems of personal meaning and action. These critics accuse systems theorists of reifying organizations by concentrating on their structures and functions and undervaluing both the proactive role of people in their creation and maintenance, and the possibility that employees may act in pursuit of individual and collective goals which differ from the formal aims of the organization (Strauss, 1978; Silverman and Jones, 1979). They argue that the actual functioning of organizations often differs from official guidelines and is dependent on a negotiated order between staff which has to be constantly re-affirmed within the context of ongoing social interactions.

The second set of criticisms of systems theories centre on issues of power and conflict and have been raised by theorists who take a radical view of social structures and social functions. These writers criticise conventional systems theories for exaggerating the level of consensus within both organizations and society and neglecting the relationship of organizations to the wider social system. They emphasise that the social order is often negotiated from structurally determined positions of unequal strength which frequently work against the interests of employees (Braverman, 1974; Clegg and Dunkerley, 1980; Forester, 1983; Reed, 1985).

These criticisms of systems theories have been refuted by some writers who have argued that such shortcomings reflect value judgements within specific applications of systems thinking rather than fundamental flaws within the theory (Wilden, 1980; Donaldson, 1985). These apologists also criticise the opponents of systems theories, arguing that the social action approach perpetuates weak analyses of social structure and that radical structuralist approaches could be re-interpreted as a form of systems theorizing. Whilst these disagreements are relevant to the ongoing debate about systems theories the crucial point for this chapter is that the main criticisms of systems theories are, in fact, accurate reflections of most versions of it and are also equally applicable to the implicit assumptions concerning the relationship between organizations and society which are generally found within both the stress and burnout literatures.

Whilst the problems involved in conceptualizing organizations have not been addressed directly within either the stress or burnout literatures, an influential minority within the stress literature have recently tackled the problem of personal meaning and criticised stress researchers for neglecting the phenomenological knowledge of their subjects (Payne, 1978; Fineman and Payne, 1981; Firth, 1985). However, these criticisms have been raised in the context of an attack on positivist methodologies rather than a discussion of the stress literature's conceptualization of the relationship between individual meaning and organizational functioning. Whilst these critics rightly emphasise the importance of individual meaning they unfortunately leave the relationship between the individual's subjective experience and the broader social context relatively untheorized. Their concerns therefore differ from those of social action theorists, as the later place greater emphasis on the inter-relationships between the differing perceptions and actions of various social groups and organizational and societal functioning.

The burnout literature has also tended to neglect the inter-relationship between personal meaning and organisational functioning. However, a fairly early study by Cherniss (1980a) is a notable exception, which combines a thoughtful qualitative analysis of the influence of both the wider socio-historical context and organizational issues on individual experience with examples of the ways in which individual action perpetuates organizational problems. Regrettably, the conceptual breadth of Cherniss' (1980a, b) writings is rarely found within the burnout literature.

Whilst the issues of power, conflict and order raised by 'radical structuralists' have been neglected by the majority of writers within both fields, there are some notable exceptions within the stress literature. Three of the most important studies were reported by Gardell (1971), Karasek (1979) and Kohn and Schooler (1982). These studies all utilized large samples and both cross-sectional and longitudinal data to investigate the inter-relationships between work conditions and occupational stress and drew attention to the effects which class-related conditions of work within industrial society have on both the individual's self concept and their subjective experience of stress. Although these three studies derive from a different intellectual tradition to Willis' (1977) research into schooling and occupational outcomes and utilize a different methodological approach, their findings are compatible with his study. Unfortunately, research of this calibre is disappointingly infrequent within both the stress and burnout literatures, and many writers have a tendency to neglect the wider implications of any socially relevant observations which they make. For example, a review of the stress literature by Glowinkowski and Cooper (1985) pointed out that sources of stress may change in response to worsening social conditions and that the traditional focus on 'role-based' stress may be less appropriate in the recession dominated eighties than when it was originally conceptualized by Kahn et al. in the mid-sixties (Kahn et al.,

1964). The review suggested that fears of redundancy and obsolescence maybe more important today, thus placing stress research firmly within a specific socio-historical context and, by implication, raising the problem of the power imbalance between employers and employees and the influence of the wider social context. However, the political implications of this observation were not pursued further within the article, which raised the issue to illustrate the problems of developing reliable measurement techniques rather than to highlight the relationship between powerlessness and stress.

One consequence of the two literatures' failure to consider the issue of organizational power in adequate depth is that they tend to recommend that the solutions to work problems, as well as their causes, should be sought through individual or interpersonal change. Although many researchers in both fields pay lipservice to the desirability of organizational change most studies then describe the implementation of techniques like individual psychotherapy, psychotherapeutically oriented staff support groups and stress management packages (e.g. Ganster et al, 1982; Rose and Veiga, 1984; Hall and Fletcher, 1984; Firth and Shapiro, 1986; Sallis et al., 1987; Ashford, 1988; / Rapson, 1982; Warren, 1982; Kanas, 1986; Kearney and Turner, 1987). Recently, several articles in both literatures have recommended that enlightened organizations institute individually oriented stress management techniques as company wide benefits packages for employees. For example, Cooper (1986) reviewed several stress management programmes by American corporations which required employees to control their diets, smoking, drinking, fitness and stress levels and concluded that the employees improved physical health was evidence of unmitigated benefits for all parties. Whilst such programmes may well have genuine benefits for employees they may also represent an extension of corporate control over staff who are now expected not only to sell their skills and time but to ensure that their total lifestyle ensures maximum corporate gain.

Both the organizational stress and burnout literatures need to develop more sophisticated conceptual analyses of the inter-relationships between the individual, organizations and society which recognise the importance of power and conflict in institutional life. As Giddens (1979, 1984) has pointed out, the nature of power relationships is often poorly perceived by members of an organization or society and may be subject to systematic distortions by dominant power-holders whose structural position in society gives them an enhanced ability to make their own sectional interests appear to others as universal ones. This obviously facilitates the continuation of structural imbalances in power relationships and mitigates against rational action to alter structural problems. From this perspective, one of the root causes of work related problems such as occupational stress or burnout may be the way in which discrepancies between the manifest and latent functions and the surface and deep structures of organizations influence the actions and understandings of participants whilst remaining inaccessible to their conscious scrutiny. At present the two fields do not deal satisfactorily with this issue because they are both based on a consensus model of rational organizational functioning derived from an implicit systems perspective on organizations.

EMPIRICAL RESEARCH

The theoretical framework adopted by most researchers has inevitably directed their empirical research towards the relationships between individual experience and discrete characteristics of specific jobs. As the various 'lists' of organizational stressors summarized in review articles within the two fields indicate, empirical studies usually identify a similar range of low-level characteristics which are conceptualized mechanistically and closely tied to particular jobs (e.g. Beehr and Newman, 1978; Glowinkowski and Cooper, 1985; Eulberg, Weekley and Bhagat, 1988; / Pines, 1982; Golembiewski, Munzenrider and Stevenson, 1986). These characteristics are seldom integrated into a more sophisticated analysis of overall organizational or societal functioning and, in consequence, whilst the organizational stressors identified within the literatures provide useful guides to the features of the work environment which can cause problems they are less successful in explaining why particular features arise or how they relate to the manifest and latent functions or surface and deep structures of the organization.

To date, the majority of empirical studies within both literatures have utilized cross-sectional questionnaire measures of perceived job characteristics. This is now changing within the occupational stress literature in response to trenchant criticisms (e.g. Kasl, 1978; Payne, 1978; Crump et al., 1980; Parkes, 1982; Brief and Atieh, 1987). These criticisms are equally applicable to the burnout literature although they have not yet been applied to it. The criticisms of empirical research raised within the stress literature have generally taken two forms. The first set of criticisms address problems of design and measurement from within a nomothetic framework. The second set challenge the epistemological implications of positivist research and advocate idiographic alternatives.

The main criticism which has been made of experimental design is that the direction of causality is difficult to infer from cross-sectional, correlational studies (Parkes, 1982). Questionnaire measures have been criticised for equating subjective and objective job conditions (Beehr and Newman, 1978), measuring irrelevant variables (Glowinkowski and Cooper, 1985), operationalizing conceptually distinct variables almost identically (Kasl, 1978) and, in consequence, identifying almost every aspect of the work environment as both a potential stressor and a source of satisfaction (Marshall and Cooper, 1981).

The stress literature has recently developed several innovative responses to these criticisms. Firstly, an increasing number of longitudinal and natural experimental studies are being reported, some of which assess stress before and after changes in the work situation. These provide better evidence of the direction of causality (e.g. Bhagat and Chassie, 1980; Parkes, 1982; Frese, 1985). Secondly, questionnaires are being tailored to specific working environments thus enabling more meaningful and precisely targeted questionnaires to be developed. Research within the nursing field indicates that these scales are reasonably reliable and have greater discriminant validity than more general measures (Overton et al., 1977; Gray, 1984; Leatt and Schneck, 1985; Dewe, 1988).

The second set of criticisms within the stress literature make the point that the universalist models and nomothetic techniques which dominate the literature neglect both specific environmental contexts and personal meanings (Payne, 1978; Fineman and Payne, 1981; Fineman, 1985; Firth, 1985; Newton, 1989). In response to this criticism, several researchers have undertaken qualitative studies involving in-depth interviews (Jick, 1979; Fineman and Payne, 1981; Fineman, 1983; McKenna and Fryer, 1984; Parry, Shapiro and Firth, 1986). This technique deals more satisfactorily with the concept of agency than positivist methodologies and these studies should provide greater knowledge of the personal meanings of stress and of variations in individual experience.

The innovations within stress research could usefully be adopted within the burnout literature in order to strengthen the field. However, neither the improvements in quantitative methods or the increasing use of qualitative techniques deals adequately with the core problem of relating the subjective experience of the individual to higher order issues concerning the functions and structures of organizations and society. These issues need addressing within a more complex framework which illustrates both the dialectical interplay between the experience of the individual and structural conditions and the relative power imbalances between the individual and the organization. These issues cannot be dealt with satisfactorily using quantitative analytic strategies which investigate stress by isolating and measuring the various presumptive elements using predetermined categories as this approach partitions reality into discrete fragments of surface behaviour and by doing so ignores and destroys both the deep structure of organizational life and the latent functions of organizational behaviour (Light, 1979). In consequence, the most that can be learnt from such techniques is which surface stressors cluster together. Unfortunately, this does not explain why particular patterns have developed or the ways in which they are maintained within a particular work environment.

Although the holistic approaches and context-specific theories advocated by the more qualitatively oriented critics of stress research are appropriate for studying both the deep structure and latent functions of organizations they have not as yet tackled these issues. To date, epistemological criticisms of this field have concentrated on the problem of meaning and have emphasised the importance of the individual's subjective experience. Whilst this point is both valid and important its emphasis within the stress literature is distinctively psychological and the field may come to over-emphasise the individual level of analysis as a result. For example, several papers by Firth and her collegues describing the Sheffield psychotherapy project on occupational stress, concentrate on the in-depth analysis of the personal histories of clients which increase their vulnerability to stress and interpret organizational events in terms of personally and historically significant meanings (Firth, 1985; Parry, Shapiro and Firth, 1986; Llewelyn et al., 1988). By analysing the personal meaning of organizational life in such depth, without presenting objective evidence concerning the work environment, Firth inevitably directs attention away from organizational issues. Whilst her analysis has value in its own right it does need to be seen as one of several directions for future research and should be complemented with studies which apply the same type of in-depth analysis to organizational issues.

To date, the qualitative studies within the stress literature and the earlier burnout literature have concentrated on depth interviews and neglected other techniques. However, as Denzin (1978) pointed out, different techniques have varying strengths and weaknesses. Whilst interviews are appropriate for understanding personal meanings they may be less useful for studying everyday actions and organizational structures since speech is not an appropriate measure of behaviour and accounts maybe either deliberately or unconsciously distorted by respondents. Light (1979) suggested that some form of direct observation enables the most accurate understanding of everyday actions and organizational functions and structures to be obtained. If observational data is then compared with interview data the analysis of these issues can be compared with the study of subjective meanings. Thus, the varying strengths of the different techniques, which are commonly seen as a regrettable source of error, may become a source of insight and a way of integrating explanations at the level of organizational function and structure with explanations at the level of personal meanings. For example, both questionnaire and interview studies of psychiatric nursing commonly report that quantitative work overload is a major cause of stress (e.g., Milne, 1983; Leatt and Schneck, 1985). However, studies which have investigated both actual and reported workload, show that nurses often have a great deal of slack in their day and that increasing staffing levels frequently leads to increased boredom, fatigue and avoidance of patients (Towell, 1975; Flaskerud et al., 1979). Complaints of overwork therefore seem to function as surface rationalizations for the avoidance and distancing behaviour many nurses use to cope with other stressors in psychiatric nursing. As later chapters in this book will show, these stressors are rooted in the highly problematic nature of psychiatry and in the deep structure of the organization.

CONCLUSION

This chapter has argued that the occupational stress and burnout literatures utilize similar theoretical models and research techniques and share a number of common problems which arise because they both adopt a psychological perspective which pays insufficient attention to the full complexity of the inter-relationship between social conditions and subjective experience. It suggests that both fields could be strengthened by incorporating concepts from the related disciplines of sociology and organization theory. This would enable the development of more sophisticated analyses of the effects which discrepancies between the manifest and latent functions and surface and deep structures of organizations have on the individual's subjective experiences of work. Admittedly, this approach to the problems of organizational stress raises complex issues and does not yield simple easily implementable solutions. Unfortunately, the fact that work problems cannot be resolved easily does not mean that they can be ignored with impunity, as facile solutions may well fail precisely because they neglect the root causes of organizational problems. In the long run, the individually-oriented analyses and intervention strategies proposed by many stress or burnout researchers may simply divert attention from organizational issues and help perpetuate the very problems they are designed to solve.

3 Psychology and social context

INTRODUCTION

The theoretical and technical problems which currently beset research into occupational stress and burnout reflect more general problems within psychology as a whole. A closer examination of the various assumptions underlying mainstream psychology may thus enable us to develop a deeper understanding of the key issues which must be addressed in any attempt to develop more meaningful accounts of the difficulties which people experience within their work environment. This chapter therefore turns from the stress and burnout literatures to a more general examination of the way in which psychology as a discipline has tackled the relationship between the individual and the social context. During recent years an increasing number of sociologically aware social psychologists have attacked the dominant theories, methodologies and research findings of mainstream psychology and proposed alternative frameworks for conceptualizing the relationship between the person and society (e.g. Georgoudi, 1983; Henriques et. al. 1984; Gergen, 1985; Moscovici, 1988; Sampson, 1988). The insights these theorists provide are potentially valuable to more applied fields such as occupational psychology. Unfortunately, their relevance for these areas is seldom emphasised within the social psychology literature which is generally written by, and for, academic psychologists. In consequence, the implications which these reformulations have for the more applied areas of psychology may be under-estimated. This chapter seeks to bridge the gap between the highly abstract concerns of many writers in the area of sociological social psychology and the more practical concerns of applied psychologists and to illustrate the ways in which this literature can help us develop an alternative framework for applied research into problems such as occupational stress. The chapter is divided into four sections. The first section examines the way in which the relationship between the individual and society has been conceptualized in mainstream psychology. The second section goes on to discuss the ways in which positivist conceptions of social science limit and distort our understanding of this relationship. The third section moves from critique to alternative and outlines the main tenets of current reformulations of psychological metatheory advanced by the more sociologically oriented social psychologists whilst the final section discusses the way in which these concepts can be used to further our understanding of occupational stress within the psychiatric system.

THE INDIVIDUAL AND SOCIETY

Many of psychology's more radical critics are, in essence, condemning the discipline's propensity for focussing on the psychological aspects of individual experience without grappling with the problem of how structural and ideological features of society influence the psyche (e.g. Pepitone, 1981; Wexler, 1983; Sampson, 1981; 1985; Gergen, 1985). One of the most common themes they raise is the discipline's failure to deal with the political and historical contexts of human behaviour. As Semin (1986) points out, mainstream psychological thought generally draws a sharp distinction between the individual and society and inplicitly assumes that whilst it is the task of social psychology to investigate the behaviour of groups of individuals it is the duty of other disciplines to analyse the constitution and reproduction of society. In consequence, many psychologists act as if society is merely a nebulous and unchanging backdrop against which distinctly psychological processes occur. By failing to examine the interplay between social structure and individual subjectivity and concentrating on the analysis of the individual as a relatively isolated entity the discipline obscures the various ways in which the structural and cultural differences within and between societies are reflected in the life experiences of different social groups.

A clear example of the problems of individualism within mainstream psychological theorising is provided by Furby (1979), in a critical review of the Locus of Control literature. Furby demonstrates that the literature contains a clear evaluative dimension which equates internality with increased efficacy and well-being. An implicit assumption underlying the belief in internality is that, in general, key events within an individual's environment actually are contingent on that person's behaviour. To perceive the locus of control of events as external is assumed to be inconsistent with reality and therefore to be a psychological problem rather than an accurate reflection of societal conditions. In consequence, a number of studies have focussed on ways of increasing internality without analysing the relationship between perceived control and actual social conditions.

As Furby points out, this strategy may be counter-productive in the case of underpowered groups and may increase their sense of guilt and self-blame whilst helping to maintain the existing status quo. For example, if someone believes that their inability to find a job is the result of their own shortcomings their response may be a strategy of educational self improvement. Unfortunately, where high levels of structural unemployment exist individual self improvement may ultimately prove self-defeating since if it is independently pursued by sufficiently large numbers of people employers may simply demand an increasingly skilled work-force to fill a shrinking labour market. Thus, a strategy which can be effective if adopted by a small number of people will have contradictory effects if utilized by larger groups. Under these circumstances an individually oriented internal locus of control is only a realistic attribute for a small proportion of the unemployed population. If adopted by the majority it might even increase individuals' sense of frustration and despair by highlighting the discrepancy between beliefs and outcome. As a group, it might be more appropriate for the unemployed to work on the principle of individual powerlessness versus collective strength and seek to increase their control of the environment through collective action designed to bring about structural changes within the labour market. As Furby's review reveals, this essentially communal perspective on the ability to control one's life is inadequately measured within the various Locus of Control scales, with the result that the worldview of politicised, but underprivileged, groups such as some sectors of the American black population, is often distorted and devalued within Locus of Control research.

Furby also discusses the inter-relationship between psychological theorizing concerning Locus of Control and psychologists' own position within the social system. In common with several other writers (Georgoudi, 1983; Gergen, 1984; Minton, 1984; Jahoda, 1986) she argues that the individualism of mainstream psychology reflects the extent to which psychological theorizing is implicitly influenced by the inherent assumptions about human nature which govern the wider social order which psychologists inhabit. Hall (1983) has argued that the dominant world view within Western culture conceptualises society as an aggregate of individuals operating within a relatively benign social order which usually provides adequate opportunities for people to develop their potentialities. Since social structures are not constraining, human behaviour is explained by internal, personal characteristics rather than by situations or relationships and failure is thus essentially due to personal shortcomings or personal pathology. Hall's analysis is admittedly somewhat overdrawn. Nevertheless, the principle of individual responsibility and individual pathology is enshrined within both the dominant culture of Western society and the various institutions of social control such as the legal system and the psychiatric system, both of which tend to view societal factors simply as mitigating or triggering influences within an essentially individual process.

A contrasting view of the individual's relationship to society was put forward by the social anthropologist Geertz (1974) who pointed out that

"The Westerner's conception of the person as a bounded, unique, more or less integrated motivational and cognitive universe, a dynamic center of emotion, judgement, and action organized into a distinctive whole and set against both other such wholes and against a natural and social background is .... a rather peculiar idea within the context of the world's cultures" (p. 31).

Geertz's comments concerning the underlying ethnocentrism of mainstream psychology are echoed by several other writers who argue that the cultural emphasis on individualism which is found within Western society is a relatively recent phenomenon, reflecting changes in social organization stemming from industrialization rather than an immutable characteristic of the human psyche (Geertz, 1979; Fox, 1985; Sampson, 1988). For example, a recent psycho-historical study of the self by Verhave and Van Hoorn (1984) argues that the demise of the mediaeval social system and world view and its replacement by a capitalist industrial system has led to fundamental changes in the concept of self. During the earlier epoch, people conceptualized themselves as one element within an agrarian community which was part of a stable, hierarchical and natural world order. This public conceptualization of self was replaced by a more individual and private concept as mediaeval communities gave way to the more atomized economic structures and social relationships of industrial society. Within the last century a concept of self based on a multiplicity of relatively discrete social roles has emerged which reflects the increasing complexity and fragmentation of modern society. Similar analyses have been advanced within other psycho-historical studies which reveal large historical variations in the concept of childhood (Aries, 1962), mother-child relations (Badinter, 1980) and family structure (Dizard and Gadlin, 1984). In addition, contemporary empirical evidence from anthropological studies shows that lay conceptualizations of psychological processes differ markedly between cultures and that structural rearrangements resulting from environmental changes like enforced resettlement may cause significant alterations in social organization, inter-personal relationships and self-concept. (Heelas and Lock, 1981; Schweder and Bourne, 1982; Gauvain, Altman and Fahim, 1984).

One implication of these studies is that axioms concerning human nature which are considered universal in Western societies, and Western psychology, may also be culture-specific. This raises the question of the extent to which cultural norms do, or should, influence the models used within psychology as a discipline. For many critics of mainstream psychology our ability to provide meaningful explanations of people's relationship to their social world is severely limited by the discipline's failure to recognize, and grapple with the effects which the prevailing norm of psychological individualism have on our theorizing and research.

The critique of individualism advanced by the more sociologically oriented social psychologists does not deny either the actuality or the importance of human agency or individual differences. However, it is designed to locate human activity within its social context. In order to achieve this, it is necessary to obtain clear conceptual and empirical analyses of the limiting and facilitating effects of structural and cultural influences. An undue emphasis upon the individual makes this difficult to achieve and results in over-simplistic analyses of the ways people relate to and perceive their social world.

PSYCHOLOGY AND POSITIVISM

Most critics link the individualism of mainstream psychology with the dominance of positivist conceptualizations of social science (e.g. Gergen, 1978; Buss, 1979; Pepitone, 1981; Sarason, 1982). During the last decade an increasing number of writers have questioned the hegemony of positivist and empiricist techniques and several have claimed that the discipline is currently in crisis as a result of challenges to the positivist ideal of hypothetico-deductive models derived from the natural sciences (Elms, 1975; Brenner, 1981; Minton, 1984). Four interlinked features of positivism have caused particular concern; firstly, the mechanistic model of human behaviour, secondly, the search for universally applicable laws, thirdly, the neglect of social context, and finally, the concept of the psychologist as neutral observer.

The first basic assumption of radical critics is that the subject matter of the natural and social sciences is qualitatively different because the former deals with unconscious and reactive objects operating within a mechanistic and unchanging environment whilst the later deals with proactive, self-aware subjects intentionally intervening within a socially constructed world (Shotter, 1974; 1980; Harre, 1979; 1986).

A second, and related, assumption is that society is mutable and that human subjectivity and action may alter concomitantly. Thus, in contrast to the universal laws of the natural sciences, many of the theoretical statements and empirical findings of the social sciences will have a circumscribed validity which is limited by the socio-cultural boundaries of the time and space in which they occur. The task of social science should be to understand these processes rather than to mimic the natural sciences by seeking universally applicable and immutable laws of human behaviour (Harre and Secord, 1972; Gergen, 1985; Sampson, 1988).

The third point made by the critics of positivism is that human behaviour is predominantly governed by the social rules or norms which people generate to understand their world or by structural features of a socially created world. Human action and subjectivity are therefore over-determined, take place within sequences which extend over relatively long periods of time and reflect upon wider cultural patterns. These aspects of human life are undervalued within most quantitative research in psychology which frequently oversimplifies or neglects these patterns in favour of a limited range of proximal variables which are easier to measure and control. As a result many empirical studies provide data which has limited relevance to real-world settings.

The final tenet is that psychological findings are not value-free. This concept is particularly important in relation to applied psychological research where findings may feed back into the policy making sphere. A clear appreciation of this relationship is seen as important in order to reduce psychologists' dependence on existing normative assumptions and increase their capacity to analyse dysfunctional aspects of the existing system (Sarason, 1981; 1982). The complexity of this issue can be illustrated by a current example of policy oriented psychological research. Browne (1986) has recently initiated a large-scale research project into parent-child interaction in child-battering families which aims to refine the identification and treatment of this problem through the detailed observation and description of parent-child communication patterns in abusive families. In itself, the aim of avoiding child-battering is entirely laudable and the project clearly has humanitarian aims. However, the research strategy is individualistic and centres on the parent-child dyad to the relative exclusion of other issues. Whilst improving parent-child relations or helping case workers identify potential abuse more accurately may genuinely help many families this type of strategy can also have negative effects. Ryan (1976) has pointed out that such approaches can inadvertently encourage victim-blaming policies in which the findings of social science research are used by policy-makers to show that problem populations have different psychological attributes to 'normal' populations. These differences then establish what the problem is and what must be changed. Policy level recommendations then advocate programmes to educate, treat or rehabilitate the individual rather than programmes to alter the social structures or environmental circumstances which may contribute to the psychological differences.

Many social scientists involved in applied research are aware that their work addresses a limited range of issues and that their proposed solutions are partial attempts to ameliorate highly complex situations. The problem is often one of ensuring that this is communicated to those people occupying positions of power over disadvantaged or marginal groups. Whilst there is no easy solution to this problem several radical theorists argue that the discipline should acknowledge more explicitly that the findings of applied psychological research are not only produced within a wider cultural milieu which influences their form but that they may also feed back into and influence that culture (Sarason, 1981,1982; Henriques et al., 1984; Gergen, 1985). Thus, in addition to examining the ways in which their theorizing is socio-culturally determined, psychologists should examine the effects which their theorizing may have on society. A thorough analysis of this issue involves going beyond simply looking at the direct effects of applied research to a more comprehensive analysis of the influence of particular modes of construing reality on social life. To give an example, several writers have suggested that we may be moving towards a 'psychiatric society' in which people's problems are increasingly conceptualized in medical or psychological terms and in which medical judgements have an expanding influence on the way we live (Conrad and Schreider, 1980; Castel et al., 1982; Miller and Rose, 1986; Turner, 1987). The reasons for this phenomenon probably relate rather more to changes in society and to the decline of other sources of moral guidance and social support than to either the proven efficacy of psychiatric or psychological techniques or the attempts of these professions to expand their sphere of influence. To some extent, this process is therefore beyond professional control. Nevertheless, it still seems important for psychologists to consider the effects on people's lives of both professional psychology and a psychologically minded social milieu. Only by doing so can psychologists hope to gain a partial distancing from the socio-cultural environment which may enable them to understand, evaluate and, if necessary, try and change, the ways in which society constructs people's consciousness and actions.

FROM CRITIQUE TO ALTERNATIVE

Radical critics of mainstream psychology initially tended to concentrate on the shortcomings of traditional approaches. Whilst this issue is important critique must be combined with the development of constructive alternatives if psychology is to advance conceptually. Several theorists within social psychology have recently addressed this task and the main tenets of an alternative theoretical framework for understanding the interrelationship between psychological and social reality are now becoming more clearly clearly delineated (e.g. Moscovici, 1972; 1984; Sampson, 1981; 1985; 1988; Henriques et al., 1984; Gergen and Davis, 1985). Although there are differences of emphasis between writers, several key themes are common to nearly all these reformulations of psychological metatheory. The three dominant themes are the indivisibility of people and their social context, the relationship between human activity and social repoduction and finally, the importance of power in social relationships.

The most fundamental proposition expounded by the theorists discussed in this chapter is that human subjectivity and action are so inextricably interwoven with the social context which people inhabit that a theoretical separation between the individual and society is conceptually unacceptable. The traditional concept of the person as a psychological entity distinct from the social milieu, though influenced by it, should therefore be replaced with an interactionist perspective which conceptualizes the person and the social context as part of an indivisible unit. This necessitates developing analyses which acknowledge, firstly, that human subjectivity and actions are constituted within and through social structures, and secondly, that people are also the producers of the social structures they inhabit.

This perspective does not imply that the individual is nothing more than a set of social roles. People experience unique configurations of social experiences and have a capacity to reflect upon and integrate their history. When this attribute is combined with the acknowledgement that most social situations contain some measure of freedom both individuality and agency become possible, although perhaps to a more circumscribed extent that some individualistically oriented theories imply. It is, therefore, perfectly feasible to examine the differences between a particular individual and others from within this perspective, provided that it is recognised that individuality is acquired within a social context and still reflects the indivisibility of the person and their socio-historical context. The analysis of individual differences thus involves the comparison of differences between socially produced people rather than a comparison of asocial, purely biological or psychological entities (Turner and Oakes; 1986).

A striking example of the way in which this approach seeks to dissolve the demarcation between conceptual categories such as the biological versus the social, is provided by Henriques et al.'s (1984) analysis of premature sexual maturation in Puerto Rican children. They report that several hundred female children have experienced accelerated sexual development which is sometimes apparent from as early as six months and has culminated in full sexual maturity in four year olds. The reason for such precocity is thought to be oestrogen supplements in the feed of the chickens which constitute the staple diet for large numbers of Puerto Ricans. Not surprisingly, these abnormal biological changes precipitate confused social relationships in which neither the affected children themselves, their peers or adults are certain how to cope with the bizarre child-woman limbo associated with accelerated development. However, it is not the biological changes themselves which lead to such confusion but the realization that social conventions predicated on normal biological patterns are inappropriate in such case. Similarly, whilst the physical changes in the children are clearly biological and are caused by oestrogen excess, the reason this has occurred is politico-economic. Finally, social perceptions of the inappropriateness of the children's biological maturation have resulted in pressure on American agri-business to alter its policies in order to halt the biological changes. The effects of the biological, psychological, social and politico-economic spheres are thus inter-related and mutually influencing within this example and do not form a hierarchy of separate levels from the biological to the societal.

A second major theme in these reformulations of psychological theory is that people should be conceptualized as creative and knowledgeable agents sustaining society through purposive and goal directed actions (Harre, 1979; Shotter, 1984). This does not imply that the form which society takes is planned or expected, for people's understanding of, and ability to alter, their situation is frequently limited by a variety of personal and structural factors. In consequence, human activity frequently takes place in a variety of unacknowledged conditions and has a range of unintended consequences which may then become embedded in the structural conditions of human existence, creating the undesired setting conditions for future action. For example, the changing age distribution of the population is the outcome of the reproductive behaviour of numerous individuals over a timespan of many years. Whilst many of today's elderly may have made personal decisions to limit their fecundity it seems less likely that they deliberately intended to alter the population structure so that they would later become popularly conceptualized as an increasing burden on the working population. The demographic changes are thus the unintended, but patterned, consequence of large numbers of individual decisions made for entirely different reasons.

In order to understand the myriad ways in which human activity may escape the control of its perpetrators it is important to interpret the psychological and structural constraints which ensure that people are both the creators and the creation of their social world. In grappling with this issue several writers have turned to psychoanalytic interpretations of human knowledgeability and motivation and sought to synthesize these ideas with sociological analyses of the superordinate social structure (Georgoudi, 1983; Henriques et al., 1984). One of the clearest recent attempts to grapple with the problem of how human knowledgeability and intention relate to the re-creation of society is provided by the former social psychologist and eminent sociologist Anthony Giddens (1979, 1984). He proposes a stratification model of knowledge which is derived from Freud's tripartite distinction between the id, ego and superego and suggests that knowledge is either unconscious, practical or discursive. Unconscious knowledge may be used purposively but is, by definition, unavailable to consciousness and cannot therefore be the object of deliberate choice. Practical, or tacit, knowledge is the most comprehensive form of knowledge and the most important arbiter of daily activity. In essence, it consists of implicit knowledge concerning ways of behaving in every day contexts which is taken for granted by the participants. Although it includes cognitive as well as behavioural elements it is generally applied unreflectingly and seldom becomes the object of self scrutiny. In consequence, individuals may not be consciously aware of contradictions within their tacit understanding or between the different types of knowledge they possess. The final level of knowledge is discursive or intellectual. It contrasts with both unconscious and tacit knowledge in that people are consciously aware of their discursive knowledge and are able to verbalize and reflect upon it relatively easily. Whilst discursive knowledge is less context bound than practical understanding it is also subject to ideological distortion and is not necessarily an accurate reflection of reality. Thus, whilst people may make conscious choices based on discursive knowledge the rationality of these decisions may be debatable. Finally, Giddens argues that the boundaries between the various forms of knowledge are mutable and that unconscious and tacit knowledge may both be transformed into objects of conscious reflection, whilst the reverse may also occur if discursive knowledge becomes deeply habituated and thereby enters the realm of unreflexive or tacit understanding.

Giddens suggests that people use their knowledge of social situations to further their core security needs. Drawing on the work of psychoanalytic writers such as Erickson (1963) he proposes that the core motive for human action is an ever-present desire for ontological security. He goes on to suggest that people attempt to meet their fundamental security needs through the routines of daily life and therefore have strong, but often unconscious, motives to reproduce the patterns of social activity with which they are most familiar. Routine is thus the 'master key' (Giddens, 1984, p.60) to the relationship between individual action and social structures as it ensures that the recurrent attempts of individuals to meet their personal security needs have the collective effect of facilitating the continual reproduction of established social norms. Unfortunately, as several social theorists have recently pointed out, the structural and ideological contradictions of our social system may become reflected in people's fragmentary knowledge of their social circumstances and in their ambivalent emotional responses towards key issues in their lives. In consequence, modern society may chronically frustrate its citizens' core security needs because its structures and ideology combine to heighten expectations and individuality whilst simultaneously denying people the means of achieving security through stable relationships and meaningful work (Lasch, 1979; 1984; Willmott, 1986). In other words, the brittleness and fragility of many people's daily routines within modern society may ensure that they supply a hollow security which does little to alleviate core anxieties. Regrettably, the chronic and deep-rooted insecurity which results from this unhappy state of affairs may well make people redouble their efforts to achieve a minimal security through their familiar routines, rather than encouraging them to seek out new options which may initially be more frightening but ultimately be more satisfying (Fromm, 1978; 1984).

The final concern of recent theorizing is to introduce the concept of socially constructed power into psychological discourse (Georgoudi, 1983; Wexler, 1983; Gergen, 1985). The analysis of this issue contains two juxtaposed elements. The first point is that the social power is unequally distributed, which ensures that the more powerful individuals or social groups within a society have a greater ability than underpowered groups to draw upon its structural resources in their attempts to further their own interests. The corollary is that power is a relative rather than an absolute phenomenon, which ensures that the underpowered groups usually have some means of exerting a degree of counter control. Power relationships between different groups thus involve a continuously shifting 'dialectic of control' (Giddens, 1984) rather that the unidirectional exercise of force. This conceptualization of power links the idea that the exercise of power is a goal-directed human activity with a recognition of the fact that power-holders may either be forced into acts which they personally disagree with as a result of their structural position or may be unable to achieve their goals in the face of opposition form underpowered groups. Such opposition is often expressed through quite minor aspects of people's daily routines and often forms part of their tacit, rather than their intellectual knowledge. Goffman's (1961) research on mental institutions provides a classic example of a 'dialectic of control' in which psychiatric patients who seem to agree intellectually with medical definitions of their illness still engage in various actions designed to undermine the depersonalizing and arbitrary aspects of psychiatric power and re-affirm their sense of self-hood. These acts may then provoke counter-control measures by harassed staff and both parties may eventually become trapped in an escalating 'dialectic of control' which may well have detrimental consequences for all concerned. If we are to truly understand the ways in which people's social context structures their beliefs, actions and emotions, we need to move beyond the analysis of the individual towards a genuinely interpersonal interpretation of the ways in which human interaction is structured through the interlocking experiences of all parties within a given social context.

RELEVANCE FOR STRESS RESEARCH

The theoretical framework developed by the more sociologically oriented social psychologists is usually expressed in highly abstract terms which provide general guidelines for approaching psychological problems rather than specific proposals for research within discrete subject areas of psychology. In order to provide a clearer illustration of the ways in which these ideas can generate fresh insights into the problems which people encounter within their work environment the final section of this chapter returns to the more circumscribed domain of occupational stress research. In the preceeding chapter stress research was criticised for utilizing oversimplistic explanatory models which pay insufficient attention to the complexity of the inter-relationship between social conditions and subjective experience; for adopting a consensus model of society which neglects the problems of power and conflict in organizational life, and for relying upon positivist research techniques which are incapable of describing the various ways in which stressful situations develop over time. These shortcomings represent fairly fundamental flaws within the theoretical models on which stress research is traditionally based. As such, these inadequacies are unlikely to be solved by reforms which merely tinker with the various parameters of the traditional research paradigm, requiring instead a more radical rethink of the basic assumptions underlying conventional stress research. The conceptual framework developed by the various writers discussed within this chapter provides a valuable source of ideas for accomplishing this task.

    The fundamental argument advanced by these writers is that people's psychological characteristics are primarily the result of their life experiences within a particular social world. This does not imply that everyone within a given social milieu is a clone since the character structures of different individuals will inevitably vary to some degree as a result of different genetic inheritances and life experiences. However, it does imply that the members of a given social group will usually have core elements of their character structure in common and perceive and respond to life in a similar fashion. If we want to understand the ways in which human action and emotion operate as productive forces in the maintenance or alteration of a given social order we therefore need to concentrate primarily upon those elements of subjectivity and action which group members hold in common, and in so doing we will inevitably pay less attention to those minor idiosyncrasies which help distinguish one individual from another. Whilst these features of the individual are crucially important if we want to enter fully into the unique experience of a specific individual they are less relevant if our main concern is to understand the collective response to a given social context.

This theoretical position suggests that if we are to gain a fuller understanding of the effects which people's occupations have on their psychological well-being we must embark upon far deeper analyses of the interrelationships between social structures and collective human experiences. Thus, if we want to understand the distinctive way in which the work of psychiatric nursing structures the subjectivity and actions of those who participate in this occupation, as opposed to understanding the individual make-up of a unique person who happens, amongst other things, to be a psychiatric nurse, we need to concentrate upon those psychological experiences which are common to all psychiatric nurses. In so doing we also need to recognize that the process of collective adaptation to the work environment involves the dynamic unfolding of collective coping strategies which may well have a significant impact upon the external work environment. Whilst such strategies may create beneficial changes within the work environment they will not necessarily have this result and may well have the contrary effect of maintaining a dynamic equilibrium which helps perpetuate the very conditions which the work-force finds unsatisfactory and stress-producing.

A second key argument advanced by many of the more sociologically aware social psychologists centres on the importance of power and reciprocity within social relationships. These writers point out that people occupying different positions within the same overall social context may well interpret that context differently as a result of their particular location within it. These incongruent perceptions may then ensure that the varying degrees of social power which different players bring to a situation are utilized in the service of divergent, or incompatible, goals. As a result, the attempts of one group to utilize their resources to escape the stresses of their situation may inadvertently exacerbate the problems faced by another group who may, in their turn, react in a manner which exaggerates the problems of the first group. The two groups of protagonists may thus become trapped within a series of increasingly adverse situations which spiral beyond the control of either party. This perspective on social relationships obviously implies that the traditional approach to stress research, which tends to concentrate exclusively on the experiences of the specific occupational group being investigated, needs replacing with a more interactional approach which locates the experiences and actions of the focal group within a matrix of intermeshed actors and events. Such a strategy will facilitate the growth of more comprehensive insights into the various ways in which the subjective experiences and coping strategies of specific occupational groups are influenced by their structural position within the work environment.

A third proposal advanced within the literature discussed in this chapter concerns the nature of social institutions. In contrast to most stress researchers, who hold an implicit model of organizations as potentially rational enterprizes with unambiguous purposes, many of the more sociologically inclined social psychologists argue that the major social institutions within our society contain a variety of fundamental contradictions which are so deeply embedded within the cultural and structural framework of our society that they constitute integral aspects of our social system. The very ubiquity of these contradictions means that they are seldom explicitly recognized or articulated by the different members of a given society or organization. As a result, the purposive and goal-directed actions of both individuals and social groups often take place in various unacknowledged conditions and have a variety of unforeseen and negative consequences which may be highly distressing for those concerned. This perspective on social institutions suggests that stress researchers must develop an enhanced awareness of the various ways in which the structural contradictions of our social institutions become reflected in the fragmented and equivocal knowledge which people have of their social circumstances and in their often ambivalent emotional responses to stressful situations. In the case of psychiatric professionals this task involves developing a detailed analysis of the ways in which the specific contradictions which characterize the social role of the psychiatric system find concrete expression within the daily actions and subjective experiences of the different participants within this organization. The next chapter will begin to address this task by discussing recent sociological interpretations of the role of psychiatry within modern society.

4 Critical psychiatry

INTRODUCTION

All societies have a tendency to respond to the disturbed, or disturbing, behaviours of individuals by developing various socially legitimated practices aimed at making such acts more comprehensible to, and controllable by, their members. The form which such practices take varies widely, for different societies interpret and deal with the same behaviours in divergent ways. Within Western society, the psychiatric system serves as a key structural and ideological mechanism for coping with some forms of socially problematic, or personally distressing, behaviour. If we wish to gain a more profound understanding of the problems of occupational stress within psychiatry we must therefore move beyond the micro-level analyses advocated in traditional stress research and develop deeper interpretations which tackle the full complexity of the interactions between psychiatry's social role and the subjective experiences of those who work within the system. Recent sociological writing within the field of critical psychiatry provides a valuable tool for tackling this task, for whilst theorists in this area have seldom been concerned with the problems of occupational stress, they have analysed the relationship between psychiatry and society in some depth. Their writings can therefore be drawn upon to develop a richer understanding of the relationship between the contradictions of the psychiatric system and the lives of all who participate within it.

The most recent literature within the field of critical psychiatry has tended to concentrate on the relationship between the forms of knowledge promulgated by the psychiatric system and the social power it possesses (e.g. Conrad and Schneider, 1980; Ingleby, 1981; Horowitz, 1982; Penfold and Walker, 1984; Busfield, 1986; Miller and Rose, 1986; Turner, 1987). The basic argument advanced within this literature centres on the claim that psychiatry serves a dual purpose within modern society and not only supplies corrective measures where behaviour is conceptualized as being problematic by the individual or society, but also helps disseminate information concerning appropriate behaviours and suitable ways of perceiving social reality. Psychiatry thus plays a formative, rather than a merely reactive, role in the way people experience and deal with the problems of social existence and may, in a very real sense, help to create the phenomena it claims to simply discover and treat.

A brief analysis of psychiatry's growing involvement with the elderly mentally infirm may help to clarify the theoretical position of many contemporary critics. There is a good deal of medical evidence to suggest that senile dementia is an irreversible degenerative condition involving organic deterioration of the ageing brain (e.g. Katzman, Terry and Bick, 1978; Katzman, 1983). However, dementia is also a complex social problem which reflects structural contradictions within modern society. On the one hand, increasing rates of social change and the fragmentation of communities and families means that Western societies have difficulty valuing or caring for unproductive or infirm members of society. Whilst on the other hand, increases in longevity resulting from both improved material living standards and advances in modern medicine mean that more old people remain physically healthy after their minds have deteriorated. Furthermore, this problem is worse amongst women, partly because their longer lifespan increases the likelihood of dementia and partly because of social factors. Many women who develop dementia are widows or have husbands who are unwilling or unable care for them at home. In contrast, a greater proportion of senile males are nursed at home by their more domestically competent wives (Allen, 1986). Thus, whilst the aetiology of dementia is physical the circumstances surrounding the increasing participation of the psychiatric sector in geriatric medicine are social and political. In consequence, critiques which simply document the negative effects of institutionalization or chemotherapy on the physical and mental health of the elderly are relevant, but partial. It is equally important to evaluate the relationship between the psychiatric sector and society when considering the issue of psychiatric care for the dementing.

Recent analyses which utilize this institutionally oriented perspective have identified three key inter-linked structural contradictions in the relationship between the psychiatric sector and society. The first, and most important, contradiction is that psychiatry is simultaneously part of the ideological and regulatory superstructure of industrialized society and an institution which aims to alleviate the personal distress which that society and its institutions help produce. A second, and lesser, contradiction is that psychiatry is simultaneously committed to the alleviation of mental illness and to identifying increasingly subtle behavioural deviations and personal distress as psychiatric problems. The third contradiction is that psychiatry simultaneously removes individual responsibility for actions and makes positive mental health the personal duty of responsible citizens. Each of these contradictions will now be looked at in greater detail.

SOCIAL CONTROL

The prime contradiction identified in virtually all the recent critiques of psychiatry centres on the tension between, and the interweaving of, psychiatry's dual mandate for helping the individual and ensuring social regulation (e.g. Morgan, 1975; Mangen, 1982; Ingleby, 1985; Scheper-Hughes and Lovell, 1986). The basic argument of these critics is that the ideology of medicalization and individualism advanced by psychiatry provides an elaborate, though not necessarily deliberate, framework for 'blaming the victim' (Albee, 1986). Such critics claim that by locating the sources of people's problems within either organic dysfunctions, or psychological dysfunctions within the individual or their immediate family, psychiatry implicitly denies the relationship between social conditions and human experience. This often leads to treatment goals which aim to adjust the individual to a lifestyle compatible with psychiatric definitions of normality. Since these definitions are derived from prevailing cultural norms, psychiatry helps to legitimate the existing social structure both by diverting attention away from competing explanations which emphasise the relationship between individual distress and social conditions and by adjusting individuals to the circumstances in which they live. The effects of this may be detrimental for patients as alternative perspectives and solutions are obscured.

The complexity of this issue can be illustrated by examining the relationship between psychiatry and ethnic minorities. In recent years several studies have shown that the Afro-Caribbean population are over represented amongst schizophrenics; are four times more likely than white patients to have reached a mental hospital through the involvement of the police; are twice as likely to be detained involuntarily under the Mental Health Act and are far more likely than whites to receive major tranquilizers and electroconvulsive therapy. (Greater London Council Health Panel, 1985; Mercer, 1986; Kushnick, 1988).

The powers which the British medical profession possesses in relation to involuntary committal are considerable and involve a suspension of civil liberties only equalled by the Prevention of Terrorism and Immigration Acts, coupled with the right to administer physical treatments such as electro-convulsive therapy and mind-altering drugs (Bean, 1986). Public concern has rightly been expressed about the illegitimate use of these powers to control ethnic minorities and, partly as a response to this concern, the concept of 'transcultural psychiatry' has recently gained popularity within the realm of psychiatric discourse. One of the key themes advanced within this branch of psychiatry is that cultural misunderstandings between white doctors and black patients may mean that cultural differences in stress reactions are misdiagnosed as psychosis. For many doctors adopting this position the preferred solution is therefore psychotherapy aimed at exploring cultural response patterns rather than chemotherapy aimed at controlling psychosis (Littlewood and Lipsedge, 1982; Jackson, 1983b; Stanley and Nolan, 1987).

Whilst this approach to the problems of ethnic groups is superficially more liberal and probably represents a very genuine attempt by many psychiatric professionals to adapt their practice to the needs of ethnic minorities, it nevertheless psychiatrizes cultural differences. As a result, it may convey the implicit message that the cultural norms of ethnic groups are pathological in relation to the dominant social culture and should therefore be adapted towards it (Mercer, 1986). This effectively depoliticizes the problem of ethnicity and thus helps undermine the rights of ethnic groups to self-determination by interpreting their behaviour as an individual problem of cultural adjustment best handled by a sympathetic psychiatric professional. Conversely, the individuals receiving treatment are expected to co-operate with psychiatric professionals since their therapy is seen as in their own best interests. The alternative perspective offered by transcultural psychiatry may thus replace the overt social control function of psychiatry enshrined within the 1983 Mental Health Act with a more covert social control function which involves a genuine collaboration between psychiatric professionals and their patients to conceptualize social reality in medical or psychological terms which reflect the prevailing cultural norms.

Perhaps unsurprisingly, some of the more radical sections of the black community have denounced psychiatry for institutionalized racism (Kushnick, 1988). Whilst this does not necessarily imply that individual psychiatric professionals are consciously prejudiced, it does mean that the patterns of interaction between the institution of psychiatry and the black population can be conceptualized as reflecting the prevailing power relationships within the wider society. By re-interpreting the inter-relationship between psychiatry and the black community in these terms radical black theorists have tried to re-assert both the concept of self-determination and the validity of not co-operating with psychiatry.

Similar interpretations of psychiatry's convoluted social role in relation to specific populations have also been advanced by many other writers, most notably feminists examining the treatment of women within the psychiatric system (Chesler, 1974; Penfold and Walker, 1984; Braude, 1988). Such writers concur in seeing medicine as a Janus-faced institution whose tremendous potential for helping the individual is too often misdirected towards obscuring the social origins of much physical and mental suffering. For such theorists the covert social control functions of psychiatry are ultimately more powerful than its ostensible mission to help the weaker members of society.

PSYCHIATRIC IMPERIALISM

The second contradiction identified within the critical psychiatry literature centres on the idea that psychiatry is simultaneously committed to the alleviation of mental illness, and to identifying increasingly subtle forms of behavioural deviation and personal distress as problems needing the expert intervention of psychiatric professionals (e.g.Booker and Imershein, 1979; Conrad and Schneider, 1980; Castel et at. 1982; Ingleby, 1985; Eaton, 1986). Such theorists argue that the remit of psychiatry has altered radically since its inception. Whilst the early psychiatrists were primarily concerned with the incarceration of highly disturbed individuals, modern psychiatry often deals with mildly difficult or distressed individuals within the community. In consequence, the former, rigid, barriers between mental illness and normality have become permeable. The effect of this, however, is less to remove the stigma of mental illness from severely disturbed individuals and more to suggest that nearly every aspect of life has pathological elements which would benefit from expert adjustment. In other words, modern psychiatry involves the pathologization of normality rather than the eradication of mental illness. This can be seen in the accelerating expansion of psychiatric categories and in the extension of psychiatry to new areas such as childhood behaviour problems, and sexual dysfunction.

The expansion of psychiatry can be illustrated by examining the proliferating categories within successive versions of that bible of the psychiatric community, the American Psychiatric Association's Diagnostic and Statistical Manual of Mental Disorders. The first version of this manual (DSM-1) was published in 1952 and contained a mere 60 categories and subcategories of mental illness. DSM II, published in 1968, lists 145 categories, whilst DSM III, published in 1985, lists over 200 separate psychiatric conditions including such disorders as tobacco or alcohol dependence, binge eating, agoraphobia with panic attacks, social phobia, panic disorder and generalized anxiety disorder. As Albee (1985) writing in the American context noted caustically:-

> "Clearly the more human problems that we label mental illnesses, the more people that we can say suffer from them. And, a cynic might add, the more conditions therapists can treat and collect health insurance payments for."

Critics of DSM-III and its more recent revision DSM-III-R (1987) have also drawn attention to the implicit value judgements contained within many of its categories (Kaplan, 1983; Bohart and Todd, 1988). Such critics argue that the implicit definition of normality against which psycho-pathology is judged reflects cultural stereotypes concerning socially acceptable middle class male behaviour within Western society. In consequence, the behaviour of other sections of society may be adjudged pathological even when it reflects the process of adaptation to adverse social circumstances. To cite one example, many critics have argued that the psychoanalytically oriented term 'masochistic personality disorder' would be disproportionately applied to women. As a result, women who engaged in ostensibly self-defeating behaviours, such as remaining with men who assaulted them, might be seen as having serious and unchangeable personality defects, rather than as being the victims of abuse. In extreme cases, such diagnoses could then be used to legitimate male violence by defining the women as unhealthy whilst their batterers remained unlabelled. Psychiatric evidence concerning the women's instability could then be cited in legal battles over issues such as maintenance or the custody of children. The expansion of psychiatric categories to new and ill-defined areas thus helps to perpetuate the soft form of social control perpetuated by psychiatry by privileging the traditional behaviour of some sectors of the population over the behaviour and experiences of other, less fortunate, groups.

The expansion of the therapeutic culture is, of course, not limited to those situations where the medical profession takes the initiative in defining new areas of human experience as psychiatric problems. It may also occur where people voluntarily immerse themselves in therapeutic encounters designed to remould and redress minor defects of the psyche. Once again, this issue can be illustrated most clearly by examining the therapeutic culture in America, where a segment of the population are heavily and voluntarily involved in seeking self-actualization through repeated therapeutic experiences. Critics of this phenomenon have pointed out that the therapeutic culture has arisen, to some extent, as an answer to the alienation of life in modern society and have argued that the relationships formed within the therapeutic setting often provide an erzatz substitute for the more enduring relationships found in more stable societies. (Illich, 1976; Lasch, 1979; 1984; Fromm, 1980; Castel et al., 1982). Unfortunately, the relationships formed in such settings often lack the depth and reciprocity of relationships forged in more communally oriented societies, for the participants are drawn to each other only by their individual psychological needs and cannot cement their interactions through the genuine interweaving of interdependent life patterns found in more communally oriented societies. The growing tendency of many middle-class Americans to redress their life problems through therapeutic experiences thus serves the contradictory purpose of superficially fulfilling some psychological needs to belong which cannot easily be met within the increasingly individualistic structure of industrial society, whilst simultaneously directing attention away from the underlying trends within modern society which militate against the formation of stable community networks. For many critics the burgeoning expansion of the therapeutic culture thus tends to repress rather than to liberate people by transposing key areas of human existence from the public to the personal arena and introducing impersonal technical expertise in place of genuine human relationships.

INDIVIDUAL RESPONSIBILITY

The final contradiction identified within the critical psychiatry literature centres on the equivocal implications of psychiatric intervention for individual responsibility. This issue has been explored in some depth by the sociologically aware British psychiatrist R.D.Scott and his co-workers in their work on 'the treatment barrier' (Scott and Ashworth, 1967; Scott, 1973; 1974; 1980; Bott, 1976; Scott and Starr, 1981). The key premise of their argument is that the cultural definition of mental illness has logically inconsistent implications for the issue of personal responsibility. As a result, various paradoxes and ambiguities are created in the relationship between patients, their families and psychiatric professionals. All parties within the psychiatric system tend to collude in denying these issues and by doing so they help maintain a system where key therapeutic concerns remain unexamined. This enables patients and their families to exploit the contradictions of psychiatry in order to avoid taking responsibility for their actions, maintain the status quo, and obtain relief from the consequences of their actions. It also enables psychiatric professionals to avoid psychologically disturbing confrontations with their patients. Unfortunately, the short term gains which all parties obtain from this strategy are frequently offset by longer-term costs which may be devastating.

The starting point for Scott's theorizing is Parsons' classic definition of the sick role (Parsons, 1951). This definition contains four elements. Firstly, the sick person is temporarily exempt from some or all of their normal social role responsibilities. Secondly, the person is also exempt from responsibility for becoming sick. Thirdly, the sick person must regard their condition as undesirable and want to recover. Fourthly, the person must, where necessary, be willing to co-operate with relevant professionals in order to recover. As Scott points out, Parson's formulation applies most clearly to acute physical illnesses in which there is a clear conceptual separation between the person's normal social identity and their temporary illness. It is less appropriate to mental illness as the latter is often diagnosed on the basis of key behaviour patterns within the person's life and is more intimately related to the individual's global personality. As Scott (1973) notes, within Western society physical illness is a role but mental illness is an identity. This concept of mental illness creates a serious paradox in the treatment of the mentally ill, for cultural definitions of mental disorder also involve the ideas of unintelligibility and lack of control. In consequence, whilst the physically sick patient can be expected to observe the norms of the sick role the psychiatric patient cannot logically be blamed for failing to comply with them and the responsibility for ensuring the success of treatment can be divested onto the psychiatric professions.

The logical contradictions between cultural definitions of appropriate sick-role behaviour and mental illness pave the way for various types of abuse. The critical psychiatry literature has generally concentrated on abuses by society and professionals and shown how the concept of mental illness may be used to deny the validity of the patients' experiences and to impose societal norms. Scott's work provides an important corrective to this by emphasising the opposite side of the coin and showing how the denial of agency inherent in cultural definitions of mental illness can supply patients with a powerful resource which they may manipulate for their own ends. In contrast to some analyses within the critical psychiatry literature, this perspective assumes that the psychiatric sector does actually meet a variety of important needs for patients, either as individuals, or as parts of a family unit, although it stresses that these needs may differ markedly from the manifest problems presented to the psychiatric sector for treatment. For example, several feminist psychotherapists have suggested that agoraphobia in women can represent a way of limiting marital conflict and that the decision to seek treatment may be covertly regarded by the couple as a way of preserving existing interaction patterns by legitimating the patient's 'illness' as opposed to being a genuine decision to try to solve the patient's agoraphobia (Llewelyn and Osborn, 1983).

The empirical research of Scott and his co-workers has demonstrated the various ways in which the denial of agency inherent in the label of mental illness can give patients a considerable degree of power over their relatives and psychiatric professionals. In the more extreme cases, where patients ostensibly warrant admission, they have a virtual licence to behave unacceptably and then disclaim responsibility for their actions. This can enable them to disguise the degree of rationality and control they possess in order to manipulate situations to their own advantage. As Scott shows, some patients may deliberately harm or degrade themselves in order to hurt their relatives through their own suffering, whilst others may utilize the opportunities for evasion and confusion which arise from the contradictions of mental illness in order to take what they want from hospital treatment and avoid those aspects they prefer to ignore.

Whilst mental patients' ostensible lack of agency can have the paradoxical effect of increasing their control over others it may also have the concomitant effect of giving their relatives a great deal of power over them. As Bott (1976) points out, behaviour which is defined as mental illness is frequently highly disturbing for other family members and may arouse strong feelings of guilt, fear and anger. These emotions can be assuaged by having the patients labelled as mentally ill, as this label locates the problems within the patients and implicitly defines their behaviour as socially unacceptable and the relatives' behaviour as normal. This label also enables families to try and control the sick members by off-loading the responsibility for them onto psychiatric professionals and gives the professionals a reciprocal obligation to take decisions for the patients and their families. Since the concept of mental illness is essentially individualistic the involvement of psychiatric professionals frequently serve to obscure the interpersonal and social context of the patient's problems, which may legitimate and intensify pathological patterns of interaction within the family. The various contradictions in the concept and treatment of mental illness may therefore exert a paradoxical effect on family functioning. On the one hand, psychiatric intervention may help bind families closer together by providing reassurance and respite. On the other hand, it may escalate dysfunctional patterns of interaction and further undermine family functioning and personal security. Under these circumstances repeated contact with the psychiatric services may become an essential way of maintaining an unstable equilibrium within the family. The psychiatric system therefore enters into family relationships as an essential third party which simultaneously binds and destroys an increasingly fragile and unstable family system.

As Scott points out, any attempts by psychiatric professionals to redefine their patients' problems in terms of personal or inter-personal responsibility rather than individual pathology are liable to provoke a hostile response as they challenge well-established personal or family dynamics. This creates the paradoxical situation where treatment which ignores the underlying meaning of the patients' problems, and is therefore unlikely to have much long term benefit, is often accepted by them but where treatment which does try to take tacit issues into account is liable to arouse strong resistance from both the patients and their relatives. Such resistance is liable to be both personally and organizationally difficult for psychiatric professionals to cope with and their response is often to avoid dealing with these issues. Unfortunately, this strategy often creates as many problems as it solves. In the first place, patients and their families are obliged to continue presenting with the same pattern of disturbances in order to obtain the relief which the psychiatric sector offers. In the second place patients, and possibly their relatives, may hit out at psychiatric professionals because they are tacitly aware that treatment does little to help them. Finally, the treadmill of re-referrals may be highly demoralizing for psychiatric staff and may undermine both their sense of therapeutic competence and any desire to help patients. As Bott (1976) points out, this may lead to highly routinized patterns of interaction between staff and patients which simply perpetuate the inherent problems of the psychiatric system.

In summary, the work of Scott and his colleagues presents a somewhat jaded account of family relationships and patient motivation which may under-emphasise the genuine desire of many patients and families to take responsibility for their problems and their real expectancy that psychiatry will offer them authentic solutions. Despite this, his work provides a valuable micro-level analysis of the way in which the contradictions surrounding the cultural definition of mental illness are reflected in the relationships between staff, patients and their relatives.

CONCLUSION

The literature examined within this chapter suggests that the psychiatric sector fulfills a complex and highly ambivalent social function, serving as both a key ideological and regulatory mechanism of modern society and as a primary resource for alleviating the misery within our society. This perspective is seldom part of the world view of the various psychiatric professions, who generally conceptualize themselves as providers of a therapeutic service based upon a growing body of professional expertise and objectively validated knowledge. For them, the problems of psychiatry are those of inadequate funding, competing philosophies of treatment and poor training. Real as these problems are, in the view of many of psychiatry's critics they are only a part of the problem, for in the final analysis it is the social role of psychiatry which undermines the often very genuine attempts of psychiatric professionals to help their patients. From this perspective, the negative effects of the psychiatric system on staff and patients will not be wholly understood unless we locate the subjective experiences of all participants within a wider analysis of psychiatry's relationship to modern society. Only by doing so can we gain real insights into the stresses which psychiatric professionals face throughout their working lives.

The succeeding chapters of this book will now move from the level of abstract theorizing to a grounded analysis of daily life within the psychiatric system and seek to forge new links between the empirical investigation of stress in psychiatric nursing and the theoretical analysis of psychiatry's role within our society. The aim of these chapters will be to elucidate the interpersonal processes which enable the structural contradictions of psychiatry to find concrete expression within the fragmented understanding and inconsistent actions of the various players within the psychiatric system. As the empirical research which follows will reveal, the attempts of different participants to ameliorate the chronic personal insecurities engendered by these contradictions often have the paradoxical effect of augmenting the problems of the psychiatric system and intensifying the very feelings they are struggling to avoid.

5 Methodology

INTRODUCTION

Recent work within the philosophy of social science has shown that the social context in which research is embedded can exert a definitive influence on the form that it takes (Ravetz, 1971; Harre, 1972; Mitroff, 1974; Rorty, 1979). It may therefore be useful to give the reader a brief overview of the social environment in which this research was located before going on to discuss the design and techniques in more detail.

The empirical research described in this book began in the summer of 1984 and continued for approximately two years. At the time I was in my early thirties and had returned to academia after working as a clinical psychologist for approximately five years. My decision to leave the Health Service and return to university to study for a doctorate was triggered by my own growing unease about the daily practices within the psychiatric system and by my desire to have a period away from full-time clinical work in which to reflect upon, and try to gain a deeper understanding of, the dynamics of the psychiatric system. My decision to undertake this research in a hospital where I had not worked previously was influenced by this desire as I wanted the opportunity to re-enter the psychiatric system as a researcher rather than as a clinician and to observe the setting without the recurrent pressures to respond to the various crises of daily life within the psychiatric sector. The study was therefore carried out in the role of a research student from a nearby university and within the various constraints imposed by the exigencies of doctoral research. The ways in which this role influenced the research design and the relationship with the research hospital will be described in more detail in the succeeding sections of this chapter which deal firstly, with the problems of gaining access; secondly, with the research design and methodology; thirdly, with field relationships and finally, with the dilemmas of supplying feedback to the hospital.

GAINING ACCESS

The various problems involved in initially gaining access to an organization can be conceptualized as both a set of practical obstacles to be overcome and as a source of data concerning the social organization of the prospective research setting (Hammersley and Atkinson, 1983; Whyte, 1988). The preliminary phase of gaining access to a research setting usually involves negotiating the terms of entry with various gatekeepers or sponsors. Within formal organizations such individuals are often in managerial positions or are union representatives. The early negotiations with these individuals frequently raise issues which may crucially influence the type of data collected during the subsequent research. One of the key problems is that such individuals are often prominent members of particular power groups within the organization. Acceptance by them may therefore arouse the suspicions of other groups within the organization who may seek to protect themselves by limiting the type of information they reveal to the researcher. A second problem is that the gatekeepers may, quite understandably, seek to influence the data gathering process in order to present the institution in a favourable light or to obtain information which may be useful to them in their official capacity within the institution. The later requirement can be particularly problematic if the researcher is initially, as I was, somewhat unsure of the directions in which the study will develop, as it may result in a commitment to provide a study which differs from the researcher's eventual conceptualization of the issues.

Within this research the initial approach to the organization was made through the Director of Nursing Services who then steered the proposal through other gate keeping bodies such as the hospital ethical committee, the unions and the Medical Director. Whilst this approach was necessitated by the hierarchical structure of the organization it had the obvious drawback of not involving the actual nurses I was hoping to study. In order to try and circumvent some of the difficulties which might arise from this strategy the clinical nurse managers of the individual units were also contacted personally at a slightly later stage and asked to obtain staff reactions to the possibility of such a project. Following this, I contacted the ward and community nurses in person and briefly outlined to them the aims of the project at two meetings which were not attended by their managers. This gave the nurses an opportunity to raise worries or queries without feeling constrained by the immediate presence of their superiors.

Gaining official access was unproblematic, although the necessity for forward planning is indicated by the six month time lag between the initial approaches and formal approval to start the project. Both the nursing management and union representatives were sympathetic to the project as both concurred in seeing psychiatric nursing as a highly stressful occupation. Whilst the initial response of the actual nurses being researched was ostensibly positive the early stages of participant observation revealed that several of them were worried about the type of information which might be fed back to their managers. They were, therefore, rather more equivocal about the project than they revealed to either their managers or to me when the formal access was being negotiated. During the early stages of the research it was therefore necessary to spend time discussing these worries and devising safeguards to ensure that the nurses who were being studied would not feel that the data being collected was a potential weapon against them. The principal strategy adopted was to agree formally with the various levels of nursing management that the nurses would be able to vet any written reports and hear the outline of any verbal presentations before they were submitted to management.

Fortunately, relatively few restrictions were made concerning the type of data which could be gathered. The only serious restriction concerned access to the patients' notes and the ward records which several members of the hospital ethical committee originally objected to on the grounds of confidentiality. This restriction was later lifted in relation to the ward research, unfortunately the research on the community unit was already completed by this stage. Some psychiatrists initially objected to the observation of their ward rounds on similar grounds, however, this restriction was re-negotiated fairly easily during the course of the research. The form which restrictions on data collection take obviously constitute data in their own right as well as being constraints on the research process. In this case the initial restrictions on observing written information have to be contrasted with the complete freedom I was given to observe the daily activities of the ward and community nurses. One implication of this juxtaposition seems to be that institutional power-holders regard written information about patients as rather more sensitive than the actual process of interacting with them.

A final condition of gaining access was to provide the Director of Nursing Services with feedback on the findings of the research. The problems arising from this requirement and the form which the feedback took are discussed in more detail in the latter pages of this chapter.

DESIGN AND TECHNIQUES

Numerous methodological textbooks have suggested that researchers should try to relate the designs and techniques they use in their empirical work to the theoretical concepts and aims of their projects (Denzin, 1978; Hammersley and Atkinson, 1983; Fielding and Fielding, 1986; Reason, 1988). The theoretical chapters of this book argued that previous research into occupational stress has failed to develop adequate analyses of the inter-relationships between individual subjectivity, action and social structure. They then went on to suggest that the critical psychiatry literature can be drawn upon to develop fresh insights into the unfolding of these processes within the psychiatric system. This kind of theoretical analysis necessitated using a research design and methodology which could investigate, firstly, the ways in which macro-level influences are implicit within micro-level encounters, secondly, the ways in which such influences can affect the processes and outcomes of everyday action and thirdly, the ways in which the contradictions and ambiguities in the structure and ideology of psychiatry lead to, and are maintained by, contradictions and fragmentation within people's understanding of their social circumstances. The richness and complexity of these processes seemed to be most likely to be captured by designing an in-depth, descriptive study with the flexibility to provide a holistic and detailed view of the unfolding of the psychiatric process over time, and by using a variety of techniques capable of tapping different aspects of social life. The research was therefore designed as an in-depth comparison of unit or ward level services within both the hospital setting and the community. The actual units studied were an acute admissions ward and a community psychiatric nursing service which was sub-divided into an acute and an elderly team. This overall design was chosen for three main reasons.

A comparative design was used in order to investigate the effects of social context and to determine whether different patient types and organizational settings create different stresses for staff. Previous qualitative research into psychiatric nursing suggests that the activities and treatment ideologies of nursing staff are not uniform and are influenced by organizational context. An American study by Strauss et al. (1964) found that as a professional group, nurses demonstrated few preferences between psycho-therapeutic, somato-therapeutic and socio-therapeutic approaches and were inclined to endorse whatever ideology of psychiatric treatment was dominant amongst their medical colleagues. Within the British context similar findings have been reported within the in-patient setting by Towell (1975), and by Baruch and Treacher (1978) and within the community setting by Sladden (1979), who suggested that community psychiatric nurses may have difficulty defining their work role in the absence of clear medical guidelines.

The ward or unit level was chosen as the primary unit of analysis because it constitutes a relatively self-contained organizational sub-system in both psychological and organizational terms, although the boundaries with the rest of the institution and the wider environment are obviously permeable. The unit level also constitutes a manageable organizational entity for a single investigator engaged in depth research. Whilst this is an essentially pragmatic consideration the problem of resource availability is a key influence on research design and is, perhaps, under-estimated in published discussions of this issue.

The type of unit chosen for study was influenced by current mental health policy and demographic trends. Community nursing was investigated because the policy of successive governments has been to phase out institutions in favour of community care. An increasing proportion of psychiatric nurses will be based in the community as this policy progresses and it therefore seemed relevant to investigate both the problems staff experience through this development and the type of treatment offered within this setting. The community nursing of psycho-geriatric, as well as younger patients, was investigated because demographic trends suggest that the proportion of elderly within the population will increase throughout this century and that the need for psychiatric provision for them will also grow. The problems of nursing psychogeriatric patients and the utility of community provisions for this group are therefore likely to become increasingly salient policy issues.

The study employed a variety of quantitative and qualitative techniques which were chosen firstly, because they enabled different facets of the research problem to be investigated in a theoretically meaningful way and secondly, because they provided corroborative evidence of the validity and reliability of the data. (See Table 5.1 for a description of the strengths and limitations of the various techniques used.) The data was collected systematically and the techniques were replicated across units where possible. In some instances the development and implementation of the various techniques was part of an evolutionary process in which prior data gathering influenced later instrumentation. (See Table 5.2 for a timetable of the research.) For example, the categories within the Activity Schedules were based on prior participant observation of the nurses activities (see Appendix A for sample forms). The six techniques used will now be described in slightly more detail.

Official Statistics

Official hospital statistics were used to obtain data concerning quantifiable information such as the sex ratios of patients and rates of admission and discharge. The statistical data for the admission ward was based on the twelve month period preceding the empirical research. The raw data used gave daily details by sex of numbers of patients admitted and discharged, bed occupancy, patients on home leave and patients detained under section. This data was abstracted from the nightly bed returns for the whole hospital as summarized figures for the various wards were not available. The statistical data for the community unit was based on the monthly unit returns for a period of six months preceding the empirical research. These returns gave details of new and repeat referrals, total caseload, number of visits, and referral source for each team.

Table 5.1
SUMMARY OF AIMS AND TECHNIQUES

Aim	Technique	Strengths	Limitations
To collect data concerning nurses tacit knowledge and daily activities within the organizational setting.	Participant Observation Diaries Ward Kardex Comments	Direct record of activity within organization.	Participant observation is ill-defined data set. All techniques yield highly complex data requiring interpretation by researcher.
To collect data concerning nurses discursive knowledge/feelings about work	Diaries Depth interviews	Direct record of nurses reflexive knowledge concerning work	Interview reports of action not equivalent to direct observation of activities
To collect numerical data on quantifiable aspects of unit structures	Official statistics Activity schedules Kardex (numerical information) Caseload records	Clearly defined data sets allow frequency and distribution of events to be calculated	Does not yield information linking patterns with symbols or meanings underlying behaviour

Table 5.2.
PHASES OF DATA COLLECTION

Techniques	Both	Community Unit				Acute Admissions Ward				
1984	July	Aug	Sept	Oct	Nov	1985 Feb	Mar	Apr	May	June 1986
Informal Participant Observation										
Formal Participant Observation										
Interviews										
Caseload Records/ Ward Notes										
Activity Schedules/ Diaries										
Official Statistics										
Follow-up and Feedback										

62

Documentary Data

The analysis of documentary data concerning patients was undertaken for two main reasons; firstly, to supplement the demographic data obtained through the official hospital statistics and secondly, because compiling written reports about patients is a key activity within the psychiatric setting which has important implications for the way patients are conceptualized and treated. Previous research using documentary data from organizational settings has demonstrated that this type of evidence cannot be regarded as an 'objective' description of the facts (Goffman, 1961; Rees, 1981; Grimshaw and Jefferson, 1987). To the contrary, the types of data recorded and the ways in which they are interpreted by others within the organization have to be conceptualized as socially produced practices which illustrate the various ways in which events are re-interpreted and acted upon in accordance with institutional norms.

Documentary evidence from the patients' hospital records was collected from the ward only, as access to the files of community patients was unavailable. Data was collected on all people having inpatient status on a specified date. The information was obtained from the ward Kardex rather than the patients' files as the latter are generally rather bulky, chaotic documents detailing the patients' complete psychiatric history. In contrast, the Kardex system deals only with the current period of hospitalization and consists of a single flip chart for each patient. This is filled in by the nurses at the end of each shift to provide a running commentry on the patients' condition and care. The nurses treatment aims are also recorded in the ward Kardex through the 'Nursing Process' details. The basic philosophy is that nursing care should be patient-centred rather than task-centred and that nurses should devise individual treatment plans for patients. Within the psychiatric hospitals the technology for achieving this tends to be a simplified version of a behaviourist psychological paradigm (e.g. Mayers, 1972; Carr, Butterworth and Hodges, 1980).

Activity Schedules/Diaries

All nurses on the ward and the community unit were asked to keep Activity Schedules/Diaries for one week. The Activity Schedules/Diaries provided both quantitative data on the amounts of time the nurses spent on various activities and qualitative data concerning their feelings about their work. The quantitative data was recorded using pre-coded numerical categories which were derived from earlier participant observation of the nurses' work and discussions with them. The form was designed to be completed simply and quickly but had an optional comments section consisting of one column for describing situations and a second for expressing feelings, these sections allowed the nurses to supplement the numerical data with verbal descriptions at their own discretion.

On the ward the forms were collected and discussed at the end of each shift which allowed any misunderstandings about coding to be sorted out immediately and comments to be amplified whilst incidents were still fresh in the nurses' memories. A similar procedure was followed in the community unit where the forms were collected at the start of the following morning.

Participant Observation

The technique of participant observation was used extensively because it provides a flexible and sensitive method for directly observing the ways in which people's tacit knowledge and everyday actions are influenced by, and help maintain, the social and organizational structures in which they are situated. The use of this strategy continued throughout the research. During the initial phase of the research it was the only technique used as it was probably the least obtrusive method of getting to know staff. At first, the field notes were written up at the end of each day to avoid discomforting staff. During later stages of the research some items were jotted down overtly and expanded later, although the majority continued to be written up from memory at the end of each session of observation.

Structured Participant Observation

One of the major weaknesses of participant observation is the difficulty of defining the total data base from which the recorded observations are derived. This raises the possibility that the observed data has, consciously or otherwise, been selectively sampled (Fielding and Fielding, 1986). In order to minimize this problem the traditional, unobtrusive methods of participant observation were combined with a more highly structured approach which involved the overt recording of all activities of a specific nurse over a clearly defined period of time. The organization of the structured participant observation differed slightly between the ward and the community settings but basically involved spending complete shifts with a specific nurse and recording that person's activities. The nurses were selected in order to provide a representative cross-section of grades, sexes, weekday and week-end work. Their activities were written up openly throughout the day and the log was shown to them and discussed with them during and at the end of the day. This technique minimized the possibility of selective sampling but inevitably increased the possibility that the nurses would alter their behaviour in response to the act of observation. This drawback was particularly salient in relation to the community psychiatric nurses. On this unit the nurses' interactions with patients were all based on individual therapy sessions and the presence of a third person was inevitably obvious. This meant that it was impossible to simply sit around unobtrusively observing the nurses' behaviour. In order to minimize the disruption to staff and avoid straining their goodwill all observations of nursing interaction with patients on this unit were carried out using the technique of structured participant observation. Luckily these nurses were all used to having students accompanying them on their activities which meant that both they and their patients found the presence of a third person less novel than it might otherwise have been.

Interviews

All nurses who participated in the study were involved in taped interviews about the problems and rewards of their work. The use of depth interviews had two main purposes. Firstly, it provided a means of discussing the nurses' feelings concerning their work in greater detail and secondly, it enabled various working hypotheses derived from other techniques to be fedback to participants and their reactions obtained.

The interviews were based on a written schedule which was used as the guide for a flexible discussion of nursing concerns rather than as a rigidly worded set of questions (see Appendix B). The interviews were carried out in the hospital during work time and lasted between one and two hours. All staff were given at outline of the interview content several days before the interviews started to enable them to think about their work and raise any worries they might have about being interviewed. The option of refusing to be interviewed or taped was made explicit. Although one or two of the nursing assistants and trainees initially expressed some reluctance to being interviewed they consented after being reassured that the data was confidential and getting positive feedback on the interview process from other nurses. By the end of the study all participating nurses had been interviewed, although one nursing assistant asked not to be taped and several others requested that the tape was turned off before imparting some items of confidential information.

FIELD RELATIONS

The empirical data described in this book involved the formation and management of comparatively lengthy relationships with the people I was studying. The qualitative research literature points out that these relationships may be problematic for researchers because of their ambiguous status as both participants within the setting and observers of that setting (Johnson, 1976; Spradley, 1980; Burgess, 1984; Reason, 1988). The converse point, that those being researched also have to cope with the researcher's ambivalent status, is made less frequently. The main issues which the literature raises in discussions of field relations concern problems of identity management, gaining trust and influencing respondents. The ways in which these issues affected field relationships within this study will now be discussed in more detail.

The research literature frequently suggests that the role of 'socially acceptable incompetent' is a valuable one within overt participatory research (Hammersley and Atkinson, 1983). This assertion is based on the argument that such a role best enables the researcher to observe the social setting and ask questions about it without generating undue anxiety in research subjects. This role came fairly naturally during the early stages of the empirical work, as I was not sure of the norms which the nurses would adopt or the ways in which they perceived their work environment. However, during the initial stages of the research I was worried that my previous background as a clinical psychologist within the N.H.S. might either make the nurses feel self-conscious if they assumed I was evaluating their work or lead them to conclude that clinical psychologists as a group were professionally incompetent if they saw me as a socially acceptable incompetent. Neither outcome seemed ideal. The solution which I adopted was firstly, to describe my former career truthfully if people asked about it but otherwise to label myself as a research student, and secondly, to simply ask questions which seemed relevant without worrying about their effects. This strategy worked satisfactorily and the nurses general reaction to finding out that I used to be a clinician was mild surprise that I should abandon this profession for student life.

The second problem which the research literature raises concerns the researcher's marginal status within the social setting being investigated. Two main points are raised: firstly, that the researcher needs to avoid over-identifying with the people being researched in order to analyse their experiences from a different vantage point and secondly, that the experience of being marginal can be highly unsettling for researchers. Speaking personally, neither of these problems arose. Whilst I often felt that I would respond in exactly the same way as the nurses if I was in their situation I seldom identified totally with the nurses' perspective or felt that I wanted to become a full member of the social setting. The relative ease with which I was able to maintain a marginal position was probably facilitated by the fact that hospital staff are used to accommodating 'socially acceptable incompetents' in the form of visiting students from various caring professions. The institutional setting therefore contained analogues of the observer role which meant that the presence of a researcher was less obvious than in some other settings.

Once the initial problems of interaction were overcome most nurses were very forthcoming about the problems they faced but, perhaps inevitably, this trust generated its own problems. There were several occasions when nurses at various levels within the hierarchy revealed things about themselves or others with the proviso that these comments be held in confidence. In some cases the information imparted concerned highly personal details of the effects of work stress on their family lives. In these circumstances it was quite easy to conceptualize the information as a private communication of distress which should not form part of the research data. In other cases however, the information was pertinent to the way the hospital functioned. Whilst it was fairly easy to remain faithful to their requests to treat this information as confidential by not revealing the actual examples they gave the general information inevitably influenced my interpretation of some events I witnessed. More generally, unguarded actions and remarks frequently revealed backstage information which participants may well have preferred not to reveal to outsiders or authority figures. Whilst such information is often crucial in interpreting social life it has to be handled with discretion to avoid causing respondents gratuitous embarrassment or harm.

Another issue which arose during the study was that of influencing the nurses' perceptions of their work. Conventional research wisdom suggests that researchers should avoid influencing respondents on both ethical grounds and to ensure that the research findings are not contaminated by communicating the hypotheses to respondents. This approach may be feasible where the interaction between the respondents and the researcher is limited, however, it becomes more problematic in studies where both parties interact over longer periods of time. The design of this study meant that I spent several months interacting with the same nurses. In many cases the nurses expended a great deal of time and effort in helping me and naturally began to reflect more on their own work and question me about my conclusions. To refuse to answer their questions seemed neither practically feasible in terms of maintaining relationships or ethically justified in view of the nurses large input to the research process. In consequence, I tried to answer their questions as honestly as possible whilst remaining within a conventional 'progressive' view of the psychiatric establishment. Although the influence I exerted was probably slight and was obviously counter-balanced by a variety of other forces it was nevertheless there and was sometimes utilized by the nurses in unpredictable ways. An except from an interview with one of the ward nurses illustrates this problem:

> *Researcher:* "Some people have said that psychiatric hospitals may do more harm than good. How do you feel about this?"
>
> *Nurse (bristling):* "I don't see how anyone can possibly think they do any harm." (Pause) "Why do they think that?"
>
> *Researcher:* "Well (pause) some people think that part of the problem is that if you take people out of their natural environment and put them somewhere that most of the decisions are taken from them they lose the ability to cope - like old people coming in and not being able to practice house-keeping skills they're already forgetting and then losing then even quicker - and sometimes you can't really deal so well with things like family problems if you take the patient out of the situation."
>
> *Nurse:* "Hmmm - I suppose that makes sense - I'll have to go way and think about that."

The nurse did indeed reflect on this issue for she came back to me a few weeks later and told me she had used my viewpoint in a successful interview to obtain a different post and that it had gone down well with the interviewing panel.

The first statement within that excerpt was taken from the interview schedule and was designed to elicit the degree of exposure nurses had to alternative conceptualizations of the institution. The nurse's own question was unexpected and should have been blocked according to the cannons of conventional interviewing. However, it was a genuine request for information and it was obvious to the nurse that I knew the reasons why psychiatry is criticised. To have avoided the question might have strained our relationship and, equally importantly, would have involved deliberately withholding information, which could be construed as a form of influence in its own right. My reply was deliberately couched in terms which were acceptable to the psychiatric establishment and obviously did the nurse no harm at her interview. Nevertheless, this example does illustrate that researchers must take account of this issue and attempt to respond sensitively to situations where they are likely to influence respondents.

FEEDBACK

One of the criteria for entry to the hospital was to supply the staff with feedback concerning the research findings. This created a number of practical, political and ethical dilemmas centring on the relationships between different interest groups and the content and format of the feedback.

A key issue which arose in the presentation of the research findings concerned the competing ends for which different interest groups wanted the data. For example, one of the primary aims of the nurses was to gain research backing for their continual claims for more staff on their particular units. In contrast, Nursing Management, faced with increasing fiscal restraints, hoped for confirmation that staffing levels were adequate. In situations like this the research findings were clearly value-laden and the problem of which interest group to support arose. A number of writers within the fields of action or participatory research have suggested that applied research should explicitly support underpowered groups (Reason and Rowen, 1981; Brown and Tandon, 1983; Borda, 1985.) This recommendation obscures several problems. Firstly, it may be difficult to identify the most underpowered group. For example, in this research it was often difficult to decide whether the nurses or patients were the most victimized group. Secondly, the aspirations of underpowered groups may not always be congruent with the perceptions of the researcher. Thus my own opinion was that the provision of more staff was unlikely to either improve services to patients or decrease staff stress. Finally, deliberately supporting one group may obscure the inter-relationship between various elements within the system and exacerbate entrenched adversorial positions rather than illustrating the manner in which the activities of relatively underpowered and more powerful members of a system inter-lock. In this instance, the solution I adopted was to agree with the nurses that the provision of more staff could enable patient care to be improved, but to add the proviso that simply improving staffing levels was unlikely to lead to this, and then try to substantiate this position with concrete analyses of the problems of structure and functioning within the units studied.

The content and format of the feedback were also influenced by more general considerations concerning the types of information the nurses were likely to find useful, and the time constraints imposed by the exigencies of a three year research grant. Generally speaking, the nurses were interested in practically useful analyses of their current working environment rather than conceptual analyses of the psychiatric sector. They also wanted feedback which evaluated them positively and made constructive and easily implementable suggestions for change. This created two problems. Firstly, there was a danger that by simply enumerating the practical problems recounted by staff the feedback would reproduce and reinforce the nurses' existing conceptualizations rather than generating new insights. Secondly, there was the problem of balancing the need to be constructive against the danger of offering the sort of facile solution which might generate a burst of short-term enthusiasm followed by later disillusionment as unacknowledged constraints negated the effects envisaged. The solution which I eventually adopted was to provide some written reports and also to hold several feedback workshops in which I tried to introduce some of the theoretical concepts within grounded analyses of the sort of problems the nurses faced. For example, a statement that several nurses had told me they felt frustrated and disillusioned when their attempts to counsel patients were unsuccessful was elaborated by an analysis which located the reasons for this primarily within the structure of the system rather than individual failings within the nurse or patient. This analysis used concrete examples from ward life to try and show that the implicit message patients received if they were treated through medication, and had all key decisions concerning their stay in hospital taken by doctors, was that they were sick and should abnegate responsibility. In contrast, the explicit message of much of the nurses counselling was that they should take responsibility for themselves. This analysis introduced the idea that both nurses and patients were involved in a system where mixed messages were communicated in a way which was perceived as relevant by the nurses, and which helped them think about both the limits and possibilities for counselling within the current ward situation and the parameters and people they needed to include if they wanted to change the ward structure. This sort of feedback played a part in facilitating minor changes within the organization. To cite one example, the nursing and medical staff on the ward decided to introduce a system in which the patient care plans of the two professions were more closely integrated as a direct result of feedback concerning the negative effects of the previous system in which the two groups formulated totally separate plans. Such changes are obviously minor. Nevertheless, they are still worthwhile, partly because they may help the institution function less coercively, but also because they encourage people to think about their social context and to conceptualize themselves as empowered to change their social circumstances to some degree.

PART II
THE ADMISSION WARD

6 Structure and routine on 'F' ward

INTRODUCTION

This chapter starts by giving some background information about the general research setting and then goes on to give a more detailed description of the ward structure and routine on the acute admissions ward. It is divided into four sections. The first section describes the town and hospital where the research took place. The second section gives some basic information concerning the ward structure and raises some of the key problems of ward organization. The third section provides an overview of ward routines by describing a 'typical' day on the unit. The fourth section complements the qualitative analysis of ward routines by providing some statistical data on the distribution of nursing activities.

THE RESEARCH SETTING

The empirical research described in this study began during the summer of 1984 and continued for approximately two years. It was carried out on an acute admissions ward and a community unit attached to a large psychiatric hospital in the North of England. Like many psychiatric hospitals in Britain the institution was originally built in the Victorian era and was situated on a sprawling site at the edge of town. It served a population of approximately three hundred thousand and had a catchment area which spread across urban and rural districts. Throughout the mid 1980's the hospital's provision of in-patient services was diminishing rapidly, in line with government plans for phasing out large mental hospitals by the end of the decade, and had decreased from over fifteen hundred beds during the early seventies to around eight hundred during the period of study. The main reduction in patient numbers was occurring in the longer stay sections rather than the acute sector. Whilst community services were being expanded to compensate for the run down of hospital-based care such services were still fairly sparse at the time of the study.

The hospital employed the full-time equivalent of just over three hundred qualified nurses and around two hundred unqualified nursing assistants. It also employed nearly a hundred student nurses on short-term contracts. The latter were theoretically 'surplus to requirements' and were officially placed on wards simply to learn, although in practice they constituted an essential element of the labour force without whom the hospital could not function.

The District Health Authority employed around four thousand people in total and was one of the largest employers in the area. Unemployment in the district had always been above the national average and nursing a highly salient career option. The local population tended to be geographically stable and many nurses[†] at the hospital were born in the area and had spent their entire careers working there. This may have facilitated the development of a rather closed community where many institutional practices were unquestioned simply because the staff had no experience of alternatives.

OVERVIEW OF THE ACUTE ADMISSIONS WARD

'F' ward was one of four admissions wards in the hospital studied. It was run by eight permanent day staff plus a fluctuating, but roughly equivalent,

---

[†] The term nurse is used generically and refers to all grades of qualified, unqualified and student nurses unless otherwise specified.

number of trainees. The day staff worked a four and a half day, thirty seven and a half hour week which was split into a 7a.m. to 3p.m. and a 12.30p.m. to 8.30p.m. shift. The nurses moved between shifts which ensured that all nurses worked with each other at some point. There were generally four nurses to a shift during the week and three at weekends. For legal and security purposes there was at least one qualified and one male staff member on each shift. The night shift lasted from 8.25p.m. to 7.05a.m. and the two staff on duty always included one male and one qualified nurse. These staff were not attached permanently to 'F' ward and rotated between the four admission wards according to staffing needs. This arrangement, together with the part-time status of most staff, meant that the night staff were not perceived as an integral part of the nursing team for the ward. In consequence, they were expected to mind patients and ensure their safety rather than to know them or contribute to their treatment.

The ward was situated on the admissions side of the hospital which was separate from, but adjacent to, the long stay side. The implicit symbolism of this spatial division was not lost on either patients or staff and several patients commented to me that they were segregated from the wider society in the same way that the longer stay patients were segregated from them. Similarly, several nurses remarked wryly that the nursing management attempted to control them through the threat of demotion to the back-wards in exactly the same way as they attempted to control recalcitrant patients with the spectre of transfer to the long-stay side.

The ward had thirty beds of which twenty were for females and ten for males. Most beds were in the two female and one male dormitories, although there were some single rooms for patients needing extra supervision. The ward also had a lounge area, dining room and kitchen, wash rooms, a nursing office, and various treatment rooms. There were no secure facilities on the ward but an adjacent ward did contain a locked observation room in which violent patients could be placed in seclusion. This architectural layout meant that the ward formed a relatively self-contained physical living space and, partly in consequence, a fairly self-contained psychological space for patients and, to a lesser degree, staff.

Patients were admitted to the ward by five consultant psychiatrists. The main criterion for admission to a particular ward was the geographical location of the patient's home, rather than the type of problems presented and, as a result, 'F' ward usually contained a wide range of patients with very disparate problems. This often created management problems for the nurses as highly disturbed or violent people were frequently mixed with quite rational individuals. This ensured that the ward routine was often dominated by the need to control the more volatile patients with the result that less disturbed individuals could get overlooked. The atmosphere of the ward was strongly influenced by the mixture of patients in residence and when the ward contained no overtly psychotic or aggressive patients both nurses and patients tended to be more relaxed and to interact on a friendlier basis than if such patients were present.

The number of psychiatrists admitting patients to the ward created various problems for the nurses. Because the psychiatrists all had equal status and were allocated roughly equivalent numbers of beds on the wards they tended to conceptualize their input to the unit in terms of monitoring individual patients rather than providing clear leadership concerning the daily running of the ward. This meant that the nurses were left to make most of the practical decisions concerning everyday ward life, although their freedom to manouevre was severely limited, firstly, by the fact that the psychiatrists' decisions concerning the admission, discharge and treatment of individual patients often had a tremendous influence on the atmosphere of the whole ward and secondly, by the fact that they needed to negotiate any changes in ward routine with all the doctors. The psychiatrists were probably unaware of the full effects of their decisions on ward life as they seldom interacted with the ward as a unit and tended to visit once or twice a week for their ward rounds. During these they generally saw individual patients for about ten minutes each in a sideroom sheltered from the actual ward setting.

An average of thirteen female and seven male patients were admitted to the ward each month. The unit generally had an average of twenty seven people registered as in-patients, of whom nearly a third would be absent on home leave. Patient numbers tended to fluctuate rather more than on the longer stay wards, which made the nurses' workload less predictable. My impression is that both the nurses and the hospital administrators tended to conceptualize patient numbers in terms of the highest figures and thus to over estimate the actual numbers of patients the nurses had to deal with. For example, the nurses frequently claimed that the ward functioned at full capacity virtually all the time and that individualized care was therefore impossible without more staff. Whilst this claim was reasonably accurate if the total number of registered patients was taken as the guide it overlooked the fact that patients frequently returned home for days or weeks before they were finally discharged.

The average length of stay on 'F' ward was six weeks, although the length varied from a few days to several months. Approximately two thirds of the patients were re-admissions and the ward seemed to serve a relatively small population who re-appeared rather regularly over the years. The nurses appeared to have rather ambivalent feelings about this. Whilst their official line was that the frequency of re-admissions illustrated the importance of having psychiatric hospitals for those people unable to cope outside, their 'backstage' conversations with each other often blamed the patients for deliberately maintaining their symptoms in order to manipulate the system. Finally, several of them commented to me privately that the number of re-admissions sometimes made them doubt the efficacy of both chemotherapy and their own nursing skills.

The core treatment regime on the ward was chemotherapy and virtually all patients were given medication which came to symbolize treatment for many of them. Since medication was prescribed by doctors and merely dispensed by nurses the ward became, for many patients, a place where they waited for treatment to occur, rather than an integral part of their treatment programme. The amount of medication prescribed by different psychiatrists varied widely and this often led the nurses to complain to each other, or the more junior doctors, that the more heavily medicated patients were so sedated that they had no idea of their true mental state. Several patients receiving the major tranquillizers of the phenothiazine group suffered severe side-effects such as tardive dyskinesia and other patients on more minor tranquillizers of the benzodiazepine group complained of drowsiness and confusion. These symptoms were often treated through further medication. The nurses tended to administer drugs routinely, without giving much thought to either the symbolic meaning of treating patients with drugs or the physical effects of drugs on the nervous system, and there were many occasions where staff linked the passivity and social ineptness of patients to their mental illnesses or personalities without considering the influence of either the ward environment or their medication on the patients' actions. In consequence, the nurses sometimes adopted rather denigrating attitudes towards patients and occasionally conceptualized themselves as morally superior.

Although the routine of 'F' ward was essentially centred on care and control the younger nurses in particular often had a firm commitment to helping patients and a desire to help them tackle their problems through psychological counselling rather than chemotherapy. Counselling sessions were generally initiated on an ad hoc basis when a nurse had some free time and tended to be unsuccessful for a variety of reasons. This often led to frustration and confusion on the part of both nurses and patients and several nurses seemed to have become increasingly disillusioned over the years and to have withdrawn from patients as much as possible. Given the numerous organizational problems within this ward in particular, and psychiatry in general, the surprising thing is, perhaps, not that some disillusionment had occurred but that many nurses retained a strong wish to help patients and responded very positively to the intermittent reinforcements they received when patients improved.

A TYPICAL DAY

This description draws upon the participant observation fieldnotes to give an overview of ward life on a typical weekday. In doing so the account necessarily emphasizes the more routine aspects of ward activity and underplays the sometimes unpredictable and turbulent course of events on this ward.

7 - 7.30a.m.

The day staff usually arrived on the ward just before seven and took part in a hurried five minute handover from the night staff. This concentrated on difficult patients or new admissions whilst other patients were dismissed rapidly with phrases like "No problems" or "Quiet Night". After this the day staff generally made coffee and went through the ward Kardex in detail discussing any recent developments and commenting on patients more generally.

7.30 - 8a.m.

Meanwhile, the first patients started getting up and drifting into the lounge in their dressing gowns for the first cigarette of the day. The television set generally got switched on by one of the nurses, causing several patients to wince behind the nurse's back. From now on the television usually provided background noise for the day's activities, although few people watched it before the evening and many patients and staff found the continual noise an irritant.

Two nurses would go to the dormitory to raise the rest of the patients, which often precipitated the first minor confrontations of the day, as there were usually a few people who objected to getting up. The staff then helped wash and dress those patients who they felt were incapable of toiletting themselves while the other patients went to the nursing office to obtain the bathroom keys. This restriction was a source of great frustration to many patients who felt that it symbolized their child-like status. For their part, the nurses were constantly aware that patients might use the relative privacy of the bathroom area to try and commit suicide and therefore attempted to monitor the amount of time the patients spent in this vicinity.

8 - 8.30a.m.

The first two staff left the ward for a half-hour meal break. Meanwhile, the majority of the patients started preparing their own breakfast and the two remaining staff either continued rousing patients or supervised people who were unable to get their own food ready.

8.30 - 9.30a.m.

The first staff returned from breakfast and the remaining two departed. The morning medication trolley was then prepared and wheeled into the middle of the lounge where a qualified staff member and at least one other nurse started to dispense the patients' drugs. Each patient would be called to the trolley in turn and watched whilst they took their medication standing by the trolley to ensure compliance. After this, those patients who were considered capable were expected to make their own beds and then go to occupational therapy unless they were being seen by a doctor later that morning. This often precipitated further minor confrontations as many patients resented being forced to participate in activities which they found uninspiring and irrelevant. Generally speaking, between five and eight patients remained on the ward for the rest of the morning.

9.30a.m. - 12noon

There was usually a lull between 9.15 and 9.45 in which the nurses congregated in the office for a second coffee break. After this, the psychiatrists and junior doctors started arriving to see or discuss patients and the most highly qualified staff member was usually tied up in the ward office or doctors' clinics for the rest of the morning. Another qualified nurse or experienced trainee was probably busy with a new admission, administration or general office work, leaving the nursing assistants or more junior trainees to talk to the patients remaining on the ward. These conversations tended to be desultory and trivial and were often difficult for the nurses. An extract from the fieldnotes of one morning's participant observation may help to convey a more detailed impression of the quality of the interaction between patients and lower grade staff:-

11.30a.m. - 12 noon

Mark (Nursing Assistant) goes to check that the dormitories and toilets are empty then returns to the lounge for another half hour. The patients are now returning from occupational therapy and the air becomes thick with smoke. Mark joins a group of four middle-aged women and tries to get them to talk about their morning. The patients respond by complaining about the tedium of occupational therapy and the conversation rapidly grinds to a halt. I join the group and pick up a magazine to avoid getting drawn into the conversation. One of the patients now starts sighing theatrically, holding her hands over her stomach and moaning about the pains shooting through her. Mark ignores her and later comments to me that the patient's psychiatrist has told them to ignore her attention seeking behaviour as innumerable tests have failed to find anything wrong with her. The woman stops complaining after about ten minutes. She now changes tack and starts making various suggestive remarks about Mark's attractive physique and his merits as a boy-friend. Two others join in and Mark becomes steadily more uncomfortable. After a few minutes he gets up and leaves, red faced, and smiling sheepishly. The women remark loudly that the poor lad's embarrassed and chuckle amongst themselves.

(extract from structured participant observation observation fieldnotes for Mark, Nursing Assistant early twenties)

12.-12.30p.m.

The patients' lunch usually arrived from the canteen on a heated trolley around mid-day. Generally speaking, two or three nurses congregated around the trolley and handed the meals out to patients, often accompanying this activity with some semi-ritualized banter centering on the awfulness of hospital food and the importance of recovering in order to escape from it. One or two nurses would then go and sit with the more disturbed patients or the finicky eaters and try and cajole them into eating. The nurses often expressed great satisfaction if a poor eater consumed a reasonably sized meal and seemed to interpret this as a sign that their nursing was effective and the patient recovering.

12.30 - 1.30p.m.

The second medication round took place immediately after lunch. Patients occasionally protested about their drugs, claiming that they had side effects; such remarks were usually countered either by explaining that medication was necessary to cure the patient's illness or by pointing out that only the doctors had the power to alter prescriptions and promising to raise the matter with the doctor provided the patient complied with the prescribed regime during the interim. The legal right of unsectioned patients to refuse medication was never made explicit and few patients were aware of it. Patients who did exercise their legal rights to refuse medication or discharge themselves were generally seen as trouble makers or 'barrack-room lawyers' who might influence other patients and exacerbate the control problems on the ward.

The second shift arrived around 12.30 and the mid-day handover started. This generally lasted about an hour and involved all the incoming staff and one or two of the more senior outgoing staff. The Kardex comments on all patients would be enumerated and the events of the last shift recounted. The focus of these meetings was usually ward centred and control oriented, centring on issues like new admissions or discharges, patients' physical health and ward based behavioural problems. At such times the patients' psychological problems tended to be discussed in relation to ward based issues rather than as problems deserving attention in their own right.

1.30 - 5.00p.m.

The patients returned to occupational therapy around 1.30p.m. and remained there till 3.30p.m. There was generally a quiet period till around

2.00p.m. and staff from both shifts tended to congregate in the office. Their conversations often centred on the patients and, in contrast to the ward oriented handovers, the staff frequently demonstrated an acute insight into the causes of the patients' problems. Unfortunately, these analyses were generally seen as irrelevant to the practical task of running the ward. From 2p.m. onwards doctors started arriving for their ward rounds and the rest of the afternoon tended to repeat the pattern of the morning. Visitors sometimes arrived to see patients during the afternoon and evenings. They were treated politely by staff and any practical queries they raised were answered to the best of the staff's ability, however, following the pattern of physical medicine, no real attempt was made to get to know them or to understand their relationship with the patient.

5.00 - 6.00p.m.

The patients' supper arrived from the canteen around 5.00p.m. and was followed by another medication round.

6.00 - 8.30p.m.

After supper the majority of patients settled down to watch television for the evening or simply sat around smoking heavily. A few visited friends on other wards or went out or home for the evening. The nurses often joined the patients to watch specific programmes but otherwise tended to congregate in the office for most of the evening. The two night staff arrived around 8.15p.m. and a brief handover occurred.

8.30p.m. - 7.00a.m.

The night staff began their shift by making themselves coffee and familiarizing themselves with any new patients. They then counted the patient numbers and checked the dormitory and toilet areas before watching television with patients or retiring to the office. The final medication round occurred around 10.00p.m. and the night staff tried to ensure all patients had gone to bed by midnight. This sometimes precipitated confrontations between staff and patients which were experienced as highly threatening by the nurses because the lower staff ratio at night increased the difficulty of controlling violent patients. Once all the patients were in bed the night staff moved to a desk in the corridor outside the dormitories and remained there until the morning. The cycle then repeated itself as the new day started.

Summary

This description of a typical day on 'F' ward raises several key themes which will be elaborated in later analyses of ward life. The most obvious point to emerge is that the basic pattern of activity on the ward was geared to the routine care of patients' physical needs within a medically oriented treatment regime which placed patients in a passive and dependent role in relation to the staff. The nurses did, however, have a sense of commitment to the patients' general welfare and the younger nurses would often choose to go and sit with patients and try and converse with them. These interactions were often difficult for both patients and nurses, partly because the hospital environment was relatively depriving for patients and they therefore had little to talk about and partly because the general atmosphere of the ward lounge inevitably limited conversation to superficial topics. Not surprisingly, the nurses tended to terminate these conversations after relatively brief periods and to retire to the security of the nursing office and the company of other staff. A more precise breakdown of the amount of time which they spent in different activities will now be provided in the next section.

THE DISTRIBUTION OF NURSING ACTIVITIES

This section provides statistical data on the distribution of nursing activities. The data was obtained from the Activity Schedules/Diaries completed by all nurses on the two day shifts for a period of one week. (Total Nurse Days / Record Forms = 52). The distribution of times spent in various activities is shown in Figure 6.1.

The Activity Schedules show that a third of total nursing time was spent in administrative duties. Whilst the ward did generate a great deal of paper work and the telephone tended to ring almost continuously during the day this activity also seemed to function as a legitimate excuse for avoiding patient contact, as administrative duties were generally carried out in the ward office which was off-limits to patients. The field notes

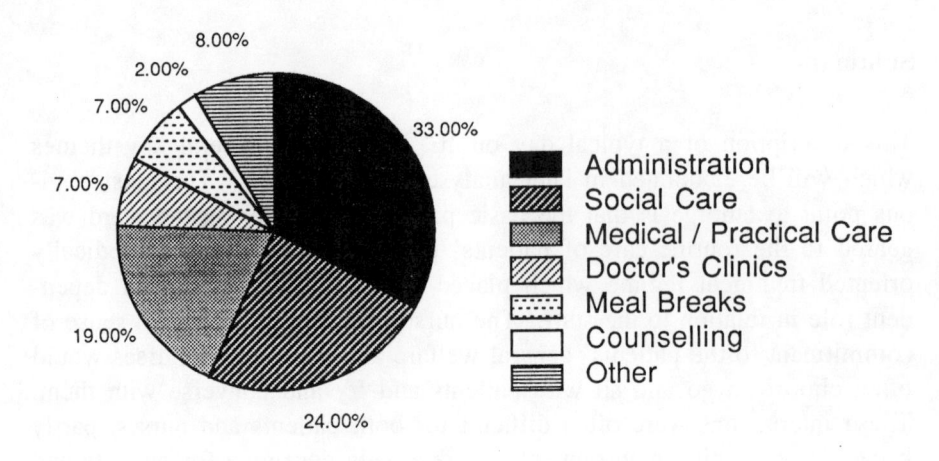

Figure 6.1: Distribution of Time in Nursing Activities.

- Administration: 33.00%
- Social Care: 24.00%
- Medical / Practical Care: 19.00%
- Doctor's Clinics: 7.00%
- Meal Breaks: 7.00%
- Counselling: 2.00%
- Other: 8.00%

indicate that administrative tasks were often carried out in a fairly desultory manner and accompanied by a great deal of chat on both work related and general topics. On many occasions the staff spent long periods reading the patients' notes or formulating elaborate care plans which were seldom operationalized. These activities seemed to give them the feeling that they understood and had responded to the patients' problems whilst enabling them to avoid actual contact with patients. An illustrative example from the fieldnotes for one weekend demonstrates the way in which the psychological and territorial separation of staff and patients was facilitated by the ubiquity of administrative tasks:-

"Saturday - Arrive unexpectedly c. 9.45a.m. and find three staff in the office chatting. Simon (student nurse) is sitting in the lounge with c.8 patients. He joins us after a few minutes. All staff remain in the office till c.11a.m. talking and filling out patients' care plans.

Arrive back after lunch c.2.15p.m. Found all five staff in office. Two doing Kardex. Two looking through a holiday brochure and discussing wedding plans. c.6 patients sitting in lounge. All staff remain in office till 3.00p.m. then two finish their shift. Other staff remain in office chatting and making out care plans till c.3.45p.m. though one nurse goes out several times to check the whereabouts of patients. Two nurses then decide to tidy the medicine cupboard and the third joins the patients in the lounge."

Although approximately half of the total nursing time was spent in direct contact with patients the majority of this time was either taken up with practical tasks such as administering medication and handing out meals or was spent in observing and socializing with patients on the ward lounge. The great majority of the nurses' interactions with patients thus concerned aspects of ward routine whilst the personal or social problems which had precipitated the patients' entry into the hospital system received relatively little attention. The seniority of nursing staff was inversely related to the amount of time they spent with patients and positively related to the time spent with doctors and on administration. This finding reflects a general tendency for patients to be dealt with by the least qualified staff whilst decisions concerning them were taken by more highly qualified staff with less knowledge of them. The consultants tended to rely on senior nursing staff for information about the patients' ward based behaviour and seldom spoke directly to the more junior nursing staff. Although these staff had more contact with patients they were rarely asked to report the content of those interactions to more senior staff and were not usually able to either contribute to treatment decisions or hear the consultants' views regarding patients' problems. In consequence, the consultants' treatment decisions were sometimes based on scant evidence and tended to relate more to the patients' diagnostic categories than to either the personal or social meaning of their problems.

In conclusion, the statistical and descriptive evidence presented in this chapter suggests that 'F' ward was organized according to a medical model in which the main treatment decisions were made by medical consultants with some input from more senior nursing staff. The main form of therapy was medication and the activities of the nurses centred mainly on maintaining ward routine and controlling the activities of the more disruptive patients. The problems and stresses which arose from this form of ward organization will now be looked at in more detail in the next chapter.

7 Life on 'F' ward

INTRODUCTION

This chapter moves from an overview of ward life to a fuller investigation of the ways in which the everyday actions and tacit knowledge of the staff and patients on 'F' ward were influenced by, and helped recreate, the organizational structure and ideology of the unit. The chapter is divided into four sections. The first section starts by illustrating the varying experiences of different grades of nurse through the presentation of the individual Diaries kept by all the nurses on one shift. The second section presents the qualitative data from the ward Kardex and the third section describes the in-patient careers of some of the people on 'F' ward during the study period. The final section summarises the main conceptual themes which can be drawn from the empirical data.

THE NURSES' DIARIES

This section discusses the qualitative data from three individual Diaries. The data is presented for two main reasons. Firstly, the forms help to counterbalance the emphasis on routine within the previous chapter by illustrating the unrelenting pressure of some shifts and the frequent unpredictability of the ward environment, both of which could increase the nurses difficulty in coping with any particular incident. Secondly, if the forms are considered in conjunction they illustrate the varying concerns which different grades of staff may have at the same point in time and thus provide a concrete example of the importance of taking contextuality into account in social science research.

The three Diaries presented here were all completed on the same shift on a week-day afternoon. The three staff on duty were a charge nurse, who was the only qualified member of staff on that shift, a second year female pupil nurse who had nearly completed her training and a part-time female nursing assistant. The afternoon in question was busier than usual, firstly because a male S.E.N. who should have been on duty was off sick and secondly, because two fairly distressed patients were admitted in quick succession. Whilst these circumstances meant that the nurses were rather more pressured than usual similarly hectic shifts were quite common on this ward.

The Charge Nurse

The charge nurse's Diary shows that he operated at the interface between the ward and the outside environment throughout the shift (see Figure 7.1). His main concern was with administrative tasks and servicing the doctors and he spent nearly all the shift within the ward office. His comments regarding his interactions with doctors during their ward rounds suggest that he adopted a deferential stance towards them and attempted to provide them with undivided attention even when their demands irritated him. The organizational problems which the doctors' rounds caused were a recurrent problem on this ward as several consultants had chosen to hold their ward rounds on the same day. Although the nurses experienced this as a recurrent stressor they had failed to raise this matter with the doctors, which pre-empted the possibility of an accommodating response from the consultants.

Brief description	General comments

12.30 - 3 p.m.

Handover till 1.30	Very hectic following a consultants ward round this morning, and me trying to catch up generally after being off for the weekend.
1.30-3.30 Dr. X ward round	Could really do without her ward round at this time as it is one of the busiest periods of the week and she requires your undivided attention at the expense of other activities.

3 - 5 p.m.

Admin and Drs clinics 3 - 3.45 Dr. Y ward round	Problem made much harder by the fact that I am the only member of trained staff on duty and am required to split myself into a dozen different places at same time. Trying to deal with Dr X and Dr Y at same time. Running around like an idiot
4.30 - 5 tea break	First time out of office due to pressure of work. Did I need it!
5 - 5.30 patients' meals given out	

5 - 8.30 p.m.

Continue with general administrative duties	As well as writing up doctors notes in the patients Kardex
5.30 - 6 Medicine round Continue to write up Kardex and arrange appointments got collared into writing up a daily diary 8 - 8.30 handover to night staff	Problem made harder by the fact that I am the only one that can dispense same and a patient missing from the ward. Found at 6.15 - injection to check, only me can check this procedure Trying to relax and watch Coronation St. but telephone just does not stop ringing. Will end up late off duty cos of amount of information to be passed on.
Unable to carry out counselling due to pressure of routine work and staffing levels	

Figure 7.1 The Diary of the Charge Nurse

By his own admission the charge nurse's contact with patients was minimal and centred on the statutory obligation for a trained nurse to dispense medication. Although the nurse remarks that he was unable to spend more time with patients due to staff shortages and routine duties these comments seem to be lipservice to the official treatment ideology of the organization rather than a reflection of his actual job structure or everyday concerns. The impression given by the Diary is that the patients did not really attract this nurse's attention until they became a serious management problem through an action such as absconding from the ward. Although his contact with them was limited the charge nurse was in an administratively powerful role in relation to the patients as he controlled the flow of information from the ward to the doctors and vice-versa. On this shift he was the only staff member whom the doctors spoke to concerning patients and was also the person who crystallized the patients' histories in documentary form by writing the doctors' notes within the ward Kardex.

The type of discrepancy which the dislocation between patient contact and decision making capacity could lead to can be illustrated by an incident which occurred on another shift and was recounted to me by one of the female staff nurses. According to this nurse, the charge nurse was asked about a depressed female patient by one of the psychiatrists and replied that she was still withdrawn and had been sitting in the lounge refusing to speak with anybody all morning. He also entered this comment in the patient's Kardex notes. In consequence, the doctor decided to increase the patient's medication. However, the staff nurse had spent several hours that morning clearing out the kitchen cupboards and had been aided by the patient who was in a much more cheerful frame of mind. Whilst the staff nurse accepted that charge nurse could not lose face by admitting his ignorance to the psychiatrist and also accepted that he simply did not have time to check on all the patients she was annoyed that he had not bothered to solicit her opinion about the patient and felt that this was indicative of the way in which poor communication between staff sometimes interfered with patients' treatment.

The Pupil Nurse

The pupil nurse's Diary (Figure 7.2) indicates that she experienced dissimilar problems to the charge nurse as a result of her different status and duties. In contrast to the charge nurse, the pupil spent most of her day

Brief description	General comments

12.30 - 3 p.m.

Admitted an overactive patient. Lady who had delusions of grandeur- thought she was The Christ re-born. Little insight into her condition.	Tried to remain calm throughout admission, took several attempts to get lady to participate with admission form etc.
Assisted with EEG	Frustrated with this lady as she is really depressed and does not see what we are doing with her in hospital. Does not wish to get better.

3 - 5 p.m.

Admitted another lady, an old patient who I've known in the past. Hypo-manic also suffers from mood swings. Believes in San Yasin (Orange people) Neglecting hygiene, stopped eating. Varying emotions -crying -laughing screaming outbursts	Mad at the thought of admitting this lady again, as only 6 weeks since her discharge. Always admitted after her Bi-sexual boyfriend has found another girlfriend - cannot cope with this. Always plays the sick role. But does have genuine mood swings, but is maintained on Lithium. Since arrival has been kissing walls, lifting clothes on lounge. Counselling her re this but little effect. Given prescribed injection.

5 - 8.30 p.m.

Looking for missing patient -suicidal risk	
Counselling lady about wandering up & down corridor naked.	
Change dressing to wrist area - patient cut own wrist last week.	

Figure 7.2   The Diary of the Pupil Nurse

dealing with patients. She describes six patients, all of whom created problems in some way - two were difficult to admit, a third seemed to want to remain depressed, another wandered around the ward naked, a fifth absconded from the ward in a suicidal state and the last had slashed her wrists the previous week. Faced with the prospect of coping with these behaviours on a daily basis, within a ward environment which meant that her practical concerns centred on care and control, it is, perhaps, not surprising that this pupil was already showing signs of incipient disillusionment and frustration.

The nurse's descriptions of patients illustrate some of the ways in which these feelings could be triggered by the contradictions of the psychiatric system as they become manifest in the everyday interactions between staff and patients. A more detailed examination of the second admission may help clarify the way in which ambiguities surrounding the relationship between mental illness and individual responsibility may trap all participants within the psychiatric system. This patient was an ex-school teacher in her early thirties who had been diagnosed as manic-depressive and was being treated within an organic model involving the long-term administration of lithium salts. The patient definitely exhibited quite severe mood swings and was generally admitted to hospital in either a manic state in which she displayed the sort of disinhibited behaviour described by the nurse, or a very withdrawn state in which she neglected her hygiene and eating and remained mute. Whilst these symptoms may have had an organic basis, the nurse's comments indicate that the patient's behaviour also seemed to be influenced by a number of social factors which were not being dealt with because her problem was officially conceptualized in biological terms. In this instance the main precipitant of a severe mood swing seemed to be a serious row with her boy-friend which had involved him threatening to leave her. The patient's hospitalization had always reconciled the couple and provided them with a needed respite in which to re-negotiate their relationship. However, it also escalated the inherent problems within the relationship by enabling him to justify his behaviour by locating their problems within her madness and enabling her to precipitate an admission whenever she felt the relationship was in danger. The long term effect of this was that the hospital had become involved in their relationship as a third party which simultaneously bound the couple together and made their relationship more unstable by ensuring that both partners could relinquish responsibility for their acts and blame the patient's illness for the problems in their relationship.

Although the patient could, perhaps, have behaved more rationally than a purely organic interpretation of her illness would imply her behaviour was probably not a deliberate dissimulation. What appeared to happen was that the social context which she inhabited facilitated certain forms of behaviour which were irrational by normal standards and which remained incomprehensible to both the patient and staff because they failed to analyse her actions within the social context of psychiatry. The patient seemed to have some inkling of this, although she was unable to express the relationship between action and context very clearly. At a later stage of this period of hospitalization, when she was lucid again, I asked her how she felt about her earlier behaviour. She replied that she was always more aware of her surroundings than the nurses realized and tended to watch herself behaving bizarrely whilst feeling simultaneously that she could, and should, control her behaviour and knowing that she could not, and did not, want to do so. She then became rather inarticulate as she tried to explain the tension she experienced at such times and ended up commenting that when a junior doctor had recently refused to admit her from an outpatient appointment, she was unsure for a split second whether she would find herself creating a scene or accepting his decision. After accepting it she realized that she had calmed down more quickly than if she had been admitted. The patient's description of her actions thus seemed to imply that when crisis situations arose she responded to cues within the immediate context in ways which she had limited control over but which she felt she could have altered if people had responded differently.

The nurse's description of this patient indicates that she too experienced some confusion and frustration about this case. While she was obviously aware of the effect of the patient's personal relationship on her behaviour, she did not seem to consider the effects of the more general psychiatric context beyond claiming that the patient always "plays the psychiatric sick role" to manipulate an admission. This statement then seemed to strike the nurse as too extreme and she immediately qualified it by affirming that the patient had "genuine mood swings" which were stabilized through lithium. The nurse's attempts to explain the patient's behaviour thus oscillated rapidly between an individually oriented psychological model in which the patient took full responsibility for her actions and a medical model in which the patient had no responsibility. The nurse's attempts to control the patient's behaviour revealed similar inconsistencies. She initially tried to quieten the patient through verbal remonstrance but then resorted to a medical model and asked the doctor to prescribe a tranquillizing injection. She later commented to me, rather bitterly, that the patient

> "was never satisfied until she's proved she's ill by making you give her an injection."

The remarks of both the nurse and the patient thus seem to indicate that they both felt trapped into acts they felt uncomfortable with for reasons they were unsure of. The nurse's descriptions of her interactions with other patients illustrate the same problems and indicate that the paradoxes of psychiatry coloured most of her relationships with them.

The Nursing Assistant

In contrast to the charge nurse and the pupil the nursing assistant described few stressors (see Figure 7.3). This may reflect the characteristics of the nursing assistant role but it also reflects a more generalized tendency for the nursing assistants to write less than other groups even when subsequent discussions of the forms indicated that they had quite strong opinions. This was probably due to their lower familiarity with written documents and lack of confidence in their own opinions.

In contrast to the charge nurse and the pupil the nursing assistant carried out a number of domestic tasks. Her other main duty consisted of chatting to patients in the lounge and "generally keeping a watchful eye on all situations". Her comments suggest that she conceptualized her main task as controlling and monitoring patients to ensure that nothing untoward happened on the ward and did not regard it as part of her job to try and find out why patients had problems or how they could be resolved. This orientation was apparent in several other diaries which showed that whilst the nurses were very concerned with preventing self-injurious or violent behaviour they generally conceptualized this task in terms of prevention and control rather than understanding or interpretation. For example, a student nurse wrote:-

> "Watching and talking to patients and checking the ward. At the moment we have quite a few potentially suicidal and violent patients. Therefore a close watch must be kept on the ward and patients e.g. dormitories, toilets and bathroom."

Violent or disruptive behaviour was generally dealt with through verbal admonishments or chemotherapy and, as the Diaries showed, the

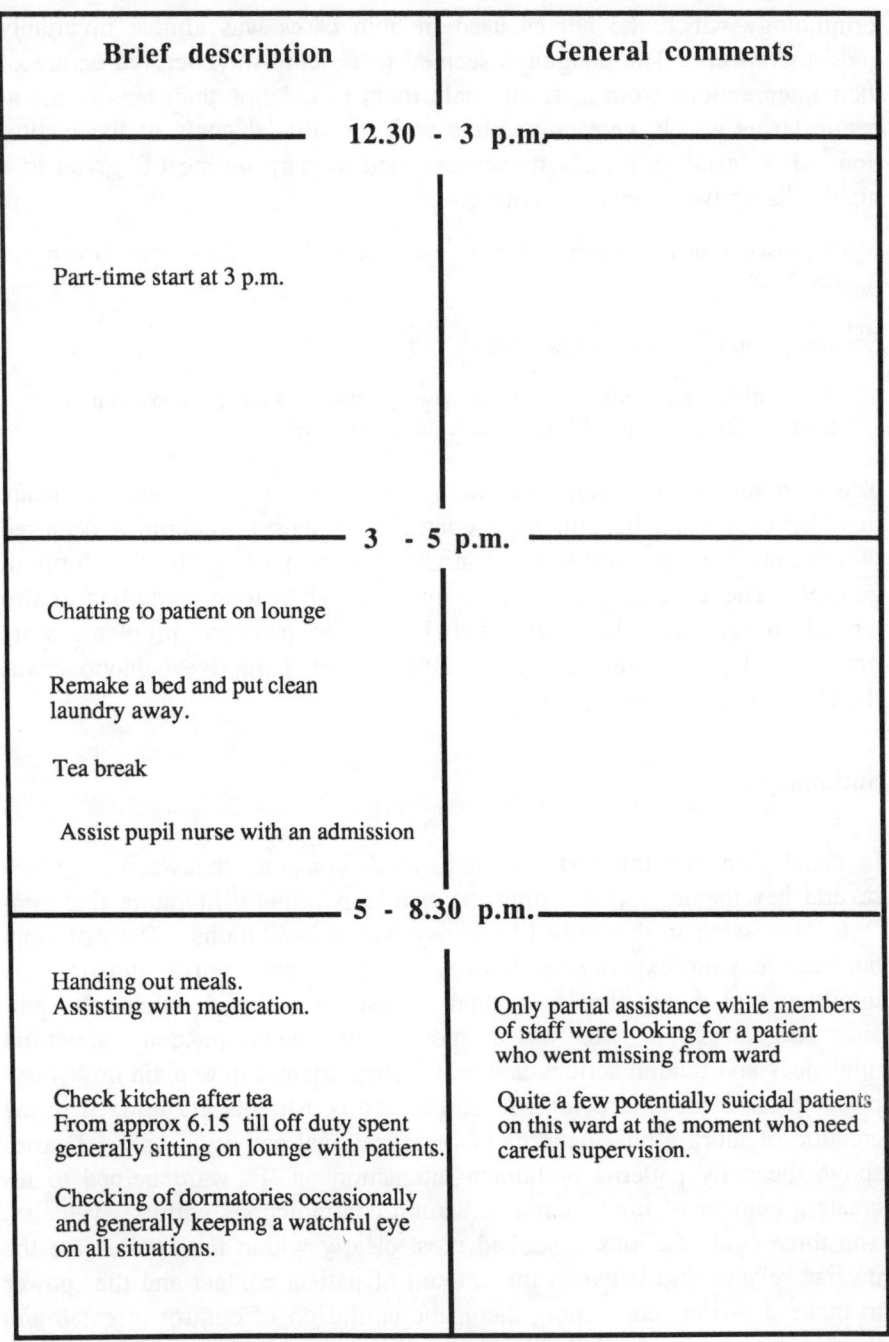

Brief description	General comments
12.30 - 3 p.m.	
Part-time start at 3 p.m.	
3 - 5 p.m.	
Chatting to patient on lounge	
Remake a bed and put clean laundry away.	
Tea break	
Assist pupil nurse with an admission	
5 - 8.30 p.m.	
Handing out meals. Assisting with medication.	Only partial assistance while members of staff were looking for a patient who went missing from ward
Check kitchen after tea From approx 6.15 till off duty spent generally sitting on lounge with patients.	Quite a few potentially suicidal patients on this ward at the moment who need careful supervision.
Checking of dormatories occasionally and generally keeping a watchful eye on all situations.	

Figure 7.3 The Diary of the Nursing Assistant

terminology which the nurses used in both cases was almost invariably quasi-therapeutic. This language seemed to obscure the coercive nature of their interventions from staff and help them to redefine their acts in therapeutic terms which were compatible with the official goals of the institution. For instance, a staff nurse described a sharp telling off given to a highly disruptive patient by writing:-

> "confused patient stripping off in lounge. Counselling difficult due to confused state."

Similarly the charge nurse wrote:-

> "Quiet night apart from one of the new admissions shouting and disturbing other residents. Required PRN medication to relax her."

The high salience of drugs as a therapeutic tool within the hospital meant that the use of medication as a control mechanism sometimes occurred without staff being aware of the highly coercive nature of this form of control. The efficacy of drugs in inducing short-term compliance also tended to reinforce the staff's belief that the patients' problems were organic and that administering drugs to counter disruptive behaviour was therefore therapeutically justified.

Summary

In conclusion, the three Diaries help to demonstrate the ways in which several key themes raised within the critical psychiatry literature find concrete expression in the daily life of psychiatric institutions. The differing, but inter-locking, experiences described by these three nurses illustrate the importance of developing contextually sensitive analyses which conceptualize organizational life as a mosaic of inter-dependent structural influences and human actions and which then attempt to explain how varying combinations of structural resources and constraints are utilized in the creation of more global patterns of organizational activity. As the Diaries show, the daily patterns of human interaction on 'F' ward helped to re-create a number of fundamental structural contradictions within psychiatry. The three contradictions described most clearly within the Diaries are the inverse relationship between the amount of patient contact and the power to make decisions concerning them, the confusion of control oriented and therapeutic activities and finally, the uncertain status of patients' responsibility for their actions. The Diaries suggest that these ambiguities were sometimes exploited by both patients and staff in order to gain various short term advantages. As the succeeding sections will show, such victories often had quite high costs for all concerned in the long-term.

THE WARD KARDEX

This section presents the qualitative data from the ward Kardex. This information complements and corroborates the Diary data by furnishing further written evidence concerning the nurses' daily interactions with patients. It also illustrates the sort of information which became documented as the patients' official histories and reveals the complexity of the relationship between the nurses' daily concerns and the way they presented these activities in official documents. As several other studies of medical records have shown such accounts are social products which have considerable implications for both the organization of medical work and the treatment received by patients. (Goffman, 1961; Dingwall, 1977; Heath, 1981; Rees, 1981).

The ward Kardex contained two types of information. Firstly, the nurses' daily comments on patients. This information was recorded by the nurses at the end of each shift and detailed those aspects of the patients' mental states or activities which the staff regarded as important. Secondly, the 'Nursing Process' plans. The Kardex data discussed in this chapter summarizes all comments on the twenty-five patients who were present on the ward on one particular day in the summer of 1985. Both the nurses' daily comments and the Nursing Process plans were analysed giving a total sample size of over four hundred items. An item was defined as a single entry of any length in the daily Kardex comments or as a complete four part statement of problem, proposed actions, objective and evaluation within the Nursing Process plans. The most striking feature of the Kardex data was the extent of the nurses' preoccupation with routine and control. Over 70% of the entries were concerned with the everyday management of patients' behaviour within the ward context, In contrast, only 1% of comments, or, to be exact, three items contained attempts to conceptualize the patients' problems from their point of view. The following examples typify the routine and control oriented emphasis of the majority of the Kardex entries:-

> "9.30a.m. x suddenly rushed into kitchen and broke a milk bottle. Shouting and screaming she was going to kill herself. Calmed down by staff and been

no problem since."

"Returned to ward (from visit to parents) Verbal outburst aimed at no particular person. Saying to stop talking about her. Counselled that behaviour unacceptable."

"Refusing medication at tea-time repeating is doing her no good etc. Please observe when taking."

In several cases the nurses formulated treatment strategies for problematic ward-based behaviour which seemed reasonably uncoercive and client-centred. However, these strategies were seldom implemented and the older and better established control oriented strategies were generally utilized in practice. For example, one of the treatment goals for an irritable and agitated patient read:-

"*Problem* Agitation. Constantly pacing up and down ward. Only sitting down for short periods at a time. Constantly complaining that T.V. and radio too loud.

Action. Encourage to talk about his problems with staff. When feels particularly agitated and anxious suggest use of relaxation.

Objective. To enable x to relax more and feel more at ease. To cope with his agitation."

The daily Kardex comments for the succeeding week contained the following entries concerning this patient:-

"Agitated this a.m. Pacing up and down ward. (Doctor) contacted - to give 100mg Largactil. Will come to ward to write up prescription sheet".

A second entry read:

"X agitated and angry. Largactil prescribed".

The majority of the comments in the Kardex were similar to those described by Goffman (1961) and suggest that the underlying ethos of psychiatry has changed little in a quarter of a century. As Goffman noted the patient's case-notes and the daily ward records were seldom used:-

"to record occasions when the patient showed the capacity to cope honourably and effectively with difficult life situations. Nor is the case record typically used to provide a rough average or sampling of his past conduct. One of its purposes is to show the ways in which the patient is "sick" and the reasons why it was right to commit him and is right currently to keep him committed ..... The events recorded in this case history are, then, just the the sort that a layman would consider scandalous, defamatory and discrediting. I think it is fair to say that all levels of mental hospital staff fail, in general, to deal with this material with the moral neutrality claimed for medical statements and psychiatric diagnosis, but instead participate in the lay reaction to these acts." (Goffman, 1971, Pelican edition, p.143 and 145.)

Whilst Goffman's account admirably describes many of the incidents recorded in the nursing Kardex his analysis under-emphases the tension between the nurses' pre-occupation with routine and control and their genuine desire to help patients. Several of the Kardex comments showed that the nurses were aware of, and concerned about, the patients' welfare and that where they could take practical steps to help patients by dealing with physical problems such as infections, hearing or visual deficits they generally did so promptly and efficiently. Similarly, the nurses were aware of improvements in the patients' mental state and often recorded these briefly in the Kardex comments with statements like:-

"Mentally very well at the moment. Home for Easter if continues to improve."

Such statements were often remarked upon with satisfaction by other nurses when they were examining the Kardex and were conceptualized as indications that the ward helped people improve.

The complexity of the relationship between the nurses' pre-occupation with control, their desire to help patients and their daily Kardex comments may be illustrated through a more extended analysis of the Kardex comments concerning one patient. This patient was in his early twenties and had been diagnosed schizophrenic. He had been sectioned after relapsing into a depressed and delusional state under the pressures of watching his father dying of terminal cancer and finding out that his girl-friend was pregnant with their child. Whilst the patient wanted the child he was understandably worried about his ability to parent adequately given his low stress tolerance and occasional outbursts of violence.

The patient's psychiatrist had decided to treat his depression with E.C.T. (electroconvulsive therapy) and one of the earlier Kardex entries for this patient read:-

"Attended (hospital) for E.C.T. this a.m. had good reaction. Slow recovery. Complained of headaches when returned to unit. Very reluctant to have any more E.C.T. To be transferred to (hospital) for repeat E.C.T. next Tuesday. If (patient) refuses then a second medical opinion will be required."

Over a two week period approximately a third of the Kardex comments concerned the patient's complaints about E.C.T. and the various legal procedures necessary before treatment could be carried out in view of his consistent refusal to agree to treatment. This issue seems to have been conceptualized as a management problem and there was no indication in either the Kardex or in the nurses' general discussions amongst themselves that his complaints of confusion and memory loss were seen as a legitimate reason for stopping treatment. The nurses' apparent lack of concern seemed to stem partly from the fact that the consultant had given them responsibility for trying to get the patient to comply with treatment voluntarily and partly from a genuine belief that such therapy was harmless. Many nurses seemed unaware of controversies concerning the value of E.C.T. and several nurses told me that modern methods of treatment had no long term side effects and that the short-term effects were amply justified by the lasting improvements in the recipients' mental state. This belief inclined staff to conceptualize the patient's complaints as exaggerations and to minimize their importance.

In contrast to the detailed statements about E.C.T. the nurses' comments about the patient's life outside the hospital were recorded very briefly and mainly to give details of the patient's location. Thus, a series of entries concerning these activities read:-

> "Gone home for day. Returning 8p.m.
> Returned to ward in good spirits.
> Visiting girl-friend today.
> Returned to ward 10p.m. Good humoured on return."

No further details of these visits were recorded by the nursing staff even though both situations were related to the reasons why the patient was admitted. Despite this, the staff were concerned about the patient's future and often speculated amongst themselves about his ability to cope with his father's death or shoulder the responsibilities of parenthood. These concerns were rarely discussed with the patient and were not seen as relevant to the Kardex. To give an example, during a quiet weekend one of the staff nurses became involved in a lengthy discussion with this patient about his worries concerning parenthood. The nurse later commented to me that she enjoyed working weekends because the pressure of routine tasks was diminished and she got more time to talk to patients. She then added that she was surprised by the amount of thought the patient had given to the problems of parenthood and the responsible attitude he was taking. When I asked if she was going to enter details of her conversation in the Kardex she replied:-

"Well no, because it's not as if anything happened is it? Besides everybody would think I was blowing my own trumpet and bragging about how I go round talking to patients."

In conclusion, the daily Kardex comments reflected the nurses' concern with routine and control and tended to emphasise the more discreditable aspects of the patients' behaviour. There seemed to be three main reasons for this. Firstly, psychiatry is geared to seeking out pathology rather than health and the nurses' attention was therefore focussed on problem behaviours rather than creditable actions. Secondly, aberrant behaviour is often both more salient and more informative than socially acceptable behaviour. For instance, if a patient goes berserk and seriously harms someone this may reveal rather more about the need for continued supervision than several days of unaggressive behaviour. Thirdly, the nurses' perceptions of appropriate Kardex entries excluded most data that was not immediately relevant to the daily functioning of the ward. The end result of this was that the daily Kardex comments tended to paint a rather unflattering picture of patients. This data then fed back into the hospital system at two levels. At the individual level the nurses' perceptions of specific patients were often influenced by earlier Kardex comments or documentary information concerning them, whilst at a more general level the type of data recorded in the Kardex influenced the nurses' perceptions of the appropriate areas to attend to and act upon during their daily work.

PATIENTS' HISTORIES

This section presents case studies of four patients to illustrate the ways in which the structure and culture of psychiatry influenced the nurses' actions and feelings towards patients over the course of the patients' psychiatric careers. The material was obtained primarily from participant observation but also draws on the Kardex and interview data. All four patients described created management difficulties for the nurses, but whilst the first two patients were disliked for this and seen as trouble-makers, the last two were secret favourites of several nurses precisely because they were so difficult. The main reason for these differing feelings seemed to be that the nurses conceptualized the first group as rational individuals who were deliberately challenging their authority whereas they conceptualized the other two patients as highly disturbed individuals whose behaviour reflected their mental illness. The nurses therefore tended to regard the first patients as abusers of the psychiatric services whilst the difficult behaviour of the last two individuals was seen as the legitimate province of psychiatry and a challenge to their therapeutic aspirations.

Psychiatry and the Courts: Michael

Michael was a voluntary patient in his early twenties who had entered the hospital about a month before the research on 'F' ward began. He had been referred by the courts as a result of a medical report in which a psychiatrist testified as an 'expert witness' that his repeated offending was caused by a drink problem which was amenable to medical intervention. Thus, although Michael was nominally a voluntary patient he had entered the psychiatric system under duress and his main objective for seeking treatment was to avoid a prison sentence. He showed little desire to alter his behaviour and treated both the staff and the ward rules with contempt, coming and going as he pleased and drinking both on and off the ward. He also encouraged other patients to go drinking with him and to challenge the nurses' authority. This worried the nurses greatly as they feared he would instigate a group rebellion against their authority.

Events came to a head a few days before Michael was discharged. In defiance of hospital regulations he went drinking on the Friday night and stole a car which he then smashed into a lamp-post. As a result, the police became involved with Michael once again, despite his protests that he was a mental patient who should not be blamed for his behaviour. They arrived at the hospital on the Saturday morning to deliver a summons to him. The nurses were quite friendly towards the police and stood chatting to them in the lounge for several minutes while Michael was being persuaded to rise and face them. The contrast between their amicable attitude towards the police and the critical response which Michael had received when his escapades of the previous night became known was observed and resented by several patients with criminal records, one of whom pointed the nurses' behaviour out to me as an example of:-

"What this place is really all about".

As a result of this incident the psychiatrist handling Michael's case warned him that he would be discharged if he drank again. This admonition went unheeded and on the Tuesday lunchtime Michael and another patient staggered drunkenly back to the ward. This behaviour infuriated the nurses who were becoming increasingly worried about his influence on other patients and the possibility that he would become violent towards them or other patients while he was drunk. They therefore contacted the patient's psychiatrist who discharged him immediately, despite the fact that he had nowhere else to sleep that night. That evening an inebriate Michael tried to return to the hospital and was forcibly ejected from the building by several male nurses. He was later picked up by the police who tried to return him to the hospital but who were told that Michael was no longer the hospital's problem. Psychiatric testimony was not used in Michael's next trial and he went to jail for his offences.

Michael's case illustrates the social control function of psychiatry and the close links between the psychiatric and the penal system. His hospitalization resulted from the social order problems he created for society, rather than from his distress or the worries of those closely related to him. In practice, the hospital, like the penal system, offered nothing but custody to Michael although by claiming to offer treatment the psychiatrist was able to present the courts with a seemingly effective alternative to custody and in doing so extend the range of behaviours classified as mental illness rather than purposive deviance.

The psychiatric label also provided Michael with a lever for denying responsibility for his actions and he seemed to regard hospitalization as a soft option to prison. This attitude was not shared by two other sectioned patients who both regretted the imposition of hospital orders rather than prison sentences, perceiving both the stigma of hospitalization and the length of stay as greater. One of them commented:-

> "they treat you like a man in prison. You're responsible for what you've done and you do your time and that's it. But here - you've got to change your whole personality before you can get out."

Not suprizingly, the nurses found Michael an extremely awkward patient and were unanimous in viewing him as 'bad' rather than 'mad'. Although they often expressed the opinion that he should never have been admitted to hospital as their job was to help the mentally ill rather than control criminals, these sentiments seemed to involve the application of psychiatric ideology to legitimate their case against an individual who was seen as a rational challenger of the system rather than a clear understanding of, and general rejection of, the social control function of psychiatry. It was noticeable that another court referred patient of a similar age, who also had drink problems, was well liked precisely because he presented rationally and was willing to listen to the nurses' advice. This man was often refered to as a 'model patient' and the nurses would remark proudly on the progress he had made in hospital. The nurses' resentment of Michael therefore seemed to be a response to his behaviour on the ward rather than his referral from the courts and the real problem seemed to be that he undermined both their authority and their therapeutic aspirations in a manner which they found difficult to combat.

Psychiatry and Fertility: Karen

Karen was a married woman in her late twenties who was admitted to the hospital after she visited her G.P. threatening to commit suicide. The reason for her despair was her husband's recent disappearance with their three children. Karen's case notes did not specify whether he had been granted legal custody of the children or whether he had simply taken them with him when he left her to live with another woman. Whilst the nurses were also unclear on this issue their general opinion was that the loss of her children reflected badly on Karen's capabilities as a mother. Karen was approximately three months pregnant with her fourth child when she was admitted to hospital. During her last pregnancy she had sustained a slight brain haemorrage which left her with nocturnal enuresis, and her consultants therefore decided that the physical risks of this pregnancy made termination and sterilization advisable. This decision appeared to have been taken fairly unilaterally and neither the participant observation data nor Karen's case notes gave any evidence that the staff had explored the implications of this issue with her.

Karen's behaviour on the ward was often difficult and the nursing staff formed a generally negative opinion of her. She smoked continuously, refused to go to occupational therapy or to get up in the mornings, often lay in her bed in her own urine and frequently wandered down to the lounge unwashed and smelling. She also criticised the nurses fairly vociferously and became friendly with other patients whom the nurses regarded as trouble-makers. This led the nurses to withdraw from Karen and deal with her in a fairly cursory manner, as the way in which she was treated on the morning of her abortion clearly illustrates. A student nurse of nineteen years had been detailed to take Karen to the local infirmary for her operation. That morning Karen refused to get up, despite repeated prompting from the nurse and lay in bed saying she was not going to have the operation. This worried the student who feared they would be late arriving at the hospital and she commented to another nurse:-

> "If she shows me up in front of Dr........ by going there dirty and smelly so he thinks we don't do our job properly I'll bloody kill her."

When Karen eventually got up she went to the lounge where she sat chain-smoking and telling everyone who would listen how scared she was of having an abortion. This eventually provoked the student to snap:-

> "Yes, well we haven't got time for melodramatics now so hurry up and get washed, so you look decent when I take you down there."

On her return from hospital Karen went round the ward telling other patients how glad she was to have been sterilized and freed of the worry of pregnancy. The nurses were privately critical of these remarks and saw them as evidence of her unfitness to be a mother. The possibility that these remarks were a defensive cover for rather more ambivalent feelings seemed not to occur to them, although an incident involving Karen and several other patients versus the staff is compatible with this interpretation. The atmosphere on the ward was fairly tense shortly after Karen's operation as a result of an acrimonious dispute between another patient and the nursing staff. This helped precipitate an incident in which the following interchange occurred:-

> *Karen (shouting):* "you lot just sit in the office all day laughing and joking and don't want to hear about our problems."
>
> *Student:* "that's not true we'd rather sit in the lounge talking to you but there are lots of other things we've got to do."
>
> *2nd patient (male sectioned):* "You don't want to tell them anything. It just goes in your file and gets used against you."
>
> *Karen:* "I'm going out with more problems than I came in with for all the help you lot have given me. None of you listened to what it's been like losing my kids or having this abortion."
>
> *Student:* "We can't help listening. You haven't talked about anything else for weeks."

At this point the student retreated to the ward office and commented that she had no intention of going back into the lounge until the atmosphere in there improved. The staff were obviously upset by this incident and several of them commented that when the atmosphere was like this they dreaded coming into work and felt that the ward was not really helping patients.

Karen's case illustrates the way in which the social control of fertility within psychiatry is mediated by staff attitudes which reflect the prevailing social norms concerning motherhood. The nurses' attitudes towards Karen seemed to be based on three key assumptions; firstly, that the loss of her husband and children was indicative of her own shortcomings as a mother; secondly, that her slovenly and awkward behaviour on the ward provided further evidence for this assumption; thirdly, that her expressions of relief at being sterilized also indicated inappropriate attitudes towards motherhood. In consequence, the nurses believed that Karen's termination was both a social advantage for the community and a physical and emotional benefit for Karen.

Karen's treatment also demonstrates the way in which the nurses' preoccupation with routine and control and their neglect of the personal meanings which events may have for patients can lead to counter-control measures by patients. Although Karen was hostile to the nursing staff and seldom volunteered her problems to them her outburst after her abortion suggests that one reason for this may have been that she resented their control oriented attitudes and felt that they should have tried harder to understand her feelings. Her attack upset several of the nurses who felt she was being unreasonable and ungrateful, as from their point of view they had indeed listened to Karen's interminable lounge-based monologues about her pregnancy and abortion, as had everybody else on the ward. Moreover, there seemed to be a mythology amongst the nurses that one of them must have discussed her feelings about termination with her. This conviction is exemplified by a reply which a student nurse gave during her interview to a question asking how she felt about abortion counselling and who had counselled Karen. The nurse replied:-

> "I'm not sure who counselled her - I mean I'm sure she was counselled - oh, we must have - I know she did talk about it a lot - she just sort of talked about it to everybody and when she came back she was just telling everybody how she felt and I know she sort of says "Hurrah" - because she was sterilized at the same time."

This perception obviously made Karen's outburst seem unjustified to the nurses and reinforced their tendency to withdraw from patients or interact with them on a routine or control oriented basis, thus maintaining or escalating the underlying problems in their relationships with them.

Psychiatry and Motherhood: Susan

Susan was in her mid-thirties and had two primary school children. Neither Susan or her husband were particularly bright and Susan had been admitted on several previous occasions when her behaviour became impossible for her husband to cope with. Her basic problem seemed to be a limited ability to deal with the practical problems of everyday life and a tendency to throw vociferous tantrums when things went wrong. This generally resulted in various members of the caring professions rushing to the family's aid, although Susan's immediate behaviour, rather than the problems which had produced it, was generally the focus of attention.

Susan's current admission was precipitated by a screaming fit she threw when her husband asked her to clean the toilet. This panicked her husband who rang their G.P., who in turn called a psychiatrist. The latter admitted Susan under threat of section on the grounds that her behaviour was a danger to her children, However, as the staff admitted privately, the grounds for sectioning her were weak and the threat was made to ensure Susan's compliance with admission rather than as a precursor to actual sectioning.

Susan resented being hospitalized and her behaviour on the ward was initially highly disruptive as the following Kardex entries show:

Entry One "Screaming on top note at regular intervals a.m. Other patients very disturbed by this. No amount of counselling quieted her. Duty Dr. informed and prescribed 10mg. Haloperidol over phone."

Entry Two "Counselled with her husband this p.m. at length. Gave an exhibition of temper tantrums. Told that this was unacceptable behaviour and that if it continues H. will not visit."

The next two entries were similar and entry five, written two days after her admission read:-

"Meeting with Dr..... Throughout interview S. continued to scream - pushing chair in office banging chairs around. Insisted on leaving hospital. Detained under section 5/2 M.H.A. in view of the risk to her children. Same explained to S. Continued to scream and shout."

Susan calmed down somewhat during the next few days, although she continued to cause problems on the ward. Two weeks after her admission her psychiatrist decided that she would respond better to the more structured regime of the behaviour modification ward. Unfortunately, when

Susan had been placed on this ward in the past the programmes had been subverted by her husband who always acceded to her pleas to return home. The staff therefore decided to seek the husband's co-operation before transferring her as the following Kardex entry shows:-

> "Case conference held ... S. is not going to get any better until she is treated away from the home environment and without interference from (husband). Dr...... to discuss with him and try and force him to come to some sort of decision - preferably separation. Children to be left in care of (husband) at present."

One week later the entry read:-

> "Discussed in Dr. ..... clinic.... Awaiting (husband's) decision on the future of the marriage.."

Susan's husband decided not to terminate the marriage and a week later two successive entries read:-

> "Continues to improve."

and

> "Presently on L.O.A. (Leave of Absence). She appears to be functioning v.well and meeting own standards adequately."

Susan was discharged shortly afterwards and returned to her family.

Susan's case illustrates several of the key conceptual themes within this research. Firstly, it demonstrates the way in which the increasing involvement of psychiatric professionals within the sphere of human relationships may escalate the presenting problems and enable an increasing range of behaviours to be identified as pathological. The quarrel between Susan and her husband was similar to numerous other domestic disputes which the couple had sorted out between them and his decision to contact their G.P. seemed to have been a fairly arbitrary choice from a range of potential responses. However, the professionals involved appear to have felt an obligation to respond to the situation as a crisis and to assume control by removing Susan. This move destabilized the situation even further and probably contributed to the future involvement of the hospital within the couple's domestic disputes by reinforcing the husband's course of action. Within a less professionalized society the relationship between Susan and her immediate family might have been stabilized through fairly constant low-key supervision by members of the extended family or community. Such individuals would have had a vested interest in defusing quarrels in order to maintain the integrity of the community. In contrast, psychiatry has an explicit mandate to deal with pathology and the training of staff may therefore result in a heightened propensity to perceive abnormality within everyday situations.

Secondly, this case illustrates the ways in which the concern of psychiatric professionals with both social control within society and control within the hospital can lead to a narrowing of vision which may again worsen the presenting problems. One of the main reasons why Susan was admitted under threat of section and subsequently sectioned was the danger she presented to her children. This thread was defined in terms of psychological rather than physical risk and the evidence for it was conjectural. Although neither Susan or her husband were stereotypically perfect parents there was no evidence that the children were physically ill-treated or psychologically disturbed by Susan's unorthodox behaviour. They visited her regularly in hospital and presented as friendly, happy, children who seemed fond of their mother and who had their affection reciprocated by her. As one nurse commented immediately after justifying the section on the grounds of potential psychological damage to the children:-

> "They're lovely kids - you wouldn't think they had a mother like Susan or a father like him."

Ironically, the possibility that the children might be psychologically damaged by seeing their mother removed screaming and struggling to hospital, visiting a psychiatric ward, or having a labelled parent simply did not occur to the nurses, as the hospital system was conceptualized as a benign environment.

Susan's treatment within the hospital also demonstrates the way in which the necessity for gaining control of recalcitrant behaviour can come to dominate staff thinking and obscure longer-term issues. Susan's activities caused the nurses numerous control problems which they could seldom resolve either by reasoning with her or ordering her to obey them and the proposed move to the behavioural ward was aimed at gaining greater control of her behaviour by placing her within a more tightly structured environment. Because Susan had previously used her husband in counter-control moves which impeded the smooth attainment of staff goals they were prepared to sanction the break up her marriage in order to prevent this. The potentially disastrous long-term effects of this move on Susan and her family were not considered by the nursing staff as the goal of enforcing compliant, socially acceptable behaviour was genuinely seen as in her best interests.

Although the nurses' responses to Susan were primarily concerned with controlling her behaviour their attitude towards her differed from their attitude towards Michael or Karen. The nurses conceptualized Susan's awkwardness and defiance as similar to the recalcitrance of a difficult child rather than as a serious threat to their authority. They were therefore prepared to be more tolerant of her activities and accepted the difficulties she caused as an inevitable part of psychiatric nursing. They also recognized that, within her limitations, Susan tried to be a good mother. In consequence, they did not censure her for her lack of parenting skills, even though they had reservations about her efficacy in this role. Finally, Susan was a rewarding patient for many nurses because she legitimated their therapeutic aspirations and reinforced their conviction that the hospital system helped patients. There were numerous practical tasks which they could perform to help the family, such as delousing them or fixing Susan's teeth, and these were always carried out promptly and with satisfaction. In addition, Susan usually calmed down after a few days in hospital and reverted to a friendly and cheerful person who got on well with the nursing staff. As one of the staff nurses said in her interview:-

> "I really like Susan because her problems are practical and you can do something about them. In the first instance she's usually presenting with some behavioural disorder and I know it will subside. She's lovely once you know her. She's not of superior intelligence so you can keep things very basic which is nice - and when she's better she knows she's better and she appreciates that you helped her get that way. You have to accept that she'll come back though."

Psychiatry and Self-Destruction: Penelope

Penelope was in her mid-forties, married to a highly qualified engineer and the mother of two teenage daughters. She was physically frail and had the emaciated, shrunken frame, hunched posture and drawn skin of someone suffering a long and debilitating illness. She was registered as physically disabled as a result of the severe long-term effects of a virus infection contracted some years previously. Penelope had been admitted to hospital four months earlier after attempting suicide. She was initially given a course of nine sessions of E.C.T. which had apparently led to a great improvement in her depression, however, her consultant advised against discharge and after some weeks Penelope regressed, becoming very negative and refusing to eat, or to speak intelligibly. Although only four months had elapsed since the start of her hospital career it proved difficult to obtain a clear account of the reasons for Penelope's admission from any of the nurses. Some nurses who had just joined the ward claimed she had been in and out of hospital for years, others offered vague and mechanistic explanations like

> "I don't think there was any reason really. You find that with these psychotic depressions, they just happen." (state enrolled nurse)

The origin of Penelope's depression was, in fact, intelligible in personal terms, as a neighbour of hers explained to me. Shortly before her suicide attempt one of Penelope's closest friends had died of cancer and Penelope had dragged herself to the funeral suffering from a bad dose of influenza which was made worse by her chronic physical debilitation. On her return home from the funeral Penelope had taken the overdose which triggered her admission to hospital.

During the week which culminated in her violent removal to the locked ward under section Penelope was the patient who attracted the most nursing attention. The incomprehensibility of her acts was frequently discussed by them and their behaviour towards her oscillated between coercion, compassion and utter frustration as the following chronology of her last week on 'F' ward illustrates. On the Tuesday lunch-time of that week Penelope ran from the ward, still in her bedroom slippers and was last seen heading towards town. After about half an hour one of the nurses rang Penelope's home and enquired, tactfully, of her eldest daughter, whether Penelope had arrived home. Nearly two hours later a householder near her home rang the hospital to say that she had arrived on his doorstep asking for a drink and transport back to the hospital. The nurses expressed amusement at her cheek and commented that her psychotic behaviour must be an act if she could talk lucidly when she wanted to manipulate people for her own ends. A community nurse was despatched to collect Penelope who eventually had to be dragged, kicking and screaming, back to the hospital.

Early that evening Penelope's husband, David, burst into the ward, furiously angry because his daughter had been upset by the nurse's telephone call. After being placated by the nurses he commented

> "Well I suppose I'd better find her and have it out with her - tell her how much she's upset the children with her latest escapade."

Afterwards David returned to the nursing office, trailed by Penelope who stood silently at the office door. Everyone ignored her and David told the nursing staff that he was going to ask for her to be sectioned to prevent her running off again. The nurses pointed out the illegality of his suggestion and David then remarked that Penelope should be chained to the walls of the local castle as madmen were in the past. The ward sister joked

"Well it would solve the problem wouldn't it?"

At this Penelope, unnoticed, shook her head mutely, turned and walked downstairs.

The following day was fairly quiet on the ward and one of the State enrolled nurses decided to devote nearly the whole day to Penelope. Penelope responded well to the individual attention and talked fairly lucidly to the nurse, who was delighted with her progress and sought me out several times during the shift to tell me how well Penelope was behaving. Unfortunately, the nurse left without communicating her actions clearly to the afternoon shift and they decided to adopt the opposite policy of ignoring Penelope's behaviour. She responded by returning to her usual place in the foyer outside the ward and answering the nurses with gibberish.

Penelope was allowed home that weekend on the authority of a senior registrar. She arrived back at the hospital on the Sunday afternoon and her husband reported that she was generally lucid and the weekend quite pleasant until the time came for her to return to the hospital when she started sobbing and pleading not to be brought back. He eventually dragged her back screaming, kicking and clinging onto the hospital railings. Her husband commented that this was highly embarrassing and the nurses commiserated with him whilst Penelope stood silently in her usual place outside the open office door. When her husband left Penelope went and sat in the ward lounge, talked haltingly with the other patients and played timidly with a baby belonging to one of the visitors. None of the nurses spoke to her although the ward was very quiet and Penelope seemed to be making an effort to integrate. After about two hours Penelope lapsed into total silence and then went to stand in her usual place in the foyer which provoked the nurses into commenting critically that she had reverted to her usual, negative, behaviour.

The next morning Penelope announced that she had decided to discharge herself immediately. She then went to the foyer and ordered a taxi to take her home. Meanwhile, Penelope's consultant had arrived to hold his morning clinic and Penelope was pulled back upstairs by two nursing assistants so that she would be ready to see the consultant. At this point her taxi arrived and the staff nurse interrupted the consultant's clinic to ask what to do, pointing out that Penelope had the right to leave as she was an informal patient. According to the nurse, the consultant seemed somewhat irritated by the interruption and, without seeing Penelope, told the nurse to send the taxi away as he would section Penelope at the end of his clinic. He then criticised the nurses for allowing Penelope to go home at the weekend saying that he had not given permission and that they had no right to make assumptions in his absence. This upset several of the nurses who felt that they could not reasonably have been expected to countermand the wishes of both the patient and her husband when the patient had informal status.

Penelope eventually entered the consultant's clinic. According to the state enrolled nurse who was helping at the clinic, Penelope was initially quite lucid and explained to the consultant that she felt much better at home and had therefore decided to discharge herself. The consultant apparently replied:-

> "We're not interested in how you feel at home - it's how you behave here that interests us"

and went on to say that he had decided to transfer Penelope to the behaviour modification ward. At this point Penelope apparently lost control and in the words of the staff nurse:-

> "She went totally berserk - started screaming and trying to hit us. She was going cyanosed - saliva dripping from her mouth."

As a result of this Penelope was transferred from 'F' ward to the seclusion room on another ward where she became noticeably calmer. Later that morning her husband rang the hospital and was told by one of the nurses that Penelope had been sectioned. This earned the nurse a reprimand from the consultant who told her that she had no right to inform Penelope's husband of this before he had seen a doctor. This upset the nurse who felt it was her duty to inform Penelope's husband of these events and that if the consultant disagreed he should have warned her to refer him on to the medical staff. Penelope was removed straight from the seclusion room to the behavioural ward and the staff of 'F' ward ceased to receive any information about her. However, one of her neighbours later told me that her husband eventually became alarmed by her treatment and pressurized the consultant into discharging her immediately her daughter's 'A' levels were over. According to the neighbour Penelope then settled down at home with the help of neighbours and friends who organized themselves into a family support group.

Penelope's history highlights the way in which a hierarchical ward structure geared to routine care and control can result in increasing tensions between patients and staff which are ultimately highly distressing for both parties. Although Penelope was frequently difficult for the nurses to handle she was also the sort of highly disturbed individual who the nurses believed they were especially skilled in helping and her recovery would have been very rewarding for several of them. One of the state enrolled nurses was particularly fond of Penelope and devoted a great deal of attention to her. This nurse had obviously thought deeply about the personal significance of Penelope's behaviour and clearly empathized with her. In her interview the nurse commented:-

> "I think Penelope's been in here too long, I think she's ashamed of being in a psychiatric hospital really, at the bottom of it - I think that's why she's so difficult at times - but I can't see why because that only keeps her in here more in the long run. (Pause). I don't know, I think she's got a lot to sort out."

The nurse's analysis was rather hesitant and she was slightly embarrassed about revealing it, seeming to regard it as a private conceptualization of Penelope's problems rather than something which could be discussed with the patient and other staff, and, perhaps, used to guide nursing responses to Penelope. When I asked her if she had discussed her ideas with Penelope or her colleagues she replied that they were not practical and she did not think anyone would find them very useful. Thus, even though this nurse obviously had clear insights into the meaning of events for Penelope she saw the appropriate nursing response in terms of inculcating socially acceptable behaviour rather than in terms of exploring Penelope's feelings with her.

The ingrained emphasis on routine and control on 'F' ward meant that the nurses often seemed unaware of the effects of their own behaviour on Penelope. There were several instances when conflict situations seemed to develop because the nurses ignored examples of co-operative behaviour and challenged difficult behaviour. To cite a case in point, when Penelope returned to the hospital after her weekend at home none of the staff asked her how it went, relying instead on her husband's interpretation of events.

Her attempts to integrate into the ward situation were similarly ignored, although her later withdrawal to the foyer drew a critical response. My own conversation with Penelope in the foyer indicated that the weekend had not been the success her husband had claimed but had been very disturbing for her and had aroused fears that her family had coalesced into a functioning unit which no longer needed her. She also confessed to being terrified of getting transferred to the behavioural unit and incarcerated in the hospital for the rest of her life. At the same time, she manifest an absolute determination not to acquiesce to the demands of staff, whatever the cost, which perhaps illustrated the extent to which the horizons of her world had shrunk and relatively trivial defiance come to represent her only means of asserting her autonomy within a world she perceived as increasingly uncontrollable.

The nurses' tendency to treat patients as objects was exacerbated by the hierarchical and medicalized decision-making structure of the ward in which consultants with very little contact with either the patients or the daily routines of the ward made far-reaching decisions concerning the treatment of patients. The events surrounding Penelope's violent departure from 'F' ward illustrate this problem and also demonstrate the power which psychiatrists wield over both patients and nurses. Penelope's sectioning caused the nurses ward management problems which extended beyond the individual patient as there were only three nurses on duty that shift and they had to cope not only with Penelope, but also with several other patients whose behaviour became increasingly volatile in response to the crisis. For example, Susan started screaming and banging her head against a wall and had to be placed in her bed by a nurse to prevent her damaging herself. Although the consultant had helped precipitate these problems by his handling of Penelope he remained aloof from them and kept one of the three nurses in his clinic which he continued to run as normal. Under circumstances such as these the nurses had little choice but to try and regain control of the ward by attending to the patients' overt behaviour and ignoring more subtle problems concerning the meaning or long-term implications of their own and the patients' actions.

The three nurses on duty that shift were shaken and upset by Penelope's departure and, although none of them challenged the consultant's behaviour, two of them commented critically on it the next day. The state enrolled nurse noted that the consultant had not bothered to see or reason with Penelope before sectioning her and having her placed in seclusion and added bitterly:-

"Sometimes I wonder if they really care at all. I could have cried when they took her away. I'm still upset - she was doing so well at the weekend."

During the same conversation the staff nurse commented that the medical staff had always told her Penelope's awkwardness was a deliberate behaviour but were now suggesting it had an organic cause and added:-

"I feel dreadful - the number of times I've told her "You know what you're doing" and now it turns out she doesn't and I've been criticising her for something she can't help."

Finally, a male nursing assistant spontaneously discussed her in response to an interview question on the spill-over from work to home life:

"I think you've got to learn to go home and not take their problems with you.... but it just depends what happens .... like Penelope, she really went off and it took four staff to hold her down, and she was punching and kicking us ... and I went home that day wondering how she was and I was upset for her because she'd been put in seclusion ... sometimes she was really nice and like I had a soft spot for her really."

SUMMARY

The aim of this chapter was to examine the ways in which the nurses' tacit knowledge and daily actions contributed to the re-creation of the psychiatric system through a detailed examination of everyday activities on 'F' ward. The empirical data which has just been presented shows that there were close inter-relationships between the ward structure, medically oriented treatment regimes, the social organization of ward life, patient care and nursing stress. This section will now summarize the key themes emerging from the empirical data and discuss the ways in which the nurses' tacit knowledge and daily actions both resolved and maintained the contradictions of the social system on 'F' ward.

The most obvious theme which emerges from the empirical data is that the nurses' tacit concerns centred on social control and on maintaining ward routine by ensuring that patients conformed to staff conceptions of appropriate behaviour. These concerns derived from several key features of the ward structure such as the hierarchical and consultant dominated decision making process, the wide range of patients, the reliance on organic treatment models, the necessity for nurses to fulfill tightly scheduled routines and staff numbers which were often too low for the nurses to cope easily in times of crisis.

However, the nurses were also concerned with helping patients to recover and conceptualized themselves as helpers rather than as agents of social control. The empirical data suggests that these two concerns were frequently incompatible and that the nurses' responsibilities for maintaining ward order often conflicted with strategies which might have helped patients understand, alter or come to terms with, the personal circumstances of their lives. Given the tension between these two concerns the question which arises is how the nurses were able to integrate them within a coherent conceptual scheme. The nurses' conceptualizations of problem patients provide some insights into the ways in which the nurses were able to integrate their concern with control with their self-image as providers of individualized help. In practice, the nurses tended to see problem patients as either 'bad' or 'mad' depending on how they perceived the rationality of their challenges to nursing authority. The first group were regarded as abusers of the system who were not only undeserving of help but who also prevented other patients from receiving the help they deserved by forcing the nurses to spend excessive amounts of time on control oriented activities. This interpretation not only provided the nurses with a rationale for neglecting the treatment needs of other patients but also enabled them to act knowingly towards this group of patients in a control oriented manner whilst retaining their self image as helpers. The second group of difficult patients tended to be conceptualized as lacking control over their behaviour as a result of their illness. This enabled many control activities such as the administration of medication to disturbed patients to be re-interpreted as treatment activities in which caring professionals took responsibility for ordering the lives of incapacitated individuals in ways which those individuals might not appreciate but which were in their best long-term interests. This interpretation neatly integrated the social control and treatment concerns of staff in a manner which maintained the psychiatric ideology of uncoercive care.

The nurses' tendency to rely on either individually oriented organic explanations of patients' behaviour or more diffuse, but equally individualistic, psychological explanations helped them to integrate their dual concern with control and treatment in several other ways. Firstly, the individualistic orientation of their explanatory models meant that their interpretations of patients' behaviour generally located the source of problems within the individual. In consequence, the nurses' attention was directed away from those features of the ward environment, their own activities, or the life circumstances of patients, which might have influenced the actions of patients. The hierarchical nature of the decision making process on the ward strengthened this tendency, both by ensuring that key decisions were usually taken by staff who had relatively little knowledge of patients and who were therefore inclined to adopt mechanistic models, and by enabling the nurses to blame consultants for over-hospitalizing patients whenever they saw that the hospital environment was having a detrimental effect on a patient. The individualistic and organic emphasis of the nurses' explanatory models also enabled them to explain away their tendency to socialize with the more verbal, less disturbed and more compliant patients by arguing that more disturbed patients needed to be treated with chemotherapy. Finally, and paradoxically, the nurses' reliance on individualistic interpretations of patients' problems enabled them to rationalize the fact that they spent very little time actually discussing the personal significance of patients' problems by allowing them to conceptualize this activity as something which could be grafted onto the existing ward structure if only more staff were provided, rather than seeing it as something requiring a more fundamental re-organization of the ward structure and ideology. The nurses' interpretations of patients' behaviours thus enabled them to combine their dominant practical concern of maintaining social control with their equally genuine desire to facilitate the patients' recovery. Unfortunately, their attempts to synthesise their two main concerns often had a number of unintended and deleterious consequences which tended to undermine the equilibrium they sought and increased the instability of the 'dialectic of control' between nurses and patients.

Although the patients' reactions to the contradictions of the system in which they found themselves differed, two main themes were apparent in their actions which in some senses mirrored the nurses' dual concerns with treatment and control. On the one hand, many patients reacted to the nurses' preoccupation with routine and control with confusion and a good deal of resentment and hostility. This was probably increased by the contrast between their initial expectancies of help and the actuality of the ward situation and by the licence which their status as mental patients gave them to act out their feelings. On the other hand, some patients found security in the ward routines and were adept at entering the hospital whenever they wanted to escape from the problems of their home lives. These patients were usually careful not to challenge the nurses' authority openly or to do so only when their obstreperousness was likely to be conceptualized as mental illness rather than awkwardness. Although these individuals often acted as model patients the nurses frequently had a nagging sense of being manipulated by them in ways which they found difficult to challenge. The responses of both groups of patients thus tended to generate feelings of confusion and futility in the nurses, which made them sceptical about the value of their therapeutic endeavours with these particular patients. In consequence, they tended to react towards patients in increasingly routinized and control oriented ways as their period of hospitalization increased. Patients, in their turn, often responded by withdrawing from staff or redoubling their opposition to them. The nurses' attempts to combine control and therapy and the patients' reactions to these attempts thus tended to lock the two groups into a series of interactions with a negative spiral of perverse consequences which were unintended by either party and highly disturbing for them both.

8 Reflection on ward life

INTRODUCTION

The two previous chapters examined the ways in which the nurses' practical understanding and daily actions were not only influenced by the structure and ideology of the ward but also helped to re-create these structures and norms through the everyday patterns of ward life. This chapter now turns to the interview data to clarify the nurses' reflections upon their working environment and daily actions. The main theme of the chapter is that the nurses' partial recognition of the ambiguities and paradoxes of everyday life on 'F' ward engendered feelings of insecurity and self doubt which, paradoxically, both contributed to the re-creation of the existing organizational system and provided a potential impetus for organizational change. The rest of this chapter is divided into three sections: the first section describes the nurses' perceptions of the problems of ward structure; the second section examines their assessments of their therapeutic competence, whilst the final section looks at their emotional relationships with patients.

NURSES' UNDERSTANDING OF WARD STRUCTURE

The two previous chapters argued that many of the problems on 'F' ward were influenced by the hierarchical and medically oriented structure of the ward. This section examines the nurses' perceptions of these issues by describing their responses to interview questions concerning the ward's therapeutic value and the decision making power of doctors. These responses suggest that many nurses had reservations about the ward organization and also reveal a tendency to blame many of the problems of ward functioning on the psychiatrists. All the nurses acknowledged that the ward tended to run on medical lines and emphasised the value of chemotherapy for psychotic and severely depressed patients. However, they all distanced themselves from a total acceptance of the medical model, either by drawing attention to the problems of ward structure and staffing levels which constrained them to act within a medical framework, or by stressing that they also tried to counsel patients about their problems. The ambivalent views which the nurses expressed about the value of the medical model can be seen in the comments of the ward sister:-

> *Ward Sister*: "I think with certain conditions we have to have the medical model. For example, with psychotics or depressives you've got to stabilize them before you can help them - but I don't believe in neurotics having the medical model - I think that's disastrous."
>
> *Researcher:* "Do you think they're tending to get it at the moment?"
>
> *Sister:* "Yes, I mean they do need tranquillizers sometimes - but it's the amount they're put on - if I were a doctor I'd be minimizing that and gearing their lives to a more therapeutic role - the doctors tend to leave patients (they say) "Oh, well she's only just come in I'll see her next week" or "She's improving a bit we'll leave her on that medication" - but that's all that's really done."

The doctors' perceived tendency to overhospitalize patients, or to admit people whom the nurses regarded as unsuitable, was repeatedly emphasised by nurses of all grades. The nurses seemed to conceptualize inappropriate referrals in terms of the challenges they posed to their authority or their therapeutic aspirations rather than simply in terms of the problems they caused on the ward. The majority of nurses saw the mixture of severely and mildly disturbed patients on the ward as an inevitable aspect of psychiatric nursing even whilst they emphasised that the mixture of patients made their workload unpredictable and directed their attention towards the management of severely disturbed patients rather than towards helping less difficult patients. The charge nurse's description of a patient whose admission he resented illustrates the nurses' predilection for complaining about the psychiatrists' naivity concerning their patients' motives.

> *Charge Nurse*: "there are individuals who cotton onto the service and bleed it dry. There was one particular lady - basically there was no real reason for her to be admitted. Since then if she stubs her toe in town she's back on the doorstep requesting re-admission - and she's not that daft that she hasn't learnt a bit of psychiatric behaviour - so she comes up and sees medical staff and starts talking about her voices - well, it's very hard to say whether she is or isn't hallucinating - but prior to her initial admission the type of behaviour that she now displays she never used to display - it's just her way of milking the psychiatric service dry - she comes into hospital for what we would class as the 5,000 mile service - while she's in she'll want her hair doing, her nails done, her eyes tested, she'll go to the dentist - and then all of a sudden the voices will disappear and X herself will say 'Well, I'm ready for going home now'."

The numerous complaints which the interviews revealed concerning the psychiatrists suggested that although the nurses' generally acted within a control oriented and medical model and were highly deferential to medical staff they had some doubts about both the efficacy of chemotherapy and the practical skills of psychiatrists. They generally justified their continuing deference to the medical staff despite these reservations on the grounds that the doctors would resent any challenges to their authority and ignore their suggestions. Whilst there was probably some truth in these observations the nurses' acquiescence also seemed to have more complex motives and to reflect not only a desire to escape responsibility for patients and to have a scapegoat when treatment plans failed but also a somewhat paradoxical awe of the doctors and desire for their approval. This was particularly evident in the comments of younger or less qualified staff. For instance, one of the recently qualified staff nurses commented:-

> "I suppose I do tend to be a bit in awe of the doctors really - I'm afraid of looking stupid if I say anything."
>
> *Researcher*: "How do you think the doctors would react if the nurses did try and put their view as equals?"
>
> *Nurse*: (laughs) "They'd say "it's not your decision - keep your nose out of it", it's not up to us to say what should be done - we can suggest and hope the doctor will take notice."
>
> *Researcher*: "How would you try and persuade a doctor to discharge someone?"

Nurse: "I think we'd say something like "we don't seem to be doing much for this lady any more - we wondered whether you thought she was ready to go" - with some of them we can sort of talk them round to thinking the same way that we do by saying things like that."

In conclusion, whilst the complaints voiced by the nurses on 'F' ward clearly had some basis in the actual conditions on the ward they also seemed to reflect a cultural tendency for nursing staff to use the medical profession as scapegoats for the perceived problems of the institution. As Turner (1987) has pointed out, these discourses form part of a socially acquired 'vocabulary of complaint' which articulates the structural hiatus between the nurses' daily responsibilities for patient care and their lack of decision-making power within the hospital bureaucracy. Such depreciations thus serve the dual functions of invalidating the existing medically oriented hierarchy and excusing the fact that nurses spend the majority of their time in activities which support the bureaucratic functioning of the hospital rather than the welfare of patients. The complementary vocabularies of outward compliance and private complaint which characterize the nursing culture thus serve the complex purpose of legitimating the nurses' public role in the reproduction of a system whose more pernicious aspects they privately resist as incompatible with their self-image as professional carers.

THERAPEUTIC SKILLS AND PERSONAL INSECURITY

The previous chapter argued that whilst the nurses often demonstrated a great deal of expertise in controlling patients and co-ordinating ward routines their therapeutic skills were less well-developed. The interview data revealed that many nurses were keenly aware of their limited therapeutic skills and were disturbed by their tendency to avoid discussing patients' problems because of their feelings of personal inadequacy. Clear grade differences in the nurses' ability to admit the limitations of their knowledge became apparent during the interviews. The student nurses, nursing assistants and the two recently qualified staff nurses were all prepared to discuss the limitations of their training, and their resultant feelings of insecurity, quite openly. In contrast, the charge nurse, sister and an experienced S.E.N. were prepared to acknowledge the limitations of the training programmes but emphasised that their own extensive practical experience meant that they had overcome these problems themselves. Paradoxically, these nurses also emphasised the status differences between qualified staff and nursing assistants and the limited role which nursing assistants could play as a result of their lack of formal training. The actual therapeutic competence and confidence of these staff was, perhaps, more debatable than they admitted, for as several trainees pointed out, the more senior staff tended to talk about their therapeutic knowledge a great deal but rarely exposed these skills to scrutiny and generally avoided any requests by the less qualified staff to observe them counselling patients.

Although the period which the nurses spent in the nurse training school averaged only six weeks a year for R.M.N.s and four weeks a year for S.E.N.s the importance of the school system in the trainees' working lives was considerable, as it was the main structure for imparting both the theoretical knowledge necessary for passing the written examinations and the correct model of action for the practical examinations. The knowledge imparted by the training school therefore tended to be conceptualized by trainees as the 'proper' way of nursing and contrasted with the tacit knowledge imparted by the ward system which was seen as the 'practical' way of doing things.

The official ideology of psychiatric nursing which was promulgated by the nursing tutors contained several contradictions. On the one hand, it advocated the adoption of a permissive and non-judgemental response to patients based on an understanding of their personal and social circumstances. On the other hand, it reinforced the hierarchical, mechanistic and control-oriented structure of ward life by inculcating medical conceptualizations of mental illness. Similarly, whilst the tutors emphasised the importance of psychologically oriented therapeutic skills they seldom provided any skills-based training, expecting the nurses to develop their practical skills within ward situations which they frequently criticised. Since little or no formal training in therapeutic skills was provided on the wards this meant that the student nurses tended to develop their practical skills by observing other trainees or nursing assistants.

The trainees did not appear to be aware of the implicit contradiction between psychotherapeutic and medical approaches, possibly because both were taught in a way which devalued the patients' personal responsibility and knowledgeability and emphasised the professional expertise of staff and the benevolent purposes of the institution. However, most trainees felt that their tutors had failed to equip them with the clinical skills they advocated and several acknowledged that they often tried to avoid discussing the patients' personal problems due to their own feelings of inadequacy. The following quotations from two student nurses illustrate firstly, the ways in which the training school helped to inculcate the dominant model of an organic and control oriented psychiatric system and secondly, the insecurities experienced by trainees who were committed to helping patients.

The first quotation comes from a male second year pupil who seemed to have resolved the dichotomy between ward-based and theoretical knowledge by discounting much that was taught in the school and emphasising only the medical and control-oriented information which was congruent with the ward environment.

> "I think the theory they teach you in school is mainly for passing exams and doesn't really relate to what you do on the ward - but they do teach you some useful things like how to deal with depression .... like they tell you how you need medication to cure it but they also tell you to look for things like razor blades in their pockets or if they're having a bath to check through the window to see if they're alright."
>
> *Researcher*: "Suppose you got someone who was depressed because of marital problems - how would your training teach you to deal with it?"
>
> *Student*: "I think your training would tell you what to do with the depression - like giving drugs and observation - because that's the psychiatric problem - it's not our job to deal with marital problems - people with those sorts of problems should go to marriage guidance."

In contrast, the comments of a female third year R.M.N. revealed a far greater concern about the effects of deficiencies in her training on her ability to relate and help patients.

> "I expected there would be more teaching on the ward - but there isn't any really, it's up to you to pick things up for yourself - I mean we get a fair among of supervision with the tablets and the injections and the Kardex and the paperwork - there's always someone to check that but nobody teaches you how to talk to patients - you just have to try and pick it up by watching the nursing assistants and the other trainees..... at first I used to try and avoid patients because I didn't know what to say - and there are still things which make me uncomfortable - hopefully it will get easier when I've got more experience - because at the moment I sort of tell myself that the reason I don't know what to do is because I'm still a student."

The students may have been able to rationalize their feelings of unease about their perceived lack of skills by conceptualizing the problem as a temporary one which would disappear with time. However, the two newly qualified staff nurses on 'F' ward could no longer use their student status to explain away their feelings of insecurity. This heightened their self doubts even further, as one of the staff nurses explained:-

> "I don't feel I was really trained to do this job. - the thing is they expect you to have all these practical skills but there's no help or guidance given - I used to go home every night worrying if I'd done the right thing because you're still wanting help you know - you're looking for someone to boost your confidence all the time ."

Similar feelings of inadequacy were expressed by a female nursing assistant with several years experience, suggesting that for many nurses' fears of incompetence do not disappear over time. Ironically, the three nursing assistants all identified their lack of formal training as a source of insecurity and expressed a desire to receive more guidance from qualified staff on dealing with patients. As this nursing assistant commented:-

> "People come on here with a lot of problems and I worry am I saying the wrong thing - because if you say the wrong thing you might be making them worse - you've got to know what to say - and I don't really - I mean it's all very well saying talk to a group of patients - but it's what to talk to them about, isn't it?... I think we need more training - if we worked more with the trained staff we could see what they were doing, learn from them .... I mean they've got these skills but we haven't so it's not us who should be telling the patients how to solve their problems."

Although the younger staff and nursing assistants were keenly aware of their lack of therapeutic skills and were eager to improve them their analyses of this issue tended to concentrate on their personal inadequacies and over-simplify the complexity of the structural problems of the ward environment. One consequence of this was that they tended to overestimate the difference which additional training or increased staffing would make to the functioning of the ward. For instance, one of the staff nurses remarked that the counselling course which she was attending in the hospital's psychology department had made her realize that nurses could transform their relationships with patients if only the ward had enough additional staff to guarantee an hour of uninterrupted counselling for each patient every week. This analysis obviously underestimated the effects of the different structural constraints involved in giving a carefully selected outpatient an hour of supervised counselling each week and working with a diverse group of patients within a hierarchical and medically oriented ward structure.

A second consequence of the nurses' failure to understand the full complexity of their social system was that they often reacted defensively when patients rejected them and blamed patients for lacking the motivation to change, without examining the wider context in which the patients' acts took place. For example, one of the staff nurses described a patient she had once tried to help with the words:-

> "These days I find I really dislike X. I feel there's nothing I can offer her. I was quite enthusiastic with her when she first came in - but she's sort of squashed me flat with negative answers everytime I came up with some thing that I felt might be quite good for her.... she knows her problems and she knows the answers - she's just not doing anything about it - she's quite happy to stay as she is really - she prefers to be the sick person, the person with the problems - so these days I try and avoid her because I find it quite frustrating."

In summary, the interview data suggests that the younger nurses and unqualified staff were aware that they often avoided discussing patients' problems because they felt insecure about their therapeutic competence and also that when they did try and counsel patients their attempts often failed. The nurses generally interpreted these failures as a consequence of either their own lack of skills or the patients' lack of motivation and neglected the impact of the structural conditions in which they interacted with patients. In consequence, they frequently became quite bitter and resentful when patients they had singled out for special attention failed to improve and tended to withdraw from these patients in order to protect themselves from further disillusionment. These actions were often subtly encouraged by the more experienced staff, who tended to reinforce the younger nurses' incipient cynicism even while they paid lipservice to the ideal of more individualized care. Whilst this may have been a defensive strategy designed to hide the more experienced staffs' lack of confidence in their own therapeutic skills it also seemed to reflect a genuine desire to help neophytes avoid some of the problems they had faced during their own early days as nurses.

EMOTIONAL RELATIONSHIPS WITH PATIENTS

The previous chapter demonstrated that the nurses often experienced a variety of quite strong emotional reactions to patients, even though they sometimes tended to act towards them in a manner which reduced them to the status of objects of routinized care. The interview data reveals more of the complexities of the nurses' emotional reactions to patients and illustrates the difficulties which many staff faced as they tried to achieve a workable and stable balance between compassion and detachment. The three key themes which emerged during the interviews were firstly, that nearly all nurses had become involved with, and hurt by, patients during the early stages of their careers; secondly, that the more experienced staff applied strong normative sanctions against nurses who were seen as becoming over-involved, and thirdly, that policies of disengagement were often only partially successful and could generate negative self-evaluations in younger nurses who were aware of, and disturbed by, their increasing cynicism and detachment.

The nurses' comments suggest that they discriminated sharply between having favourite patients and forming close emotional relationships with patients and that they saw the two situations as having different legitimacy. All the nurses admitted either having favourite patients or preferred types of patient and described the reasons for their preferences in terms of personal similarities or feelings of professional efficacy engendered by the patients' positive responses to treatment. Whilst several nurses commented that having favourites was not strictly professional, and stressed the importance of treating all patients equally, most nurses seemed to conceptualize their preferences for particular individuals as important evidence that they still cared about patients as people. Paradoxically, their limited failure to observe an organizational norm centring on the impartial and equal treatment of all patients seemed to be an important way of reinforcing professional ideals concerning individualized and personal care. As the ward sister commented:-

> "I suppose everybody has their favourites if we're honest about it - we wouldn't be human otherwise would we? But I think there's a big difference between having a soft spot for a patient and getting over-involved with them - you have to ensure that it's not obvious and that you treat them according to what they need and not how you feel."

In contrast, all the nurses conceptualized close emotional involvement with patients as something which should be avoided and emphasised the importance of detached concern. The problems of achieving an appropriate balance between compassion and objectivity were particularly salient for younger staff and several of them expressed a reluctance to achieve the degree of detachment shown by the more experienced staff. A female S.E.N. with several years experience, who was seen as an important role model by several younger staff because she still cared deeply about the patients, remarked:-

> "I think you learn by experience - at first you do tend to get too involved and it often doesn't work - and you do get hurt a lot - especially when you're

young - because if you care you try so hard and you think you're doing so well with them and then they let you down and you feel so hurt - and you keep analysing where you might have gone wrong - and sometimes you try everything you can think of and nothing works and you keep wondering why - but I think some people just give up and withdraw completely because they've been hurt so much - I've tried to learn how to care and not get too involved - even if it does mean I still get hurt sometimes."

This attitude contrasted with the more critical attitude towards 'over involvement' which was adopted by the sister and the charge nurse. Ironically, the sister's comments indicated that one way of controlling nurses who seemed to be deviating from socially acceptable norms was to label them as having psychiatric problems themselves:-

"(Over involvements) never been a problem for me - but I've seen it with other nurses and it's usually with patients they identify with - they're probably not aware of that - but that's what happens - it's usually the vulnerable ones with problems of their own who identify with patients - and it's usually the neurotic or manipulative patients they get involved with - and they just suck them dry - if I ever see that happening I usually have a word with them for their own good..."

As a result of repeated disappointments when patients failed to improve and strong normative sanctions against over-involvement or innovation many nurses did withdraw from patients. However, as the comments of several nurses indicated this process had its own costs and could lead to both a negative self-concept and a decreased capacity to relate to key individuals in the nurse's private life. The long term effects which such actions could have on personal relationships and self-esteem were described by a male nurse:-

"After a busy day or when patients have been playing up I tend to go home very tense - and my wife's just had a miscarriage and she's very depressed just now - and it tends to be "Oh God, no, I've heard all this before" - I feel I've just come home from work and it's starting over again as soon as I walk through the door - and the guilt adds to my stress really - because if I've got time for anyone it should be my wife - I know I should sit down and talk it through with her - let her know I care - but the last think you want when you go home is somebody hammering at you again - I do worry about it really - because my first wife was a nurse up here too - and I think a good 70% of our problem was that we turned off from each others problems because of the work up here."

In summary, the younger nurses on 'F' ward faced strong normative pressures against emotional involvement with patients from more experienced staff. Whilst these norms helped to protect the individual nurse from stressful emotional experiences they also helped to maintain pre-existing patterns of interaction between staff and patients and to ensure that the staff remained a cohesive group who defined ward situations in similar terms. This was particularly important to staff security as they frequently felt that the patients' view of ward life undermined their authority and their attempts to help. However, the process of disengagement could also create unintended problems by lowering the nurses' personal feelings of self-worth and professional efficacy.

CONCLUSION

In conclusion, the interview data suggests that the nurses on 'F' ward had a partial realization of the discrepancies between the official ideology of psychiatric nursing and the practical knowledge they used to organize their everyday activities within the ward situation. This knowledge often made them feel uncomfortable and could trigger attempts to alter their daily pattern of work activities. However, as the nurses' insights tended to form a piecemeal and individualized critique of discrete problems of organizational structure, patient characteristics and nursing action, rather than a coherent analysis of the whole range of factors influencing ward life, their attempts to improve the quality of care tended to under-estimate the structural inter-relationships between various problems and to have a highly individualistic orientation. As a result, their attempts to help patients were often unsuccessful, which caused particular stress for those nurses who genuinely cared about patients and sought their main job satisfaction through helping them. One solution to these feelings was to adopt a more instrumental attitude towards work. This attitude tended to be reinforced by the more highly qualified and experienced staff on 'F' ward, who cautioned the more idealistic staff about over-involvement with patients and the impracticality of changing the ward environment. The potential for change which was inherent in the nurses' partial understanding of the problems of their working environment thus became channelled into the maintenance of existing patterns of interaction and facilitated the re-creation of the very system many nurses found dissatisfying and stress-producing.

PART III
COMMUNITY PSYCHIATRIC NURSING

9 Structure and routine on the community unit

INTRODUCTION

Proponents of community care claim that the move into the community is a fundamental ideological and structural advance in psychiatric treatment. In contrast, detractors dismiss it as merely a change in location. The main aim of the next three chapters is to examine the work environment and perceptions of the community psychiatric nurses in the light of these competing claims and highlight the similarities and differences between the ward and community settings.

This chapter is divided into five sections. The first section outlines the differing explanations which advocates and critics advance for the historical development of community services. The second section presents some background details on the development of community services within the research hospital. The third section provides some basic statistical data on the unit and the penultimate section provides a descriptive account of the nurses' daily routines which draws out the qualitative differences in the work of the two community teams. The final section compares the community teams to the ward and highlights the key structural differences in work organization within the different settings.

FUNDAMENTAL CHANGE OR SUPERFICIAL ALTERATION?

The historical reasons for the growth of community care have been examined from three competing perspectives. These are firstly, traditional histories of psychiatry which chart its development in terms of medical achievements; secondly, revisionist histories of the institution which concentrate on the relationship between psychiatry and the state, and thirdly, historical accounts written within the European tradition initiated by Michel Foucault, which emphasise the constitutive power of psychiatry within modern society.

Traditional histories of psychiatry are often written by, and for, the medical and nursing professions (e.g. Mora, 1975; Carr, Butterworth and Hodges, 1980). Such accounts generally adopt an idealized perspective which depicts psychiatry as a purely medical enterprise drawing authority from a scientific knowledge base, humanitarian ideals and proven efficacy in healing the mentally ill. From this perspective the history of psychiatry and the various changes in societal reactions to the mentally ill illustrate incremental advances in knowledge and skill and the gradual fruition of a more enlightened and humanitarian system. These accounts are not necessarily complacent and often make reference to past critics of the system in order to assert that the shortcomings that they describe are being overcome within an improved system. Thus, whilst these accounts often accept that both the past and the present systems are flawed and that psychiatric knowledge is imperfect, the basic aims and functions of psychiatry are accepted as self-evidently beneficial. In consequence, proposed solutions generally advocate increases in resources in order to allow further scientific advances to be made and better services delivered.

Histories of community psychiatric nursing written from within the nursing profession generally echo this theme and claim that the growth of this branch of nursing represents an important development in both service provision and the professional standing of psychiatric nurses (e.g. Hunter, 1974; Sladden, 1979; Carr, Butterworth and Hodges, 1980, Pope, 1985). The basic argument advanced in such accounts is that the growth of community psychiatric nursing originally occurred as a result of three factors:- first, the growing realization of the iatrogenic effects of institutionalization which was documented in the fifties and sixties by writers such as Barton (1959), Goffman (1961) and Wing and Brown (1970); second, the discovery in the fifties of a range of psychoactive drugs which enabled mental illness to be treated outside the institution; third, the 1959 Mental Health Act which emphasised the importance of orienting psychiatric services away from the institution and towards the community. These developments are said to have created a demand for community-based psychiatric nursing. Whilst the early services set up in the fifties and sixties (e.g. May and Moore, 1965; Greene, 1968) revealed their institutional origins and generally involved the follow-up of discharged patients and the administration of depot injections, advances in treatment are claimed to have created an expanded role for community psychiatric nurses as independent professionals administering a range of medical and psychological treatments. This has been reflected in the development of one year post-qualification training courses in community psychiatric nursing and in the increasing separation of their professional identity from that of hospital based psychiatric nurses.

Orthodox accounts of the development of community care have been strongly criticised by opponents of psychiatry (e.g. Scull, 1977; 1985; Baruch and Treacher, 1978; Brown, 1985; Ramon, 1985; Busfield, 1986; Baron, 1987). Whilst these critics have generally concentrated on psychiatry as an institution or on the medical profession their criticisms are equally apposite to conventional justifications for the growth of community psychiatric nursing. The basic argument of these critics is that the conventional histories of psychiatry present it as a self-contained and benevolent system and ignore the relationship between psychiatry and the state, thus obscuring the various ways in which the development of psychiatry was influenced by socio-economic and legislative parameters. This helps to legitimate the psychiatric system by highlighting its scientific and humanitarian role whilst neglecting its more political implications.

In contrast to traditional accounts, revisionist histories emphasize the relationship between the socio-economic structures of modern society and the rise of psychiatry. From this perspective, recent moves into the community were precipitated by the desire of government to reduce welfare costs by running down large institutions and by the ability of the various welfare professions to manipulate policy changes to their own advantage and use them to expand into the community setting. As such, community care represents a change in location rather than a change in practice. Some of the more vociferous critics of psychiatry have tended to suggest that the rhetoric of advancement traditionally associated with putative changes in care is nothing but a smokescreen designed to mislead the general public. For example, Sedgewick (1982) argued that:-

> "What is particularly striking about the long history of psychiatric medicine is its capacity to produce quite different rationalizations for a relatively constant practice."

Such a stance probably underestimates the complexity of the relationship between the accounts which people give of their actions and alternative analyses of these events. Whilst the aims of psychiatric professionals are unlikely to be as selflessly dedicated to the common good as conventional accounts imply, the assumption that such accounts are nothing but cynical cover-ups is equally problematic. As Giddens (1984) has pointed out, the level of understanding which people have of their social context is both incomplete and variable. Given that psychiatric professionals such as community nurses have already had to come to terms with a critique of their work centring on the problems of institutionalization, it may be difficult for them to see beyond this and become fully aware of the various problems surrounding the much vaunted solution of community care. Thus, changes in practice which critics of the system perceive as minor may genuinely seem quite radical to participants within the system.

The third perspective on psychiatry's move into the community is provided by the European tradition which derives from the work of Michel Foucault (Castel, Castel and Lovell, 1982; Miller and Rose, 1986; Turner, 1987). Theorists utilizing this perspective reject the traditional rhetoric of community care as a myth, but also repudiate the argument that the ideology of community is simply a rationalization for either the minimization of welfare expenditure or the extension of the social control apparatus of the state. In contrast to the two previous perspectives, they link the development of community care to changes in the ways in which society conceptualizes itself and to the growth of the idea that many problems result from neither mental illness nor social conditions but from minor and remedial failures of individual subjectivities. They argue that the increasing psychiatrization of society means that the psychiatric sector is now developing an expanded role which stretches beyond the confines of the hospital and increasingly involves the fine-tuning of the psyche in order to achieve the optimal adjustment of the individual to society. This policy is seen as as going beyond traditional concepts of social regulation since it is concerned with the promulgation of positive mental health and regulated subjectivity as a mutually beneficial goal for both the individual and society. However, theorists within this tradition regard this development as an undesirable change which is unlikely to facilitate genuine improvements in people's quality of life.

Although these three perspectives on the development of community care are based on conflicting assumptions it would be counter-productive to dismiss any of them entirely. Whilst it would be unduly naive to assume that mental health professionals are solely concerned with the best interests of their clients it is probably equally misguided to assume that their manifest therapeutic aims are nothing more than a disguise for unadulterated self-interest and oppression, and that any innovations within the system are automatically pernicious. Whilst many of the problems with which psychiatry deals might be more appropriately dealt with by fundamental social change this does not necessarily mean that the limited or inappropriate solutions proposed by the various psychiatric professions signify bad faith or that they cannot help people cope better with life's problems. Nor does it mean that the expansion of the psychiatric system should automatically be rejected on doctrinaire grounds. Similarly, it is probably unreasonable to see the expansion of psychiatry as part of an inevitable power/knowledge spiral which is so inexorable it is almost beyond value judgements or human control. The contemporary psychiatric sector involves a variety of professional groups, settings, techniques and client populations and has a variety of complex and equivocal effects. It does, therefore, seem appropriate to try and develop differentiated analyses of the multiplicity of effects which psychiatric growth may have. In some instances, the expanded community sector may provide genuine help with few hidden drawbacks, whilst in other cases the increasing propensity to define normal behaviours as pathological may have deleterious consequences for people so defined. One of the future tasks of those who analyse the psychiatric system should, perhaps, be to supplement global analyses with more detailed and contextualized accounts of its effects in different settings.

DEVELOPMENT AND STRUCTURE OF THE UNIT

The pattern of development which the community unit in the research hospital underwent was typical of many community services in Britain. The service was started in the early seventies and was initially staffed by ward-based nurses who made follow-up visits to discharged patients in an attempt to reduce the 'revolving door' syndrome by increasing the degree of community support. By the mid-seventies six full-time community posts had been established and the unit was seen as a key area for further expansion. At this time the referral system followed the pattern within the rest of the hospital and patients went from their G.P.s to consultant psychiatrists before being referred on to the community nurses. The psychiatrists then remained nominally in control of the case and decided when patients were ready for discharge. This system changed in the early eighties when the nurses began accepting direct referrals from G.P.s, a development which initially aroused some hostility from the psychiatrists. Whilst their objections were couched in terms of the importance of medical responsibility and expertise for patient welfare the shift in power relationships between G.P.s, psychiatrists and nurses may also have contributed to their unease.

The community nurses had an expansionist philosophy of care and had actively solicited referrals from G.P.s and psychiatrists in order to strengthen their case for increased staffing levels. This strategy had initially been highly successful and had resulted in rapid service expansion. However, when the research started cutbacks in the hospital budget had created a situation where the Director of Nursing Services was becoming increasingly reluctant to finance further expansion and was beginning to question the nurses' working practices and to suggest that they needed to manage their caseloads more efficiently. This created a good deal of antagonism between nursing management and the community nurses. The nurses' feelings seemed to stem not only from a genuine feeling that management did not understand the pressures they worked under, and gave them little support in coping with the increasing referral rate, but also from a sense of outrage that managers who lacked the superior qualifications of the community psychiatric nurse should presume to evaluate their work.

The problems which the nurses encountered in managing the referral rate illustrate the dual role of patients as consumers of psychiatric services and commodities to be processed by that service. The problems also demonstrate the way in which the nurses' genuine desire to help their patients and their other key goal of enhancing their professional power through service expansion often became fused in both their thoughts and acts. Whilst the patients were the manifest consumers of the nurses' services and had generally triggered their referrals by visiting their G.P.s it was the later who decided whether, and to whom, to refer them. This gave the G.P.s a tremendous amount of power within the psychiatric system as they effectively controlled the initial access to patients of all psychiatric professionals. Since the number of patients treated by a professional group tends to be a key criterion for resource allocation, the nurses were understandably reluctant to risk alienating either the G.P.s or the psychiatrists by suggesting they limited the rate of referrals, or by admitting that they were unable to help some patients. As the succeeding chapters reveal in more detail this frequently created various stress producing dilemmas for the nurses as they tried to balance the exegencies of interaction with their patients with the organizational need to please the referral agents.

By the time this research began in the summer of 1984 the community service had grown to fourteen nurses supervised by a clinical nurse manager. All staff were qualified and around half had taken the one year post-qualification course in community psychiatric nursing. In contrast to ward based nurses, who were usually allocated to particular wards by nursing management, the community nurses had all chosen to work within the community setting and had gained their posts in competition with other nurses. These factors may account for the nurses' high level of commitment to the cause of community nursing and for the friction between community nurses and ward based staff. Whilst the contact between the two groups was relatively limited the opinions which both parties expressed about each other were generally negative. The ward based nurses frequently saw the community nurses as arrogant and felt that they conceptualized themselves as a separate and superior group. For their part, the community nurses were often disturbed by the attitudes which ward based nurses displayed towards patients and were resentful of imputations that community nursing was a soft option with office hours and large travel expenses.

At the time of the study the community nurses were divided into an 'acute team' dealing with patients of under sixty-five years and an 'elderly' team dealing with patients of sixty-five and over. The nurses each carried individual caseloads of around thirty-five patients. As on the ward, approximately two thirds of the patients seen by both teams were female. The average age of acute team patients was fifty-five (Range fourteen to sixty-five) and nearly three quarters were diagnosed as suffering from anxiety or depression while the remainder were usually classified as schizophrenics. In contrast, most patients seen by the elderly team were in their seventies or eighties and diagnosed as dementing. The majority of patients seen by the acute team had been receiving treatment for under a year whilst most patients visited by the elderly team had been seen for around two years. As with the ward, a substantial proportion of patients had been re-referred to the community nurses on several occasions and had lengthy histories of involvement with the psychiatric service.

THE DISTRIBUTION OF NURSING ACTIVITIES

This section provides statistical data on the distribution of nursing activities. The data was obtained from the Activity Schedules/Diaries completed by all community nurses throughout the course of one week (Total Nurse Days/Record Forms = 64). The overall distributions of activities are given in Figure 9.1. One of the clearest findings of the Activity Schedules was that the nurses spent a far greater proportion of their time in direct patient contact than ward based nurses of the same grade. In contrast to the ward situation, where the most senior staff performed an essentially administrative role with circumscribed patient contact and lower grade staff carried out the majority of patient care, the community nurses spent approximately 40% of their time with patients. As the interview data will show, the possibility of increased patient contact within a different organizational context was an important motive for moving into the community for many nurses who had become disillusioned with the potential for helping patients within the ward environment.

Although the community nurses spent more time with patients than the ward-based nurses the majority of their time was still taken up with various activities concerned with the maintenance of institutional functioning such as record keeping, meetings and liaison with other professionals. Administrative duties were a pre-occupation of all nurses on the community unit and a recurrent source of stress recorded in their Diaries. In practice, virtually all the administrative work of nurses in both teams involved writing case notes for their own files. Although these files were sometimes looked at by other nurses they were not as crucial a mechanism for transmitting shared meanings or information as the ward notes, and the importance which the nurses attached to writing length casenotes at the end of each visit thus seem disproportionate to the practical value of such notes and to reflect their initial socialization within an organizational culture where record keeping was of paramount significance. As Garfinkel (1967) noted organizational records are often less important as literal accounts of events than as symbols of the fact that the relevant personnel

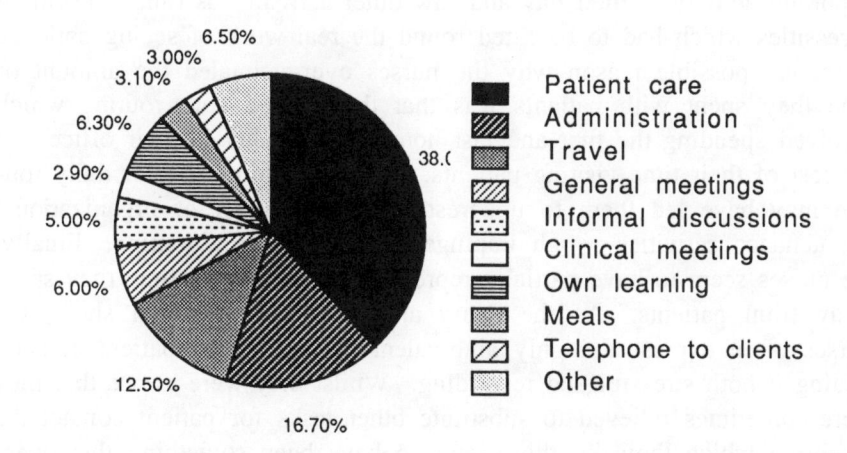

Figure 9.1: Distribution of Nurses Time

Pie chart segments:
- Patient care: 38.0%
- Administration: 16.70%
- Travel: 12.50%
- General meetings: 6.00%
- Informal discussions: 5.00%
- Clinical meetings: 2.90%
- Own learning: 6.30%
- Meals: 3.10%
- Telephone to clients: 3.00%
- Other: 6.50%

have performed their job competently. This aspect of record keeping may have been particularly important to the community nurses as their actual interactions with their patients were invisible to their superiors.

The nurses' concern with filling in their patients' casenotes was counter-balanced by a marked reluctance to provide G.P.s or psychiatrists with written feedback about their patients. This was a source of some irritation to the nurses' immediate superior who had been forced to field a number of complaints about this from doctors. The nurses tended to justify their behaviour in terms of lack of time and the assertion that most doctors preferred verbal feedback, however, the nurses' manager commented to me that she believed that the nurses frequently avoided sending letters because they were unsure of the adequacy of their therapeutic skills and were reluctant to expose themselves to negative evaluations by using the more formal medium of the written word. Ironically, the nurses' frequent failure to provide written feedback to other professionals seemed to have higher salience for their superiors than the casenotes which they meticulously tried to complete at the end of each day.

Many of the nurse seemed genuinely surprized when the results of the Activity Schedules were fed back to them and it became apparent that they had considerably overestimated the total time they spent with their patients. There seemed to be several reasons for this. Firstly, the ideology of nursing conceptualizes the main task of the nurse as direct patient care. As a result, the nurses perceived direct patient contact as the most important activity in their day and saw other activities as time consuming necessities which had to be fitted round the real work of seeing patients. A second possible reason why the nurses over-estimated the amount of time they spent with patients was that they had a core routine which involved spending the first and last hours of their day in their office and the rest of their time visiting patients. This perception of their daily routine may have led them to underestimate the number of organizational maintenance activities which impinged upon their core routine. Finally, the nurses seem to have partially repressed the amount of time they spent away from patients. As the Diary and interview data will show, the nurses often expressed highly ambivalent feelings about patient contact, finding it both stressful and rewarding. Whilst they were aware that they were sometimes relieved to substitute other tasks for patient contact the extent to which they did this seems to have been something they were unwilling to admit it fully even to themselves.

A TYPICAL DAY

This section draws upon the participant observation fieldnotes and Diaries to give an overview of the community nurses' routine on a typical weekday. The basic structure of the acute and elderly teams day was similar and involved a nine till five Monday to Friday week with a half hour lunch break. The crucial difference between the working day of the two groups of nurses appeared to be qualitative and to reside in the extent to which emotional or practical concerns predominated during the nurses' interactions with patients. The patients of nurses in the acute team expressed more emotional distress and expected the nurses to solve their problems rather more than the patients seen by nurses in the elderly team. Concomitantly, the nurses in the acute team seemed to be more affected by their patients' emotional states, to experience a greater sense of responsibility to solve their problems and a greater propensity to feel judged by their patients. In contrast, the patients of nurses in the elderly team made relatively few emotional or practical demands, although they were often pathetically grateful for the nurses' company. In response the nurses seemed surer of their value for patients and more concerned with providing support and practical assistance than with curing the patients' problems. The various demands on these nurses appeared to create less stress for them, even though the situations they had to deal with were sometimes objectively more serious than the problems faced by nurses in the acute team. To cite a fairly typical example, the nurses in the acute team often seemed to become disturbed or agitated by hysterical telephone calls from patients demanding immediate home visits whereas nurses in the elderly team coped with the prospect that their dementing patients might inadvertently start serious fires with relative equanimity. The basic structure of the nurses' working day will now be described in more detail.

9 - 10.30 a.m.

The nurses' working day usually began and ended at the research hospital which was the administrative base for the service. The first hour and a half of their day was generally spent in the communal office on activities such as writing patients' casenotes, arranging appointments, making telephone calls, collecting drug supplies and discussing patients with other nurses. This part of the day served an important social function similar to the lengthy handover periods and office-based conversations on 'F' ward and help develop feelings of group solidarity amongst the nurses.

10 a.m. - 4 p.m.

If there were no meetings the nurses generally spent the main part of their day visiting patients. The great majority of patient contacts took place in the patients' homes, although some of the nurses in the acute team saw a minority of their patients in G.P. surgeries. The nurses in the acute team tended to make appointments to see patients at specific times whereas the nurses in the elderly team generally visited their patients on a less formal basis. This meant that nurses in the acute team sometimes faced greater pressures to maintain a pre-ordained schedule than nurses in the elderly team. The Activity Schedules showed that out of a total of 126 patient contacts scheduled by the acute team nurses during the course of one week eleven proved abortive because the patients were either not at home or failed to attend their appointment. Similar figures were recorded by the elderly team where fourteen visits out of a total of 117 were to patients who were not at home. This caused relatively few emotional or practical problems for nurses in the elderly team who generally went on to other visits and then revisited the patient at a later stage. In contrast, the failure of acute team patients to keep appointments sometimes made the nurses question their own competence and the value of the treatment they were providing, as well as creating a gap in their schedule which it was difficult for them to occupy constructively or pleasantly.

A second scheduling problem faced by all the nurses was that interactions with clients could take longer than envisaged. The reasons for this varied from social demands made by lonely clients, through emotional crises in patients' lives to the practical problems of co-ordinating interactions with other health or social service groups. Once again there were differences between the two teams in the frequency with which different types of problem were raised. Within the acute team the most commonly cited reason for unexpectedly lengthy visits was the emotional state of patients. A typical diary comment was:-

> "Client upset - mixture of marital/sexual probs identified. Lots more time to sort out/reassure client than anticipated. Mixture of satisfaction (at helping) and stress re did not finish till much later than expected."

In contrast, the elderly team usually explained disruptions to their schedule by recounting difficulties in co-ordinating the activities of different professional groups.

The final causes of disruptions to the nurses' planned routines were emergency or unscheduled visits requested by doctors or patients. Once again clear differences between the two teams were apparent in the reasons why such visits occurred. The Activity Schedules showed that eight of the eleven visits classified as emergencies by nurses in the acute team occurred in response to telephone calls from distressed patients whilst the others were in response to requests from G.P.s. In both situations the interaction patterns between the professional and patient sometimes seemed to involve the escalation and dramatization of emotionally fraught situations rather than essential interventions in crisis situations. On several occasions the nurses in the acute team significantly disrupted their routines in order to make immediate visits to patients who had rung them in emotionally distraught states rather than trying to calm them over the telephone or arrange more convenient visits. In contrast, the three emergency visits reported by the elderly team were all initiated by G.P.s in response to marked physical or mental deterioration in the patients. A typical example of these problems was given by a nurse on the elderly team who wrote in her diary:-

> "Emergency visit - G.P. worried about patient's physical state. Spent one and a half hours clearing up chronic diarrhoea. Feel v. concerned re patient's physical state. Report back to G.P. on emergency visit. Arrange hospital admission. Kept late because of telephone calls to/from other agencies involved in case. Satisfaction at sorting problem out but some stress because routine of afternoon disrupted."

4 - 5 p.m.

The nurses generally returned to the hospital around four o'clock and spent the last hour of the day in various administrative tasks. The general mood of the nurses in the two teams often seemed rather different at the end of the day. The nurses in the acute team often appeared tense and rather frenetic and their conversations concerning the various trials, tribulations and triumphs of their day sometimes had a slightly hysterical quality, as though the emotions projected at them by patients were now being re-enacted and released within the office environment. The nurses in the elderly team usually seemed quite calm in comparison and appeared concerned with communicating relatively objective accounts of their patients' problems rather than descriptions of the emotional atmospheres they had faced throughout their day.

This description of the daily routines within the community unit suggests that there were important qualitative differences in the work of the acute and elderly teams which centred on the effects which differing ratios of emotional and practical demands had on the nurses' mental equilibrium. It also suggests that disruptions to their routine could be stressful for the nurses. The reasons for this seemed to involve both pragmatic considerations and more fundamental security needs. At the most obvious level disruptions to their planned routine frequently involved the nurses in extra work or made them unable to meet scheduled commitments. However, such disruptions sometimes seemed to trigger deeper insecurities which were associated with the emotional character of the nurses' interactions with patients and with feelings that they could not control or predict their environment. Although the level of unpredictability within the community nurses' environment was probably less than that of the ward based nurses such disruptions had to be faced by the nurses on an individual rather than a collective basis. In several instances this seemed to increase the nurses' vulnerability to stress by removing the psychological support of shared experiences and responsibilities.

COMPARISON OF THE COMMUNITY UNIT AND 'F' WARD

The preceding descriptions of the structure and daily routines of the community unit suggest that it differed from 'F' ward in several crucial respects. The three most important differences between the two settings centred on variations in the structure of the nurses' relationships with doctors, patients and other nurses. Ironically, the nurses sometimes seemed to compensate for the anxiety which these differences aroused through actions which helped to re-create some of the structural conditions which they had once found so problematic on the wards.

One of the most obvious differences between the ward and the community nurses lay in the structure of their relationships with medical staff. In contrast to ward-based nurses the community nurses carried individual caseloads and were theoretically empowered to accept or discharge patients as and when they deemed appropriate. This was an important source of professional status for the community nurses and they often emphasised that their responsibility for patients was of a greater magnitude than that of ward based nurses when they were negotiating with nursing management. However, in practice the nurses' daily interactions with doctors mirrored the power relationships within the ward setting to a greater extent than either the formal structure of the unit or the nurses' self presentations implied. The nurses rarely, if ever, challenged the doctors' reasons for referring patients and seemed to regard it as axiomatic that patients should enter treatment after being referred. This view appeared to be shared by many medical practitioners who seemed to expect their referrals to be accepted unquestioningly. A similar situation seemed to arise in relation to discharges and the nurses frequently appeared reluctant to discontinue seeing patients before receiving medical sanction for this course of action. The most obvious reason for this behaviour was that the nurses were keen to keep patient numbers high and maintain the goodwill of the medical profession in order to increase the size of the community unit. However, the nurses' former socialization within a hierarchically organized, medically dominated, organizational structure also seemed to influence their behaviour and make them reluctant to challenge medical authority.

This tendency was probably exacerbated by feelings of insecurity which the nurses sometimes seemed to have concerning their own judgements, as such doubts may have inclined them to collude in maintaining a situation in which professional responsibility for patients remained ambiguous. Thus, whilst the nurses claimed the status of independent professionals and were prepared to shoulder the responsibility for the routine management of their caseloads they tended to transfer the responsibility for difficult cases and for the acceptance and discharge of patients back to the medical profession. This situation also benefited the doctors as it enabled them to retain status differentials by claiming that they had ultimate responsibility for patients but freed them from the majority of decisions concerning patients. The actual relationships between the community nurses and the medical profession were therefore rather closer to the patterns which prevailed within the rest of the hospital than the nurses' claims of independent status implied. Thus, although the nurses' increased freedom to manage their own caseloads could, perhaps, have diminished some of the problems of medical power complained of by the ward nurses they still seemed to have problems in defining their authority relationships with the medical profession.

The second major difference between the ward and the community setting centred on the structure of the nurses' relationships with patients. As the previous chapters showed, patient care on 'F' ward was the collective responsibility of a number of nurses, all of whom tended to interact with patients in order to ensure the maintenance of ward routines rather than to understand the personal significance of their problems. In contrast to the ward-based nurses, the community nurses had sole responsibility for the patients on their caseload and generally saw patients on an individual basis in their own homes. The necessity for ensuring the maintenance of order and routine was therefore greatly diminished and the nurses were able to concentrate more on the personal meaning of their patients' problems. The nurses regarded this as a key difference between the two settings and found the increased personal contact with patients an important source of both satisfaction and stress.

Whilst the differences between the two settings should not be underestimated, the wider context of psychiatry created various similarities in nurse/patient relationships within the two settings which did not appear to be recognised by the nurses. This was most obvious in relation to patients whom the nurses conceptualized as having organic disorders such as schizophrenia, as in these cases they tended to perceive their task in routinized and control-oriented terms which involved administering medication, providing long-term support and ensuring that the patients' behaviour conformed to socially acceptable standards. However, as the next chapter will demonstrate, problems of routinization and control often arose in the nurses' interactions with their other patients. Such problems often seemed to occur because the nature of the patients' relationship to psychiatry was regarded as unproblematic by the nurses. As a result, issues relating to the 'treatment barrier' described by Scott (1973) were rarely explored and the full significance of the patients' problems and of their relationship to the nurse often remained unexamined. This could lead to quite long-term relationships characterized by an oscillating 'dialectic of control' in which the patients repeatedly recovered and relapsed, and the nurses recurrently withdrew from, and returned to, the treatment of the same group of patients.

The last key difference between the community and ward nurses lay in the pattern of their relationships with other nurses. Within the ward situation the nurses worked as a hierarchical team with collective responsibility for patient welfare. This facilitated mutual support amongst staff but also had the drawback of sharpening the divisions between staff and patients, encouraging critical staff group interpretations of patients' behaviour and stifling innovation. In contrast, the community nurses operated as individual practitioners and seldom worked with other nurses during periods of direct patient contact. Once again, this structural alteration was a source of both satisfaction and stress for the nurses, for whilst they enjoyed having the freedom to manage their own caseloads they missed the social contact of ward nursing and the opportunities to share the responsibility for difficult patients. Paradoxically, their attempts to deal with this issue sometimes re-created some of the problems and ambiguities concerning responsibility found within the ward situation. One crucial way in which the nurses seemed to compensate for their lack of collegiate contact was by forming closer relationships with patients or keeping preferred patients on their caseloads. Unfortunately, the structure of psychiatry meant that nurse-patient relationships within the community were still implicitly predicated upon the notion that the patient remained in need of expert advice and, as a result of this assumption, quite normal problems of everyday life could inadvertently be pathologized by the nurses and the sort of advice which one friend might give to another was sometimes reconceptualized by both parties as an activity which necessitated specialist psychiatric skills. A second major strategy which the nurses used to counter the insecurities generated by their individual responsibility for patients involved responding rapidly to putative emergencies and arranging for their colleagues to provide cover for difficult cases during their absences. Unfortunately, both these strategies sometimes had the effect of escalating the patients' demands on the psychiatric system and exacerbating the nurses' feelings of insecurity and personal responsibility. These problems will now be described in more detail in the subsequent chapters.

10 Life on the community unit

INTRODUCTION

This chapter moves from an overview of the community unit to a more detailed illustration of the ways in which the everyday actions and practical knowledge of the nurses and patients in this sector were affected by, and helped to recreate, the organizational structure and ideology of the unit. The chapter is divided into three main sections. The first section illustrates the qualitative differences in the work of the two teams by presenting individual diaries kept by staff in each team. The middle section details the case histories of patients seen by each team and analyses the problems these interactions caused staff. The final section summarizes the main conceptual themes suggested by the empirical data and draws out the differences between the work of the two teams and between the work of the community and ward based nurses.

THE NURSES' DIARIES

This section discusses the qualitative data from two of the nurses' Diaries. The data is presented for two main reasons; firstly, to enable the similarities and differences between the two teams of community nurses to be illustrated more clearly and secondly, to highlight the contrasts between the ward and community environments.

The Acute Team

The Diary of the Charge nurse on 'F' ward suggested that within the hospital setting the more highly qualified staff had an essentially office based, administrative role in which patient contact was limited and routinized. In comparison with that Diary the writings of the nurse in the acute team, shown in Figure 10.1, revealed a greater sense of involvement with patients as individuals, and greater feelings of personal responsibility for their treatment. Her Diary also suggests that the distribution of power between nurses and patients was more evenly balanced than within the ward situation and that patients had a greater capacity to influence the nurses by making rational objections to the way in which the system operated. In this case the nurse was clearly disturbed by the negative reaction of some of her patients to the presence of a student nurse and was inclined to regard their objections as legitimate criticisms rather than as evidence of mental illness. The nurse's remarks concerning her trainee's awkwardness with patients also highlight the differences in the style of interaction between patients and community and ward based nurses. Trainees were generally given their community placement in the final stages of their training when they were virtually qualified. Once qualified they usually moved immediately into positions as staff nurses within the hospital and were often amongst the more highly trained staff on the ward. Despite this, the community nurse clearly perceived her student as lacking both the confidence and the experience necessary to talk to patients about their problems.

This nurse's comments concerning the G.P. who telephoned requesting her to contact an emergency referral illustrate the similarities in the way both community nurses and ward based nurses tried to influence doctors. Although this nurse was annoyed with the G.P. both for exaggerating the urgency of the patient's problem and for not informing her of it earlier in the day she felt that it would be inappropriate for her to communicate

Brief description	General comments

─────── 9 a.m. - 12 p.m. ───────

Informal liason with GP. Pick up messages, relay information etc.	
Client with bulimia and anorexia in chaos	Stressful session. Students lack of self confidence/ experience creating barrier to her interaction with clients, little spontaneous conversation.

─────── 12 - 3 p.m. ───────

Client not at home. Telephoned me later, does not wish me to visit with student	
Staff meeting	Mixed feeling impatience/ irritation. Some nit picking. I felt meeting too long, tended to go round in circles. Frustration

─────── 3 - 5 p.m. ───────

Students mid-placement review and feedback session.	
Interrupted by urgent call from GP requesting that I contact new referral as matter of urgency. Same done, problem not as urgent as GP had assumed. Visit arranged for next week.	Annoyed! Had been at surgery A.M. but no message to contact re opposite despite client seeing GP this A.M.

General Comments
End of third week of student attachment, am beginning to feel the strain of having another person alongside for approx. 7 1/2 hours daily X 5 days.
Student interested, but lack of confidence and/or inexperience is proving a barrier to her involvement. Despite encouragement, long silences during some CPN/client interaction is proving anxiety provoking for some clients, & CPN. Some clients refusing joint visits. Some clients reluctant - but tolerant. Some ringing to see how long before I can visit alone, all adding to stress.

Figure 10.1 The Diary from the Community Unit AcuteTeam

her opinions to him directly as she might antagonize him if she did so. The strategy which she adopted to deal with this situation was simply to ring his surgery early the next week and inform his receptionist that she had contacted the patient as he had requested, but had postponed her visit till the next week as the patient agreed that an immediate visit was no longer necessary. Whilst the nurse commented to me that she hoped this message would make the G.P. realize he had over-reacted the tone of her response seemed rather too circumspect to convey her intended message with any clarity. Her response thus reveals clear similarities with the ways in which the nurses on 'F' ward tried to influence doctors and illustrates the re-creation of the same pattern of authority relationships within the community setting.

The Elderly Team

Generally speaking, the Diaries of the nurses in the elderly team were less colourful than those of nurses in the acute team and contained fewer descriptions of stressors or of emotional reactions to the work situation. The Diary of the sister in the elderly team, shown in Figure 10.2, summarized most interactions with patients with the rather sparse description "Routine Visit". This term was used by several other nurses in the elderly team to describe those visits where their basic role was to call on the elderly person once or twice a week and check that they still appeared to be coping adequately. Such visits seldom seemed to cause the nurses immediate emotional or practical problems, although the nurse's comments do indicate that some visits could be problematic by noting that one of her patients was confused, nervous and anti-social when she visited. However, the nurse added in conversation that she rarely found such behaviour upsetting as she generally attributed it to the effects of dementia rather than to deliberate awkwardness or personal rejection. This attribution was similar to the attributions which the nurses on 'F' ward frequently made concerning the difficult behaviour of psychotic patients and suggests that both the perceived reasons for the patients' actions, and the actions themselves, influenced the nurses' emotional responses to the problems they faced. In general, the nurses in both the ward and community settings seemed to find it easier to cope with difficult patients once they had denied the validity of the patients' actions by disassociating the concept of agency from the patient. Unfortunately, one negative effect of this attribution was that such patients could become unrewarding to work with because their approval or gratitude no longer had much value either and

Brief description	General comments
9 a.m. - 12 p.m.	
Meeting to discuss clients attending the day centre	
Routine visit	
Routine visit	rushing visits a bit due to meeting at 1p.m.
Routine visit	Client not too well and depressed, GP informed.
12 - 3 p.m.	
Staff meeting to discuss workloads	Prolonged meeting. Some irritation and stress.
3 - 5 p.m.	
Routine visit	Client very on edge and confused today didn't want me to stay.
Admin.	

Figure 10.2   The Diary from the Community Unit ElderlyTeam

such patients therefore could not meet either the nurses' need to have their professional competence confirmed by others or their needs for human contact during their working day. As the next chapter will show this problem was raised in a number of interviews and seemed to be a key issue for staff seeing elderly patients.

In conclusion, the two Diaries presented here suggest that the main qualitative difference between the working environment of nurses in the acute and elderly teams lay in the nature of their relationship with patients. Considered as a whole, the Diaries of the nurses in the acute team indicated that they found their relationships with patients more emotionally stressful than did nurses in the elderly team. There seemed to be two main reasons for this; firstly, the 'dialectic of control' between nurses and patients was more evenly balanced within the acute team and the patients had a greater propensity to make emotional demands on the nurses by contacting them in distressed states of mind and demanding instant succorance. Secondly, the nurses in the acute team set more optimistic, change oriented goals for patients and therefore invested greater personal significance in the responses of their patients to treatment. Whilst this meant that their work could contain more sources of satisfaction than the work of the elderly team it also meant that the environment they experienced was subjectively less stable and was often experienced as more pressured. In comparison with the Diaries of the nurses on 'F' ward the Diaries of the community nurses revealed a heightened concern with patients as individuals and a decreased emphasis on control oriented activities and the maintenance of organizational routines. However, several diaries suggested that the nurses still returned elements of their earlier socialization within a medically oriented and hierarchical organizational structure and indicated that their resultant inability to question medical authority could sometimes exacerbate their feelings of stress.

PATIENTS' HISTORIES

This section presents four case histories. The case studies were chosen to illustrate the different types of relationships which may occur between nurses and patients and show how these relationships were influenced by an interaction between the patients' characteristics, the nurses' needs and the ideological and structural environment of community psychiatric nursing. The material was obtained primarily from six days of structured participant observation of the nurses' interactions with patients and from general discussions about these patients over the succeeding weeks. Fourteen visits made by nurses in the acute team were observed and twelve visits by the elderly team. All patients seen by nurses in the acute team were contacted by the nurse several days before the visit and asked if they minded having an observer present and the option of refusing was made explicit. The patients of nurses in the elderly team were generally not informed of the impending visit but were asked on the doorstep if they minded having another person present. Most of these patients assumed that I was one of the students who frequently accompanied the community psychiatric nurses. No patients refused to allow their visit to be observed although two nurses commented afterwards that they felt some patients were less forthcoming than usual.

Two patients from the acute team are described. The first study illustrates the way in which the nurses' preference for working with friendlier and more attractive patients could facilitate the pathologizing of everyday problems in living. The second case study investigates the ways in which some patients sought to remain in treatment and highlights the similarity of the 'dialectic of control' within the ward and community settings. The third case study describes a patient seen by the elderly team and illustrates both the routine and practical nature of these nurses' interactions with patients and some of the problems of responsibility and risk-taking which those nurses faced. The final case study describes an extended family network of two sisters and their mother who were all involved with the community services and the research hospital. This study highlights the way in which the family has become a site for expert intervention (Lasch, 1977; Donzelot, 1979; Cohen, 1985) and also shows how the essentially individualistic orientation of psychiatry may contribute to the breakdown of family structures.

The Acute Team

Y.A.V.I.S. Patients: Pamela

Once of the best documented findings within the psychotherapeutic literature is that therapists tend to prefer working with patients who are young, attractive, verbal, intelligent and successful (Yalom, 1975; Brown and Pedder, 1979). As Pamela's case shows the 'YAVIS' syndrome was one factor influencing the expansion of the community psychiatric nursing services to new groups of patients whose problems were far removed from traditional concepts of mental illness.

Pamela was in her late thirties, had a daughter of ten and was married to a bank employee. She had been to see her G.P. two weeks earlier to ask for medication for an irritable bowel and had mentioned that she thought her symptoms were probably triggered by the stress of various marital problems. The G.P., whom the community nurse described as 'enlightened and caring', had then referred the patient to the community nurses. Prior to the initial visit there were some indications that Pamela may have been ambivalent about treatment, as on the first occasion that the nurse telephoned her to arrange a home visit she said she was unsure when she was free and promised to ring back to arrange a date whilst on the second occasion that the nurse contacted her she apologized for not returning the earlier call and stated that perhaps she should forgo any further appointments as she was sure the nurse had more important problems to deal with. The nurse interpreted these remarks as indicating that the patient was a considerate and self-effacing person who generally put others first and commented to me just before the initial interview that she was looking forward to meeting the patient.

When we arrived at Pamela's house she invited us into the lounge and offered us coffee. She accompanied this with a few social remarks asking whether we encountered any problems finding the house and then commented that she was rather surprized her G.P. had referred her to a Community Psychiatric Nurse as she had not really gone there seeking psychiatric help and had only intended to get something to help her deal with her physical symptoms. The nurse responded by pointing out that physical symptoms are often linked to psychological distress and suggested that the patient might feel better after she had discussed her marital problems with a third person. The patient then replied that she had been discussing her problems with several friends and commented that she felt they had probably helped her as much as anyone could. In response, the nurse pointed out that Pamela had still not resolved her problems and went on to say that because friends were not properly trained they often gave bad advice which could be influenced by their vested interests in seeing the marriage either fail or continue. Pamela then revealed that she and her husband were attending marriage guidance together and suggested that this was probably an adequate level of professional involvement. In response the nurse pointed out that marriage guidance counsellors were volunteers with a limited amount of training and added that marriage guidance aimed to save marriages rather than provide help for the individual whereas she was there to help the patient decide what was best for her as an individual. At this point the patient disagreed with the nurse and said quite firmly that she did not feel it was appropriate for her to consider her own needs without also considering the effects her actions would have on her husband and child. After some discussion on this issue the patient recounted her family history and described the problems in her marriage in more detail.

At the end of her hour long interview the patient thanked the nurse for coming, said she felt better for talking to her and that she felt she was probably exaggerating her marital problems and could sort them out without further help. The nurse responded by saying that she felt the patient needed the opportunity to talk to someone who would be concerned with her individual needs and the patient agreed to a second appointment with the words:-

"Well, if you really think it's necessary ....?"

In the car afterwards the nurse remarked that Pamela seemed a very pleasant person and added that she was glad she had managed to overcome Pamela's reluctance to have further appointments. I asked her why she thought the patient was reluctant to see her again and she replied that some patients tended to feel that they were wasting the nurses' time and that it was important to re-assure them that emotional problems were just as important as physical ones, and that they should seek help at an early stage in order to prevent their problems from worsening.

The nurse saw Pamela the following week and then Pamela rang the hospital and left a message for the nurse saying that she felt she could cope with her problems alone and did not require any further visits. I asked the nurse how she felt about this and she replied that she always felt disappointed when people dropped out of treatment before their problems were resolved and wondered if she had failed them in any way. She added that she had liked Pamela as an individual and would probably have enjoyed visiting her over a longer period.

Pamela's case illustrates the way in which several key themes identified within the critical psychiatry literature find concrete expression within the everyday interactions of health service professionals and their patients. One of the clearest issues to emerge centres on the relationship between the move into the community and the expansion of psychiatric jurisdiction. Pamela originally visited her G.P. seeking treatment for a physical problem which she identified as having an emotional cause. Her remarks during the interview suggested that she may have preferred her G.P. to simply treat her physical complaint and leave her to cope with her marital problems. If the community services had not existed the G.P. would probably have adopted this course of action, as Pamela was clearly not the sort of person who warranted in-patient psychiatric treatment, however, the existence of a community service designed to deal with patients' emotional problems seems to have triggered a referral to that service. Thus, as Cohen (1985) remarks, the creation of community services designed to minimize the effects of labelling and institutionalization may have had the paradoxical effect of pathologizing problems which would previously have been regarded as a normal part of life and encouraging health service professionals and patients to re-define them as issues needing expert intervention.

The superiority of professional intervention was explicitly stated by the nurse when she pointed out that friends should not be relied on because they may give biased advice. At the same time, the nurse denigrated the value of other, rival, counselling organizations such as marriage guidance by identifying their staff as volunteers without adequate professional training. Ironically, the nurse herself admitted to me after the initial session that her expertise in marital problems was derived from her personal experience and from several years work as a community nurse. Her perception that her own advice would be more valuable than that of either a layperson or a marriage guidance counsellor thus seemed to be based primarily on her position within the Health Service rather than upon the personal possession of a clearly identifiable skills base.

Although both the nurse and the doctor may have unwittingly conspired to foist professional help on a reluctant patient they both seemed motivated by a genuine desire to help her rather than a cynical intention to extend the sphere of professional domination. Both Pamela and the nurse concurred in seeing the G.P. as a conscientious and caring doctor who tried to treat his patients as individuals and to take account of their personal situation as well as their physical problems. Similarly, the nurse struck me as genuinely concerned with both Pamela's problems and those of her other patients. She was, however, a firm believer in the ideology of preventative community care and saw this as an unmitigated benefit to the community as a whole. In consequence, she did not consider the possibility that her interventions or the expansion of community care might yield a mixture of beneficial and negative effects for either her individual patients or the wider community. For instance, she seemed unaware that by raising some of the quite real dangers in relying on advice from friends she was also implicitly making a more general statement undermining the value of naturally occurring social support systems.

Pamela's case history also highlights the generally more personal and equal relationship between nurses and patients within the community setting. In contrast to the ward situation, where the physical environment and access to resources were controlled by nursing staff, the physical environment of the patients' homes was controlled by them which gave them a greater degree of power in relation to the nurses. In addition, various social norms concerning the offering and acceptance of hospitality helped normalize the process of interaction between professional and patient. One result of this was that the community nurses often seemed to have more regard for their patients as individuals than nurses on the ward and to want to form relationships which contained elements of friendship on both sides. This process was probably intensified by the nurses' relative isolation from other staff throughout their working day. Paradoxically, the nurses own friendship needs and their desire to retain contact with valued clients sometimes seemed to heighten the probability that their patients' problems would be pathologized and conceptualized by the nurses as requiring continued psychiatric intervention.

The Treatment Barrier: Joan

Although the nurses seemed to prolong some patients' involvement with the community sector because of their own friendship needs there were other patients whom they found quite irritating but whom they remained involved with for fairly lengthy periods of time. These patients probably formed the largest single grouping within the acute team's caseload and six visits to patients of this type were observed out of a total of fourteen visits. The 'treatment barrier' described by Scott (1973) seemed to be a key feature of these patients' involvement with the psychiatric sector and to cause a variety of problems for the community nurses.

Joan's history was fairly typical of patients within this group. Joan was a married woman in her early fifties with two adult children and a husband who was a long distance lorry driver and who was away from home two or three nights a week on average. She had a history of agoraphobic and hypo-chondriacal symptoms and panic attacks extending back approximately eleven years. During this time she had been seen by a variety of health service professionals such as psychiatrists, psychologists and community psychiatric nurses and had a history of slight improvement followed by relapses whenever help was withdrawn. She was on tranquillizers which she tended to misuse by taking additional tablets whenever she felt agitated and her initial symptoms may therefore have been compounded by the physical and psychological symptoms of benzodiazepine dependence, as this frequently resembles patients' original anxiety related complaints (Lacey and Woodward, 1985). Joan's latest referral to the psychiatric community nursing service had occurred approximately six months previously and had been triggered by the fact that she was visiting her G.P. on a daily basis complaining of a variety of physical symptoms. Since being referred to the service her visits to the G.P. had declined to approximately one a week. This pleased both the doctor and the community nurse and the later argued that her own hour long weekly visits therefore represented a considerable saving to the Health Service as she earned rather less than a G.P.

When the nurse and I arrived at Joan's immaculately clean and tidy house she welcomed us both and offered us tea or a cold drink. She then began discussing her various physical symptoms and complaining of feeling tired and of being unable to sleep the previous night. The nurse tried to re-assure her by pointing out that the temperature had been in the eighties over the last few days making everyone lethargic and sleepless. Joan responded by citing other aches and pains and the nurse again tried to counter-act this by pointing out that the numerous tests she had undergone had revealed no organic cause for her problems. Joan reiterated by noting that her gynaecological problems had not been investigated for over a year and the nurse was eventually trapped into suggesting that if Joan really felt that she had a physical problem she should visit her doctor. Joan agreed to do so and added in passing that she would mention to the doctor that the nurse had told her to visit.

After this Joan changed the subject and started talking about relationship problems she was having with her sister. This broadened out into a description of the way her whole family failed to support her and the problems of coping with panic attacks on her own. She then raised the issue of the emergency weekend visit which another community nurse had made to her the previous week after she telephoned the service in a panic.

The nurse re-assured her that she understood that such attacks could be difficult to cope with and that she did not mind Jean telephoning the service in an emergency and Joan then suggested that she would find it easier to manage if the nurse increased the frequency of her visits. The nurse demurred on the grounds of work pressure and said she felt it was time to leave, whereupon Joan raised several other issues which delayed our departure for another twenty minutes.

Once outside the nurse drove her car round the block out of Joan's sight, parked, sighed and announced she needed a short break before driving to her next appointment. She then commented that she found that visiting Joan always made her feel very tense as the patient talked virtually non-stop and seemed to think she could spend all day with her, and added:-

"I find her irritating because she's hooked into a medical model and expects everything done for her but she does improve a bit when someone's seeing her so I suppose it's worth it."

Joan's history illustrates the way in which the expansion of the psychiatric system is influenced by the behaviour of patients as well as psychiatric professionals and shows how contradictions centring on the problem of patient versus professional responsibility may be exploited by patients within the community, as well as by the patients on the ward. Both Joan's G.P. and the nurse seemed to conceptualize themselves as having a professional obligation to try and alleviate her problems and, as a result, Joan was able to pressure her doctor, who appears to have responded by passing Joan onto a variety of other Health Service professionals. As a lower status employee the nurse was therefore under two sets of obligations to continue seeing Joan and was susceptible to pressure from both the G.P. and the patient.

The nurse's problems in dealing with this patient may have been exacerbated by the conceptual model which she used to interpret and treat Joan's problems. The community nurses had generally rejected an organically oriented medical model in their dealings with patients who they did not regard as psychotic. However, most of them seemed to have replaced it with a rather simplistic form of behaviour therapy which shared many of the attributes of the medical model in so far as it seemed to be applied mechanistically with the nurses sometimes acting as if specific presenting problems automatically warranted particular technical solutions. Thus, in Joan's case, the nurse had given the patient a relaxation tape and a handout on anxiety management even though she knew that the same strategy had failed several times before. During the session the nurse repeatedly reiterated the value of these aids and emphasised that they would work if only the patient would use them, and in response Joan usually apologized and promised to try and use them more regularly in future. Wider issues concerning the personal meaning of the patient's actions or the social context in which they occurred were not raised by the nurse during the session and later discussions suggested that they did not form part of her therapeutic framework despite the fact that she had an intuitive understanding that Joan's problems would not be resolved by the techniques she was applying. To give an example, one of the comments which the nurse made after the visit was that she felt Joan's problems were exacerbated by loneliness and boredom. Whilst the nurse had tried to tackle this by encouraging Joan to socialize more and was aware that Joan probably used her as a substitute friend she seemed surprized when I asked her if she had ever raised this issue with Joan and replied she had never considered discussing the nature of her relationship with patients with them. She added that the idea made her feel uncomfortable and that she felt such actions would violate her professional obligation to maintain a detached relationship with patients. One consequence of this perspective was that the double-bind situation in which both Joan and the nurse were trapped seemed to be unrecognized by the nurse. This made it more difficult for her to resolve the contradictions within her relationship with the patient and facilitated the continuation of a recurrent pattern of improvements, relapses, professional withdrawal and re-referral which seemed to be becoming increasingly entrenched.

Although the nurses tended to find patients like Joan exasperating such patients also filled various organizational and personal needs. At the organizational level, the doctors were clearly glad to rid themselves of the responsibility for such patients and were more likely to support the expansion of the community services because of this. At the individual level, such patients both fulfilled and thwarted some of the nurses' security needs within the work situation. On the one hand, patients like Joan clearly wanted the nurses' involvement and visits to them generally conformed to a relatively predictable and undemanding routine which helped meet some of the nurses' basic security needs within the work situation. On the other hand, such security was frequently undermined both by the periodic crises such patients underwent and by their skill in subtly undermining the nurses' suggested interventions. As a result, the nurses often seemed reluctant to discharge such patients for a variety of organizational and personal reasons even though such patients tended to irritate them by continually thwarting their therapeutic aspirations.

The Elderly Team

Mental Deterioration and Marital Dissolution

In contrast to the nurses in the acute team many of the interactions between elderly team nurses and their patients centred on the provision of practical support and supervision for patients with varying degrees of mental and physical deterioration. The case of Arthur and Doreen exemplifies this type of relationship and illustrates the way in which the increasing mental and physical infirmity of those patients could raise complex questions concerning their ability to remain within the community. In some of these cases the nurses' dual mandate to provide both care and control, coupled with the demands of competing interest groups, could create quite volatile situations which were often disconcerting for both the patient and the nurse. The role of the psychiatric services in the dissolution of Arthur and Doreen's marriage illustrates some of these issues.

Arthur and Doreen were an elderly couple in their late seventies who had been referred to the community nursing service by their G.P. approximately eighteen months previously. They lived in a two bedroomed retirement bungalow and had two married children who lived in different parts of the country and whom they saw approximately twice a year usually for a period of several days. The couple had been referred because Arthur had succumbed to recurrent bouts of severe depression over the last few years, which had necessitated several admissions to the research hospital in a withdrawn state in which he refused to eat or speak. According to the nurse, Doreen had initially coped with Arthur's problems reasonably well on her own but had become increasingly frail herself over the last two years and now found it difficult either to look after Arthur or to function without him. Arthur had been re-admitted to the research hospital a week before the observed visit and was still in a withdrawn state, with the ward reporting great difficulty in getting him to eat. He was visited everyday by Doreen who was apparently becoming increasingly upset herself. The community nurse was visiting her every other day to monitor her physical and mental state.

On the observed visit the nurse and I arrived around lunch-time and found a neighbour talking to Doreen. The neighbour commented that she was about to make Doreen a sandwich and confided to the nurse that she was worried about Doreen as she had been wandering round her garden in the small hours of the previous night talking to herself and seeming rather confused. Once her neighbour had gone Doreen offered the nurse and I coffee and biscuits, which the nurse agreed to on condition that Doreen ate with us. Over coffee Doreen seemed restless and upset and repetitively asked when Arthur was coming home. The nurse explained that Arthur had to stay in the hospital until he began to eat again and Doreen replied that he always ate at home and would eat if they were together. The nurse then asked whether Doreen was sleeping and the patient replied she was not bothering to sleep any more but dozed on the sofa when she felt tired. After some general conversation and re-assurance about Arthur the nurse and I left and the nurse called at the neighbour's house to ask if she would mind some sleeping pills for Doreen and give them to her each night. Later that day she rang the G.P. to inform him that Doreen had regressed and to ask him to contact her family, explaining to me that in circumstances like this she felt it was important to keep the patients' doctors fully informed of their condition in order to avoid later accusations of neglect.

The nurse's fears proved justified as one of Doreen's sons visited his mother during the next week and later rang the doctor and the nurse to harangue them for failing to take adequate care of his mother and to demand that she now be placed in care. The nurse was clearly upset by both the son's accusations and his suggested solution and commented that it made her feel really angry when families separated elderly couples unnecessarily. She added:

> "Really you can't win in situations like this. Sometimes you know you've got to admit the person if they're in a really bad state and their partner can't cope - but you feel so cruel separating old people like that."

The eventual outcome of this case was that Arthur's depression lifted after several weeks in hospital and he was allowed to return home. Unfortunately, Doreen had reached a stage where Arthur's return failed to stabilize her behaviour and she eventually had to be admitted to the research hospital herself. Doreen's son arranged for Arthur to be placed in a nursing home near them and the couple were separated for the foreseeable future. The nurse was obviously upset by this and commented that she would have been willing to continue trying to keep the couple together if their G.P. had been more willing to stand up to family pressure.

This case history illustrates two of the key structural contradictions in the provision of care for the elderly and shows how they could effect both the nurses' actions and their experiences of stress at work. The first contradiction centres on the effects which the individually oriented structure of hospital care had on the marriage of Doreen and Arthur. From the nurse's description of Arthur's physical and mental condition it seems reasonable to infer that he needed some form of supervised care which Doreen was unable to provide and that the hospital was providing a necessary service by admitting him. However, because the hospital contained no facilities for treating the couple as a unit this meant that Arthur's admission precipitated a crisis in Doreen's physical and mental state. This was a clear source of conflict for the community nurse as her role as intermediary between hospital and community services meant that she was one of the professionals responsible for initiating Arthur's entry into hospital. Whilst both the ward based and community nurses recognized the couple's mutual attachment and were prepared to bend the hospital rules to allow Doreen hospital meals with Arthur they were unable to provide the more comprehensive provision which would have enabled the couple to remain together throughout Arthur's hospitalization and which might have helped prevent Doreen's deterioration.

This case history also illustrates some of the problems of professional responsibility which could perturb the nurses in the elderly team. In contrast to the ward situation, which provided continuous supervision, the community nurses saw their patients for relatively limited periods. This heightened the possibility that the more vulnerable patients might injure themselves in the nurse's absence and that the nurse would then be criticized by the family or other professionals for providing inadequate care. Such condemnations could be quite emotional in content and could upset the nurse more than the actual accident itself. As one nurse explained in her interview:-

> "I had a patient once who injured her leg and no-one found out for several days - and you always feel bad when something like that happens - but usually I can accept it - but then the son 'phoned up and started shouting at me for neglecting his mother - and I felt shaky and upset for days even though I knew it wasn't my fault really."

In order to avoid this type of incident several nurses in the elderly team admitted that they were sometimes over-protective towards their patients and were more inclined to favour admission where they felt the family or G.P. were unsympathetic towards them. Thus, the nurses' professional responsibility for their patients well-being could result in paradoxical outcomes where the provision of support services which were designed to help patients live in the community for longer might also hasten their admission because the professionals involved were unwilling to tolerate the risks of allowing patients to remain within a setting where they might injure themselves.

Family Problems and Individual Solutions: Helen's Family

The final case history documents the way in which several members of the same family may become involved with the psychiatric services as patients and again demonstrates the way in which the individually oriented organizational structure of both community and hospital services precludes an effective response to the the problems of the family rather than the individual. The case study describes the lives of Helen, her sister Mary and their mother Martha, all of whom were patients of the community nurses or the hospital during this research. The major events in each individual's life will be outlined separately although they unfolded concurrently.

Helen

Helen was a married woman in her late thirties who was in the last month of pregnancy when the research on the community unit started. Although she was diagnosed as schizophrenic and had been on depot injections until her pregnancy her community nurse had reservations about this diagnosis and felt that many of Helen's behaviour problems were simply ways of drawing attention to her chronic insecurities. Helen had first come to the attention of the psychiatric services five years previously when she had visited her G.P. in a distraught state threatening to kill herself and her two young children. Her despair seemed to have been triggered by the fact that her husband had recently left her to live with their next door neighbour and the strain of seeing them together was more than she could cope with. Helen's G.P. took her threats seriously and arranged for her to see a psychiatrist who admitted her to the research hospital. Helen's behaviour apparently deteriorated quite dramatically whilst she was in hospital resulting in a period under section, a fact which was raised in a custody case about a year later and which resulted in Helen's husband gaining custody of their children and Helen losing access to them.

During one of her several subsequent periods of hospitalization Helen had met an older man in his early fifties who did some voluntary work at the hospital. The two married a few months later and Helen unexpectedly became pregnant within a year. The community nurse, who had known Helen for about three years, felt that she had become more stable since her marriage but doubted her ability to cope with a new baby and regretted the fact that Helen and her husband had rejected the psychiatrist's suggestion that the pregnancy be terminated. She described the marriage as "a union of lost souls really" and said that Helen's husband treated her like a child and encouraged her tantrums and dependency by alternately indulging her and panicking and demanding psychiatric help to deal with her.

Helen's forthcoming pregnancy meant that a social worker and health visitor became involved with the case in addition to the psychiatrist, community nurse and G.P. and this multi-agency involvement resulted in several lengthy case conferences before the birth of the baby. The nurse found these frustrating as she felt they were often rambling and inconclusive and once remarked to several other colleagues that:-

> "Someone should do something about organizing something for that family - because unless someone does something she's going to lose that baby."

This remark was reponded to sympathetically by the other nurses, several of whom either commented that the doctors and social workers should be taking a more directive role or empathized with the nurse's worries concerning Helen's future.

Around the time of her child's birth Helen's case was transferred to another social worker who arranged for a specialist foster mother to work with Helen on a daily basis in her own home in order to to monitor Helen's parenting skills and reduce her anxiety level. This system worked well at first but, unfortunately, the foster mother fell ill after working with Helen for approximately two months and Helen then reverted to her former behaviour patterns, making wild and hysterical accusations against numerous people and refusing to cope with the baby on the grounds that her husband loved the baby more than her. Her husband took time off work to try and resolve the crisis but was unable to manage and in the end the baby was taken into care and Helen was re-admitted to hospital where she regressed rapidly after learning that her husband had rejected her and that she was unlikely to regain custody of her child. When last heard of she was on the locked ward of the hospital and seemed unlikely to be discharged in the near future. The community nurse, who visited Helen several times during the initial phases of her hospitalization, was distressed by this outcome and returned from one visit virtually in tears and remarked:

> "It seems so unfair that she's lost everything twice. I feel I've failed her somehow. I keep wondering if it could have been different if only I'd said something different."

Helen's history demonstrates the way in which several of the major stresses faced by the community nurses were influenced by both the structure of their work and their own perceptions of their responsibilities towards patients. One of the clearest themes to emerge from the participant observation and discussions with Helen's nurse was her strong sense of involvement in this case. This involvement was facilitated by an organizational structure which had enabled the nurse to work with Helen on an individual basis for several years and was an important source of satisfaction for the nurse. However, such involvement could also be a source of stress and disappointment when cases went wrong and could result in strong feelings of insecurity. As Helen's nurse commented in her interview:-

> "Sometimes with difficult cases like Helen's it's difficult to know whether you've made the right decision - and then sometimes I wish there could be two of us - just for a bit of support for me really - because I'm not really sure myself whether I'm doing the right thing quite often - and I feel if other people were there they'd understand what I'm talking about more."

One consequence of the nurse's mixed feelings of responsibility and therapeutic insecurity was a tendency to respond to telephone calls from Helen or her husband by immediately rushing over to see them or by asking colleagues to visit them at weekends or during her holidays. This may have helped to exacerbate the interactional problems between Helen and her husband by enabling both of them to avoid responsibility for their actions by escalating disputes into crises and then calling on the psychiatric services to arbitrate. The nurse's belief that she was then responsible for controlling the situation and restoring domestic calm may then have triggered other actions by her which further escalated the situation. Helen's final period of hospitalization, for example, was in some senses initiated by her community nurse who called the psychiatrist out on an emergency visit after her own attempts to calm a domestic dispute failed. Whilst this solution may have had a variety of short-term gains for those involved the longer term costs for Helen were quite high.

A final problem illustrated by Helen's history is that of multi-disciplinary co-ordination in complex cases where patients gather increasing numbers of helping professionals to them over time. In Helen's case the large number of professionals involved resulted in a number of inconclusive case conferences marred by status disputes between different professionals and agencies and divergent opinions concerning the best way of handling her problems. These enabled Helen and her husband to play various professionals off against one another by exploiting inconsistencies in the strategies adopted by different groups and facilitated the development of an ill-coordinated, crisis oriented response to the couple's problems. Whilst the community nurse recognized this problem and often criticised the lack of group decision-making in this case she tended to adopt a fairly passive role herself and generally relied on other professions to co-ordinate Helen's care plans.

Mary

Helen's sister, Mary, had also been a patient of the community psychiatric services for several years. She had originally been referred by her G.P. for phobic symptoms but was now being seen for a more generalized inability to cope with everyday stressors. Her dependence on the community psychiatric nursing service was exemplified by an incident which occurred during the weekend participant observation when she rang the community nurses in a distraught state because the local council had sent a circular to all their tenants warning them that dogs should not be allowed to run free on a nearby grassy area without being supervised. The nurse visited the patient that morning in response to her call, re-assured her that the circular did not mean that her dog would have to be destroyed and sympathized with several other worries concerning her family. Mary then relaxed and chatted to the nurse and myself in a normal and friendly manner for the next half hour. As we left the nurse commented to me that he had a soft spot for Mary, even though her histrionic behaviour often irritated him, as he felt that she was basically a friendly and pleasant person who could have a more fulfilled life if only she could overcome her symptoms.

Mary and Helen tended to upset each other and both had a propensity for ringing their respective community nurses after family rows. This could occasionally lead to tension between the two community nurses as when Mary's nurse only half-joking asked Helen's nurse to "try and keep your patient from upsetting my patient and doubling my workload."

This remark upset Helen's nurse who took it as a personal criticism of her ability to handle her patients properly. The force of the criticism was increased by the status differences between the two nurses as Helen's nurse had not yet gone on the one year postgraduate course in community psychiatric nursing whereas the other nurse had done so.

Martha

Many of the disagreements between Helen and Mary centred on their widowed mother, Martha. At the time the research started Martha was in her early seventies and had just been admitted to one of the psycho-geriatric admission wards in the research hospital. Prior to this she had lived with Helen for a brief period of several months during which time she had been a patient of the elderly team. Helen had apparently chosen to have her mother living with her because the later was becoming slightly forgetful and physically frail. Not surprisingly, the relationship between Helen and her mother deteriorated in the relatively cramped confines of a council flat and Martha was admitted to the research hospital around the sixth month of Helen's pregnancy because the professionals involved feared that Helen may have started hitting her. These fears were based on a number of hysterical threats which Helen made but not on firm evidence that Martha had actually been battered.

Martha was admitted to a psycho-geriatric ward where the majority of other patients displayed few physical or intellectual abilities and where the nursing ethos emphasised basic physical care centring on such activities as feeding, washing and toiletting of patients. The rest of the time most patients sat in the rows of chairs around the edge of the ward common room staring blankly into space. Conversation between the patients was minimal and the nurses made little attempt to encourage communication. As one third year student remarked to me:-

> "When I first came on this ward I was really keen and tried to talk to them and do things with them - but now I just can't be bothered - there's a limit to the number of one way conversations you can take."

From various conversations I had with Martha during a period of research on this ward it become apparent that she was bored and unhappy on the ward, worried about her future and fearful that the psychotropic medication she had been placed on was making her memory worse. She commented during one conversation:-

> "I know the nurses are very kind and everyone's doing their best for me but no-one ever tells me what's going to happen to me."

She then started to weep quietly and continued:-

> "I just want to go home - I look at the other patients - and I know it's not their fault but I'm frightened of being like them."

Helen and Mary both came to visit Martha whilst she was in hospital and tried to involve the staff in several arguments between them concerning the best way of providing for their mother's future. The ward based nurses regarded these disputes, coupled with the fact that both sisters were patients of the community nurses, as clear evidence that the two sisters were unstable and not acting in their mother's best interests. The hospital therefore applied to the courts to become Martha's legal guardian which gave the hospital staff effective control over her future. Although most of the staff concerned recognized that Martha was ill-suited to a geriatric ward and initially talked of arranging sheltered accommodation for her these plans never materialized and by the end of the research Martha was still in hospital and had regressed quite considerably in her mental acuity. This was regarded by several nurses as evidence that she had a rapid onset form of dementia and the possibility that her restricted environment or medication may have contributed to her intellectual decline was not raised by them.

One of the clearest themes to emerge from the description of this family's involvement with psychiatry is that the problems of various members were treated by a variety of Health and Social Service professionals on an individualized basis which paid little attention to the emotional and practical involvements which family members had with each other. Psychiatry's neglect of family context has been demonstrated in other empirical research (e.g. Baruch and Treacher, 1978) and has been identified by several theorists as an example of the way in which the increasing involvement of the state in the realms of private life is hastening the dissolution of family ties (e.g. Lasch, 1977; Donzelot, 1979).

This case history illustrates some of the ways in which this process may be influenced by the practical concerns of the various staff involved in dealing with problem families. The organizational structure of both the hospital and the community services was predicated on the concept of individual care which meant that it was structurally problematic for the nurses to interact with different members of an extended family. This structure was linked to organic or psychological treatment ideologies which were also individually focussed. As a corollary of this the tacit, or practical, knowledge which the nurses used to organize their everyday experiences was also individually based and tended to involve giving common-sense advice to family members about how to interact with others rather than more detailed analyses of interaction patterns within families. Finally, the nurses generally conceptualized themselves as working within a benevolent institution which existed to help troubled individuals or to take key decisions for individuals who were unable to act in their own best interests. In consequence, they tended to see the faults in the interaction patterns within this family and to be aware of the potential harm to the more vulnerable members in it without being aware of the damage which the psychiatric system itself might inflict. Thus, for the nurses the choice was between a pathological family and benign institutions rather than between troubled family care and poor state provision. Given the potentially serious damage which could have resulted if Helen had battered her baby or her mother it is, perhaps, not surprising that the professionals involved eventually opted for the ostensibly safer course of placing the baby and Martha in state care rather than the more risky strategy of continuing to support the family in the hope that they could eventually resolve their problems. However, this strategy was not without costs for the nurses involved as their very genuine desire to help their patients resolve their problems successfully was frequently frustrated by the tactics they used to minimize the risks within problematic family situations such as this.

DISCUSSION

The aim of this chapter was to describe the practical knowledge which the community psychiatric nurses used to organize their daily activities and to show how they attempted to deal with the stresses caused by the structure of their working environment. Although there were clear differences between the ward and community setting which should not be undervalued there were also enough similarities between the structure and ideology of the two settings to lend some credence to Cohen's blunt assertion that:-

> "the same old experts have moved office to the community and are doing the

same old things they have always done." (1985, p.75)

The result of this was that many of the paradoxes and ambiguities which caused problems within the ward setting were re-enacted within the community environment.

One of the key structural contradictions identified within the critical psychiatry literature centres on psychiatry's dual mandate to help the distressed individual and control socially problematic behaviour. Within the ward situation this obligation caused problems at two distinct levels; firstly, key decisions concerning issues such as admission, discharge and sectioning sometimes seemed to be taken for reasons of social control rather than in the patients' best interests; secondly, the nurses' concern with the maintenance of ward routines meant that they generally sought to control the problematic behaviour of their patients rather than understand it. The effect of this was often to exacerbate the patients' problems and provoke behaviours designed to undermine staff authority. This could be highly distressing for the nurses, partly because such behaviours were often very difficult to deal with but also because many staff genuinely cared about the patients and had a strong desire to help them.

Although the nurses' obligation to maintain control over their patients' activities was diminished within the community setting the nurses still experienced problems resulting from the tensions between their desire to help individual patients and their duty to maintain social order. This was particularly apparent in the nurses' relationships with patients like Helen where there was a possibility that the patients' behaviour might seriously harm a third party. However, it could also occur in relation to patients whose behaviour was socially unacceptable in other ways and in response to pressure from other parties, such as relatives, for the nurse to take responsibility for containing troublesome situations. Given the professed distrust of most of the community nurses for hospital care it was ironic that the nurses on 'F' ward complained on several occasions during the research that the community nurses had a tendency to exaggerate their patients' problems and exacerbate them by seeking admission for relatively trivial reasons.

A second criticism of psychiatry is that both the conceptual models used by practitioners and the organizational structure of the institution mimic the individually oriented ethos of general medicine and neglect the interpersonal and social context of patients' problems. This tendency was clearly apparent within the ward situation where the physical structure of the institution segregated patients from their families and where both the treatment regimes of organic psychiatry and the nurses' informal interpretations of patients' behaviour tended to concentrate on individual pathology. In comparison with the ward based nurses the community nurses had an enhanced appreciation of their patients' home circumstances and family relationships. However, as the case studies showed, the treatment ethos and structure of the community services mirrored that of the ward in some ways and still focussed on the amelioration of individual problems through the medium of expert intervention. In consequence, the service still had severe difficulties in dealing with the inter-personal or social context of some patients' problems.

A third contradiction identified within the critical psychiatry literature centres on psychiatry's propensity to define an increasing range of behaviours as pathological rather than simply seeking to ameliorate or contain severe disturbance. Within the hospital environment this outcome often occurred because the personal and social context of patients' problems was neglected within the organic and control oriented treatment ethos of the ward. The situation was rather different within the community as the nurses often had a rather better understanding of their patients' personal lives and tended to conceptualize them as people with 'problems in living' rather than mental illnesses. Despite this, their actions towards their patients were still predicated on the dual assumptions that they were responsible for their patients' well being and that they were there to provide some form of specialized treatment which would solve their patients' problems. These assumptions helped create two contrasting situations which both contributed to the pathologization of patients' problems. Firstly, the nurses sometimes responded to their feelings of social isolation and responsibility by maintaining relatively long-term and routinized relationships with patients who caused few problems and with the more socially attractive individuals on their caseload. Whilst these patients often seemed to receive quite sensible advice and emotional support from the nurses one of the wider implications of re-defining such essentially normal activities as treatment and as the province of psychiatric experts may have been to implicitly devalue the actual or potential existence of such resources within the general community. Secondly, the nurses sometimes became involved in prolonged relationships with patients who seemed to have little real intention of relinquishing their presenting symptoms. Whilst the nurses were often aware of this at an intuitive level, they were seldom able to combat this problem, both because of structural constraints on their freedom of action and because their conceptual framework tended to locate problems solely within the patient or their family. This meant that the nurses seldom analysed their own and their patients' actions as reciprocally influenced patterns situated within the wider context of community psychiatry.

In conclusion, whilst there were clearly important differences in the everyday actions and tacit knowledge of the ward and community nurses several of the key problems identified within the ward situation were re-created within the community setting in different guises. As a result the nurses still experienced many of the stresses faced by the ward nurses.

11 Reflections on the community unit

INTRODUCTION

The two previous chapters described the structure of the community unit and the pattern of daily activities within it. The key point which emerged from these chapters was that many of the structural problems of the ward environment were re-created within the community setting, even though the work of the two groups of nurses was superficially quite different. This chapter now turns from the observational data to the interview data and examines the nurses' reflections on their working environment.

The main theme which emerged from the interviews with the nurses on 'F' ward was that their partial realization of the problems of ward life could lead them to take actions which were designed to improve the quality of care but which sometimes had the paradoxical long-term effect of re-creating the very problems they sought to ameliorate. This chapter argues that a similar process often occurred within the community unit. Whilst the community nurses had a clear understanding of many of the problems of institutional life their interpretations of their own work environment often under-estimated the similarity between the deep structures of the ward and community settings and, as a result, the nurses often failed to appreciate that many of the problems they encountered had similar causes to problems within the ward situation. In consequence, they too experienced feelings of insecurity and self-doubt which, as this chapter will show, frequently led them to act in ways which re-created the very problems they sought to escape.

This chapter is divided into three sections. The first section examines the reasons why the nurses perceived community care as radically different from institutional care and discusses the relationship between this perception and their reasons for choosing to work within the community. The second section examines their feelings of therapeutic competence whilst the third section examines their emotional relationships with patients. The feelings of the nurses in the acute team are generally discussed in the first part of each section followed by a description of the feelings of the nurses in the elderly team.

SEEKING A RADICAL CHANGE

This section examines the relationship between the nurses' reasons for entering community psychiatric nursing and their belief that the community environment provided a radical alternative to institutional care. In contrast to some critics of psychiatry, the community nurses were unanimous in perceiving community care as fundamentally different from institutional provision. Their reasons for believing this were based not only on the criteria they used for evaluating the institution but also on the personal meaning which changes in psychiatric practices held for them. Although the community nurses generally had a clearer understanding of the problems of institutional care than the nurses on 'F' ward their analyses were still partial and were usually based on a limited rejection of the treatment model of organic psychiatry and a critique of the effects of institutionalization on patients. From this perspective, there were significant differences between the ward and community settings as psychotropic medication was used less routinely and the nurses spent more time trying to understand the personal meaning of their patients' problems. However, as recent critiques of psychiatry have pointed out, such analyses are partial because the relationship between psychiatry and society is regarded as unproblematic and key issues such as the relationship between social control and individual help, the medicalization of life and the problems of expertise and responsibility are still ignored. One consequence of the exclusion of these parameters from the framework the community nurses used for evaluating the similarities and differences between the ward and community settings was a tendency to concentrate on the more obvious differences between the two environments and undervalue the deeper similarities between them.

The community nurses' personal experiences of working within the two settings also influenced their beliefs about them, and their descriptions of the personal meaning of the differences between the two environments provides a clear illustration of the reasons why participants within the psychiatric system may perceive fundamental changes where critics see continuity of purpose. One of the most graphic illustrations of the personal impact of the changes which have taken place within psychiatry was provided by a nurse within the acute team who had worked intermittently within the research hospital for over thirty years. Her testimony not only illustrates the magnitude of the changes which had taken place within the research hospital but also reveals how the community nurses' failure to perceive the underlying continuities within the structure of psychiatry could cause them to respond to changes in their work with initial enthusiasm followed by growing disillusionment, a response pattern which mirrored the sequence disclosed within the ward setting. The nurse described conditions within the hospital at the start of her career in the following terms:-

> "When I started here in the forties it was the old institution where all the doors were locked, knives and forks counted and locked away after meals, where there was no private clothing at all - it was literally the era of the ticking shift and mass baths. When I came back (after a twenty year break) I was amazed at the changes - and it took me about six months to adjust to the fact that doors were now open, and that people were wearing their own clothes, that where previously I'd worked on a ward where we had a hundred beds in a massive dormatory there were now only thirty beds on a ward - I felt very insecure at first because previously it had been the old institution where the nurses walked about like prison warders with big bunches of keys hanging from their belts - I liked it eventually - I felt it was much better for patients and staff - but at first it made me feel very odd."

Although this nurse felt that conditions within the institution had changed dramatically during her twenty year absence she still became disillusioned with institutional work and eventually sought to escape from it:-

> "Before I came here I spent three years on a long stay ward and at the end of that I felt I'd given all that I had to give to that type of patient - I'd become

institutionalized myself - I knew I just went in and did what I had to do routinely - it had got difficult to care anymore, and that made me feel quite bad about myself - so I gave my notice in but the matron suggested I went into the community instead - and when I did I thought this is for me - challenge, responsibility, a chance to use my own initiative - I felt as though my work had some meaning again."

Whilst this nurse still regarded community work as radically different from ward-nursing she revealed at a later stage in her interview that she was now experiencing many of the negative emotions which had led the ward based nurses to reject patient contact:-

"I often find I want to pull away from the client - this year at times I've been listening to clients and experiencing anxiety symptoms myself when a little voice inside me has been saying "I must get out" - and it's not specifically that I've got to get on to the next patient - it's just that the general stress has been so much that I need time to myself and I feel a need to get away. They don't have this on the wards - if the going gets too heavy you can always make an excuse - you know - "I've got to put the linen away, and give out the medication". We have no way of escaping ..... and sometimes if I've put a lot of effort in and they demand more and more then it begins to feel like "You're taking my blood" - and it's not good to get into that position where you feel you've given someone a pound of flesh - because you really find it very difficult to go on working with them."

Whilst the intrinsic rewards which community work seemed to offer through increased personal contact with patients were probably the central determinant of most nurses' decisions to move into this area, the enhanced prestige attached to this area of psychiatric nursing was also a highly salient factor for many nurses. Most of the community nurses were in their thirties or early forties and the majority saw their move into the community as a way of improving their employment prospects whilst remaining within the clinical field. Several of these nurses argued in their interviews that their extra training and responsibility should entitle them to a higher renumeration than ward based nurses. They also argued strongly for the enlargement of community psychiatric nursing teams and the importance of preventative psychiatric intervention through the recognition and treatment of problems in the early stages of their development. While several of the community nurses were fiercely condemnatory of the hospital system these same nurses were almost evangelical in their advocacy of community services, conceptualizing their own work as a radical innovation in the way the mentally ill were treated. To give an example, a sister in the acute team commented:-

"I think people enter the hospital system too easily - and it can do more harm than good - people learn how to be patients - they get to know the route in and some of them use it too easily - and it sets a dangerous precedent because the next time there's a row at home it's "You're mad, you should go back and get yourself sorted out" or they escape into hospital away from the problem - that's why what we're doing is so important - because we're going into the family which is where the problem lies."

In response to a later question concerning the effects of fiscal restraints, the same nurse replied:-

I think the cutbacks are having a bad effect on our morale - because we're all working hard to maintain services at their present level - and we're not able to get into preventive work with the G.P.s - we'd like to be saying to them "Give me more (patients) sooner" - and seeking out people who need help at an earlier stage - instead we're running around just to keep services at their present level."

The nurses' strong belief in the value of community services thus enabled them to amalgamate their twin goals of helping patients and obtaining professional advancement within the same conceptual framework. Whilst these aims were not necessarily contradictory both the participant observation data and other comments which the nurses made during their interviews suggested that the two aims sometimes co-existed more uneasily than the rhetoric of community care implied. This issue will be examined in more detail in the succeeding sections.

THERAPEUTIC SKILLS AND PERSONAL INSECURITY

The ward data revealed that many nurses felt uneasy about their therapeutic competence and tended to avoid patient contact because of this. This section shows that the community nurses experienced similar feelings of inadequacy and demonstrates that such feelings were heightened by the unavoidability of close patient contact, their strong feelings of personal responsibility for their patients and their twin goals of helping patients and improving the professional status of psychiatric nursing.

In contrast to 'F' ward where the sister and charge nurse were reluctant to admit feelings of therapeutic inadequacy but seemed to avoid patient contact, all the nurses on the community unit admitted having doubts about their ability to handle the wide range of problems which they encountered within their work. Such feelings appeared to be particularly intense within the acute team, partly because the range of problems faced by the nurses in this team was generally greater, but also because these nurses set more optimistic goals than nurses in the elderly team and were therefore more inclined to question their therapeutic skills when patients' problems failed to disappear.

Whilst the nurses all felt that the community unit should cater for all types of patient most of them also believed that it was impossible for the individual nurse to gain sufficient expertise to deal with a truly generic caseload. However, as their comments show, the nurses were often reluctant to suggest that the referring agent sought a more suitably skilled person to deal with the problems. To some extent this reflected the pragmatic problem of finding more appropriately skilled personnel, but it also seemed to reflect the nurses' reluctance to risk negative evaluations by admitting their inability to deal with some problems. The complexity of this issue is revealed by the comments of a charge nurse in the acute team:-

> "I think we're taking on too much taking everyone. My honest feeling is we ought to specialize more. However, because of the generic quality of our work I'd probably take them on because there isn't anyone else..... .I find other professionals' criteria for deciding whether to see someone or not is very rigid. One of the best parts of our function is that we try and be prompt and go out to the person as quickly as possible.... certainly the G.P.s are making happy noises about that which is a good thing from our point of view."

A similar example was given by another nurse in the acute team who cited several cases of adolescent glue sniffing referred to her the previous year, and commented:-

> "I've got to call on life experience in dealing with adolescents - and as the mother of three sons I've a certain amount of experience but no special skills - but I don't think I can say I'm not expert enough to deal with that and just leave them - I feel that any help is better than no help at all."

These two quotes illustrate the way in which the nurses' very genuine desire to help patients and their generic role within the psychiatric service trapped them within the paradoxical situation of having to draw upon experiences which were common currency within the general population in order to provide a service which was legitimated through the concept of expert knowledge. Thus whilst the nurses may well have been able to give cogent advice and re-assurance based on their own experiences their position as a psychiatric professionals was based on an alternative source of legitimacy. Ironically, the stresses created by this paradox may have been greater for the more highly qualified nurses who had taken the post-qualification certificate in community psychiatric nursing as they had less justification for admitting areas of inadequacy. However, as the nurses who had taken the course pointed out, the course concentrated on academic teaching and contained a relatively limited skills training component and, as a result, whilst all the nurses felt the course had increased their understanding of psychiatry, several nurses experienced difficulty in translating the theoretical components of the course into practice. As one nurse commented:-

> "(The Course) certainly broadened my horizons. I had the opportunity of looking at other facets of life (but) I would have liked to have seen much more skills training really ... so we could practice some of the theory that we learnt - in many ways the thing that I got from it was that you can prepare a better argument for why you're doing what you're doing - it goes back to the point that a lot of people don't understand what we're trying to do. We have to educate people about the importance of community care."

The nurses' feelings of insecurity were often compounded by their strong sense of personal responsibility for their patients and by the high standards they set themselves. All the nurses mentioned that their initial training had inculcated an almost parental sense of responsibility for their patients which could make it difficult for them to accept that patients had to take some responsibility for their own lives. A sister in the acute team explained:-

> "It's very hard for nurses to say that patients have to take responsibility for themselves - I think it stems back to the old idea that the nurse is someone who cares and who does things for people - I still have difficulty coming to terms with not being able to do anything for people - I always wonder if there's something I missed - and patients have expectations of you - they expect you to solve their problems and they find it hard to accept that sometimes you just can't."

Whilst the nurses in the elderly team had an equally strong sense of responsibility towards their patients their goals were generally less optimistic and more practically oriented than those of the acute team. In consequence, they generally seemed to feel less troubled by uncertainties concerning their ability to help patients, although they tended to experience the same insecurities as nurses in the acute team when they faced patients with similar problems to those seen by the acute team. A nurse in this team explained:-

> "I prefer the sorts of problems we deal with really - although I know a lot of people don't... I mean, you might think that if somebody had been sick or had diarrhoea that was really disgusting - but I wouldn't mind that at all - I'd wash

them and make them comfy and feel I'd done something really useful but that lot (i.e. the acute team patients) I couldn't do with them at all - they're always ringing up demanding attention - besides I wouldn't know what advice to give to people like that."

Although the nurses in the elderly team seemed to experience fewer emotional problems they still suffered from feelings of insecurity concerning the value of their activities. These derived in part from the fact that their work carried less status than that of nurses in the acute team. The lower status which psychiatric nurses accord work with the elderly has been noted by other writers (e.g. Towell, 1975) and seems to reflect not only the inferior status of this group within society but also the more obviously mundane character of the interactions with such patients. During the course of this research the qualifications of the nurses in the elderly team increased as more nurses completed the postqualification training course and these nurses increasingly claimed that the focus of their work had shifted from the direct care of the elderly to advising families on management techniques and counselling bereaved families. These activities were seen by the nurses as involving educative and psychotherapeutic skills which were more highly valenced than more obviously practical activities.

The insecurities experienced by the nurses in the two teams illustrate some of the issues surrounding the concept of therapeutic skills within psychiatry. The problems dealt with by nurses within the acute team often involved complex emotional situations which could be difficult for the nurses to resolve or articulate precisely. This could create insecurity in the staff since it was difficult for them to admit openly either that they were unable to perceive the solutions to the patients' problems or that the solutions lay in improved social conditions rather than psychiatric intervention. One strategy for resolving this dilemma seemed to be an assumption that such problems were resolvable if the professional involved possessed specialist therapeutic skills denied to the uninitiated. This enabled the process of interacting with patients to be mystified and its status enhanced and also obscured the complex problem of defining precisely what the nurses were doing during their interactions with patients. However, this strategy also had the negative effect of increasing the insecurity of staff since the imprecision surrounding the everyday use of the concept of therapeutic skills made it difficult for the nurses to feel genuinely confident that they possessed the specialist skills they claimed. Thus, whilst the various therapeutic literatures on helping undoubtedly contain useful ideas concerning the process of interaction with distressed individuals the concept of psychotherapy also plays a key role in legitimating and mystifying the activities of psychiatric professionals.

EMOTIONAL RELATIONS WITH PATIENTS

The ward data indicated that many nurses experienced difficulty achieving a workable balance between compassion and detachment and illustrated the process through which younger nurses were socialized away from close involvement with patients. The interviews with the community nurses suggested that the problem of involvement was re-enacted within the community setting in a more intense form and that the organizational structure of the unit meant that this issue remained a perennial problem for many nurses. As a sister in the acute team explained:-

> " I think people become emotionally enmeshed with clients - I think it happens far more than on the wards ... you don't get to know their back-grounds on the ward - a lot of staff who've been on the wards and start on the community meet patients who've been in and say "My God, I never realized this was the home situation when I met them on the ward, how awful - no wonder they couldn't cope."

The nurses' initially high levels of involvement often resulted in intense disappointment when patients failed to respond or seemed ungrateful for their efforts. This problem was particularly pronounced in the acute team and one solution adopted by the nurses, which often seemed to occur without conscious planning, was to withdraw from disliked patients. A male nurse in this team explained:-

> "I think you tend to put off visits to patients you dislike - you space the visits out - decide you can leave them a few more days - not consciously, but I think you do cut it down. - I can think of one woman who I really disliked seeing - because whatever you said was wrong.... and in the end it got such a pain that I'd put off seeing her - in the end I didn't go and see her for nearly five months..."

Whilst the community nurses experienced various pressures which sometimes tended to make them withdraw from, or blame, their patients the relative social isolation of their work was a powerful counter force inducing closer personal relationships with patients. Once again, this was particularly apparent within the acute team where the nurses often described their favourite patients in terms which suggested that the dividing line between personal and professional involvement was difficult to maintain. For example, a sister in this team remarked:-

"The thing that makes people more rewarding is if they're more motivated - there's a lassie I've got at the moment that I could well envisage getting on very well with socially, it's a shame really that I'm visiting her because we get on really well and could be friends, but you've got to put a limit on in a professional relationship - she was going to ask me to the christening of her daughter - but I said I didn't think it would be right."

The final point raised by all the nurses in the acute team was that their closer relationships with patients made community work more emotionally draining than ward work and caused greater problems in their relationships with their own families. A charge nurse in this team explained:-

"I think if things are going wrong in your home life - then this job can make it very difficult ever to put things right. In some jobs you could go into work and do something really calm and unemotional - and then you could probably face home problems better because of it - but in this job if you've had a bad day and then you come home and there's an atmosphere there's no time to get your balance back - and it can be very hard to cope with."

Whilst the nurses in the elderly team also experienced problems in achieving the appropriate levels of involvement with their patients, their difficulties centred round the level of responsibility they felt for patients and were associated with far less emotion. As a nurse in this team remarked:-

"It's always a temptation to get over-involved - you find you're visiting someone three times a week because you're worried they can't cope - and the reasons seem valid to you but when looked at by your colleagues they may feel you're becoming over-protective and should pull back slightly."

These nurses also reported far fewer negative effects on their home life and indicated that where spill over effects did occur they were generally the result of emotionally fraught interactions which resembled those experienced by the acute team. According to another nurse in this team:-

"The effects of work vary - the dementias don't bother me at all - though it was a problem at first - I used to worry about them all the time - but now I've accepted that they used to live like that before I came along and if they do have an accident like a fall I probably couldn't have prevented it .. I think it's the agitated depressions that make me feel exhausted - somebody you don't feel you can do much with and you're going on and on repeating the same things and they simply won't try."

The dividing line between professional involvement and friendship also seemed easier for the nurses in this team to maintain, probably because the differences between them and their patients were greater.

However, several nurses in this team mentioned that the social isolation of their work, coupled with the type of problems they dealt with, could lead to feelings of loneliness and depression. The different characteristics of this team's work thus carried their own costs as the following quotation indicates:-

> "You're on your own in the community - you've no-one to discuss anything with - sometimes I think it might be nice to work with acute patients because of that - because it can get depressing working with the elderly all the time - you look at them and you think someday we'll be old - will we go like this - forgetting things - it can be heart-breaking to see them."

To summarize this section, the interview data suggested that the community nurses, like the ward-based nurses, often experienced difficulties in managing their emotional relationships with patients. These problems were greater within the acute team where the 'dialectic of control' between nurses and patients often re-created the 'treatment barrier' (Scott, 1973) found within the ward situation. The nurses' relative isolation from their colleagues created additional problems for them as their friendship needs were poorly met within the work environment. This difficulty was particularly intense within the elderly team as the social and intellectual differences between the nurses and their patients were greater.

CONCLUSION

In conclusion, the interview data suggests that the community nurses saw community services as a radical alternative to institutional care and concentrated on the differences between the two settings rather than their similarities. The main advantages which they saw community care having for patients were firstly, that patients were not hospitalized; secondly, that psychological models rather than medication were used and thirdly, that patients were seen by the same nurse throughout their treatment and were able to develop a personal relationship with that individual. From their own point of view the two chief merits of community work were closer relationships with patients and opportunities to improve their personal status and that of the nursing profession.

Whilst differences between the two settings certainly existed there were various similarities between them which the nurses underestimated. The three key similarities between the two settings were that the nurses dealt with generic caseloads within a structure where the medical profession retained a large degree of control over the entry and discharge of patients from treatment; that the nurses felt responsible for solving their patients' problems and were expected to do so by many patients, and that the treatment models used were individualistic and neglected the effects of the psychiatric context on the relationship between nurses and patients. As a result of these similarities many problems within the work situation were repeated in the community setting and the nurses often felt manipulated by their patients and uncertain of their therapeutic skills. This could lead to feelings of insecurity which were exacerbated by the nurses' relative isolation from their colleagues, their strong feelings of personal responsibility for patients and their desire for enhanced professional status. These problems seemed particularly intense within the acute team as their patients' problems were more diffuse, the level of expressed emotion from patients was higher and the patients were a more socially valued group whose positive evaluations were important to the nurses. In contrast, the elderly team generally had more practical problems to deal with, clearer authority relationships with their patients and lower expectations of success. They were, however, more prone to feelings of boredom and loneliness and also to feelings of inferiority deriving from the lower status of their work.

Nurses in both teams attempted to deal with the insecurities created by their work by visiting patients frequently, developing routinized relationships with patients and maintaining contact with preferred patients. Whilst this strategy helped alleviate their anxiety by giving them a greater degree of familiarity with their patients' problems and increasing the predictability of their working environment it also had the paradoxical effect of concommitantly increasing their doubts about their own competence and escalating many of the problems within the 'dialectic of control' between them and their patients. This meant that the nurses' attempts to solve the various problems they faced often had a similar outcome to those of the ward-based nurses and helped perpetuate the various contradictions of the psychiatric system.

PART IV
CONCLUSION

12 Conclusion

This study set out to examine the effects which the organizational structure and ideology of the psychiatric system have on the daily actions and subjective experiences of psychiatric nurses and their patients. In contrast to most previous studies within the stress literature, which have implicitly assumed that we do not need detailed analyses of social structures in order to understand individual experience, this study has adopted an explicitly interdisciplinary perspective which emphasizes the reciprocal interplay between the structural and ideological features of a given social environment and the knowledge and activities of various participants within it. By using this perspective the study tried to demonstrate that the problems of occupational stress in psychiatric nursing cannot be fully understood through either a theoretical stance which isolates individual experience from the structural context in which it takes place, or a theoretical approach which regards people as mere puppets of inexorable structural forces which operate without their involvement. As the research revealed, the daily enactment of the psychiatric process occurred through the active and purposive involvement of the people concerned and through numerous individual decisions and choices which were made within particular sets of structural conditions and influenced by the ideology and culture of the psychiatric system. The various ways in which the social context of psychiatry influenced the patterning of social relationships will be discussed in the next section of this chapter. The book will then conclude by exploring some of the implications which this approach to occupational stress has for practical interventions within welfare organizations.

SOCIAL RELATIONSHIPS IN THE PSYCHIATRIC SETTING

One of the ways in which the empirical research sought to highlight the interactions between structural conditions, stress, coping and systemic reproduction was through an examination of the various sets of relationships in which the nurses were involved. The findings of the study suggest that the nurses' relationships with their colleagues, other professionals and patients were not simply a function of their individual personalities but were strongly influenced by the positions that the different protagonists occupied within the psychiatric system and by the structural contradictions of the system. Whilst there were clear differences in the actions and experiences of nurses and patients the research showed that there were also some ironic parallels between their experiences. Both struggled to make sense of a contradictory frame of reference and to utilize the contradictions for their own benefit; both sought the solutions to their problems from within a psychiatric framework and both experienced a sense of bewilderment and betrayal when their attempted solutions failed; both experienced feelings of personal failure and perceived the major influences on their lives as outside their control and finally, both tended to respond to these feelings with coping strategies which intensified the very problems they sought to ameliorate. The various ways in which the ambiguities and paradoxes of the psychiatric system influenced the nurses' relationships with their patients, nursing colleagues and the medical profession will now be examined in more detail.

Relationships with Patients

The three key contradictions described within the critical psychiatry literature were most apparent within the nurses' relationships with patients. The overt social control function of psychiatry was most obvious within the ward setting and was characterized by activities such as the control of patients who had been committed under section and the use of medication to subdue disruptive individuals. Whilst this aspect of the nurses' role was less obvious within the community it still existed and the nurses were sometimes responsible for initiating proceedings which eventually brought people into hospital against their will. The more overt social control functions of their work were often recognized by the nurses and were frequently disliked by them as such activities tended to conflict with their self-image as helpers. In order to reduce the discrepancy between the two activities the nurses utilized various rationalizations which enabled them to reframe such activities as either legitimate sanctions directed at rational, but morally reprehensible, individuals who were abusing the psychiatric services, or as therapeutic activities designed to help irrational individuals who were morally blameless, but who had forfeited their right to self-determination because of their mental illnesses. The therapeutic terminology of psychiatry was particularly important in legitimating the latter perspective as it enabled socially unacceptable behaviour to be reconceptualized as mental illness and its control interpreted as treatment, thus integrating the social control and treatment concerns of staff within a framework which maintained the psychiatric ideology of uncoercive care. The clinical terminology of psychiatry therefore seemed to function not only as the expression of a shared organizational perspective but also as a mechanism through which the nurses could acquire a degree of emotional immunity from the more overt contradictions of the psychiatric system.

In addition to identifying the overt social control function of the psychiatric system, the critical psychiatry literature argues that the institution fulfills a more pervasive covert or 'soft' social control function by promulgating individualistic explanations and treatment strategies which obscure the social implications of many patients' problems. This form of social control operated not only through the models which the nurses used to interpret their patients' problems but also through forms of work organization which segregated patients from one another and individualized their relationship with psychiatry. The nurses' desire to segregate patients was particularly apparent within the ward setting where the physical structure of the unit placed patients in close proximity with one another and sometimes led to the formation of social and emotional links between patients. The nurses generally regarded such relationships with suspicion and saw the development of group solidarity amongst patients as a potential threat to their authority. In order to deal with such threats they tended to categorize group leaders as rational 'trouble makers' who should be excluded from the ward and to see other attachments as self-evidently pathological because they occurred between disturbed individuals. This enabled them to rationalize their attempts to undermine such relationships as being in the patients' best interests. Although the nurses tended to discourage relationships between patients they were equally suspicious of social isolates and patients who had difficulty co-existing amicably with their wardmates. From the nurses' point of view the ideal relationship between patients seemed to be one in which patients co-existed peaceably and communicated with each other in a distant and superficial manner. The group context of the ward was thus fragmented and the proximity of other individuals in similar circumstances became a mechanism for re-affirming the solitary nature of each patient's transactions with psychiatry rather than an opportunity for developing shared understanding and mutual support.

The individualized nature of the nurses' relationships with patients was equally evident within the community setting where the nurses each carried their own caseloads and interacted with each patient within a series of isolated relationships. Whilst the nurses were aware that many of their patients had similar problems and that these problems often centred around social isolation, and feelings of intense loneliness and personal inadequacy they were reluctant to bring their patients into contact with one another in order to explore such problems and offered a variety of rationalizations for this ranging from lack of suitable accommodation to the probability of medical opposition. Such problems certainly existed but rarely appeared insurmountable and more fundamental reasons seemed to be firstly, that the nurses' immersion within the individualistic models of psychiatry meant that in practice they seldom paid much attention to the value of bringing patients together and secondly, that the prospect of group solidarity between patients was quite threatening for the nurses as it raised the possibility that their authority and therapeutic expertise would be challenged by the group. The nurses' own insecurities, which derived in part from the social isolation of their work organization, thus contributed to the maintenance of interaction patterns which obscured both the social implications of patients' problems and the possibility of socialized solutions. A classic example of this occurred on one of the local council estates where several nurses were involved with a number of single parent families in which the mothers were suffering from depression and anxiety. Whilst the nurses recognized that their patients' problems were often very similar and that they were often exacerbated by structural constraints such as social isolation resulting from relocation to a new area, lack of safe play areas for children and lack of local shopping facilities, they made no attempt to introduce their patients to one another or to become involved in the development of community level networks and continued to operate within an individualized framework in which they conceptualized themselves as the key source of support for their patients. Not surprisingly, this burden of responsibility often worried the nurses and they regarded the estate as a difficult area to work in because it consisted of numerous problem families with a high referral rate.

The second major contradiction identified within the critical psychiatry literature centres on the idea that psychiatry is simultaneously committed to the alleviation of mental illness, and to identifying increasingly subtle forms of behavioural deviation and personal distress as problems needing the expert intervention of trained psychiatric professionals. This paradox was particularly evident within the community setting where the nurses often seemed to regard the whole community as potential clients, a perception which resulted in a curious amalgamation between therapeutic imperialism and a siege mentality in their attitude towards their work. On the one hand, the nurses not only saw opportunities for professional advancement and expansion through extending their services to new populations but they also believed quite genuinely that people would benefit both from easier access to therapeutic help whilst their emotional problems were still relatively minor and from preventative exposure to psychiatric precepts before they developed problems. On the other hand, the nurses' perception that the whole community consisted of potential clients was extremely anxiety-provoking for them as they felt that the demands on them were potentially limitless and that their workload could easily escalate beyond all control. This fear was exacerbated by the lack of clear boundaries on caseload sizes within the community unit and by the individualized nature of the work organization. As a result of this perception the nurses tended to avoid direct contact with the communities in which they worked and utilized the medical profession in the dual capacity of gatekeepers who limited the number of referrals they received, and advocates who could advance their case for professional expansion. Whilst this strategy helped to contain the nurses' anxieties concerning the potential size of their caseloads it also had the effect of reinforcing their tendency to equate community care with the care of individuals within the community and exacerbating their neglect of the communal aspects of their patients' problems.

The third contradiction identified within the critical psychiatry literature centres on the equivocal implications of psychiatric intervention for personal responsibility. Within this research one of the most striking features of nurse-patient relationships within both the ward and community settings was the degree of ambivalence which both parties revealed towards the asymmetries of responsibility and dependence which characterized their interactions. Ironically, the nurses' perception of the 'model' patients involved an amalgam of responsibility and compliance which was very similar to nursing management's conception of a good nurse and more generalized images of the ideal citizen. For the nurses, the perfect psychiatric patient was very similar to the ideal patient of general medicine and was someone who coped with their problems without constantly demanding help, but who was co-operative and grateful for any help given, and who showed a capacity for insight and the ability to make constructive changes in their life as a result of the advice the nurses provided. For nursing management, the ideal nurse was also somebody who coped with problems without complaining, showed understanding and compassion towards patients without becoming too involved and welcomed organizational change when it occurred but refrained from criticising the organization at other times. Unfortunately for the nurses, their patients were, almost by definition, unlikely to conform to their ideal and as a result the nurses often became disillusioned and developed a more cynical view of patients as both manipulative and irresponsible. This perception could be disturbing for the more committed nurses as it conflicted with their own desired self-image as dedicated helpers.

The tortuous relationship between responsibility, compliance and control was most apparent within the ward setting where the structural organization of the unit meant that access to virtually all resources was controlled by staff and key decisions concerning patients were taken by staff without involving the patient to any significant degree. This left patients with few areas of discretion in which to exercise autonomy and self-determination and many responded with passive compliance to ward routines. The nurses generally interpreted this as evidence of the patients' immaturity of character and often criticised the patients' reluctance to accept responsibility for their own behaviour without seeming to recognize that the avoidance of personal responsibility exhibited by many patients was, to some extent, a learnt behaviour intensified by the organizational structure of the ward and cultural norms concerning appropriate sick role behaviour. Whilst the nurses were often irritated by the passivity of patients and their reluctance to accept responsibility for their own lives they generally responded in a highly coercive manner towards those patients who rebelled against their authority, and often displayed a marked degree of ambivalence towards patients who acted in a rational and self-determined manner even when this did not involve direct challenges to their authority. This was noticed by many patients and some of them explicitly stated that they felt themselves to be trapped within a situation where their powerlessness made any form of protest dangerous. Whilst these patients often complained amongst themselves about conditions on the ward and the apparent failure of staff to help them solve their problems they were careful to avoid alienating staff through direct confrontations. The patients' passivity and the nurses' authoritarianism were thus two facets of an overall nurse-patient nexus which was heavily influenced by the organizational and ideological constraints of the ward environment.

Whilst nurse-patient relationships within the community setting were less authoritarian than relationships on the ward they were still characterized by high levels of dependency on the part of many patients and ambivalent responses towards this by the nurses. On the one hand, the nurses often experienced the demands which patients made of them as highly stressful and found it difficult to cope with the high levels of responsibility which they felt for their patients' lives. In consequence, the negative emotional characteristics of the nurses' relationships with patients generally assumed greater salience than their actual problems and within both the community and the ward setting the individuals whom the nurses conceptualized as problem patients tended to be those who made most demands on them and were least grateful for their services, rather than those who had the most intractable or disabling problems. On the other hand, the nurses often encouraged the growth of dependency in a variety of ways and frequently seemed to derive a good deal of satisfaction from it. For some community nurses their patients' dependency seemed to function as confirmation that they were providing a valuable and worthwhile service and to help compensate them for the lack of more objective criteria concerning the efficacy of their work. Thus, nurse-patient relationships within the community were also influenced by the attempts of each party to utilize the contradictions concerning responsibility to meet differing sets of needs and interests and the desire of many patients to abnegate responsibility was once again complemented by the nurses' desire to feel valued and needed by their patients.

Relationships with Nursing Colleagues

The nurses' relationships with their patients were also affected by the sort of relationships they had with their nursing colleagues and those, in turn, were heavily influenced by the setting in which the nurses worked. The nurses on 'F' ward operated as a hierarchically organized team with shared responsibility for the daily management of a group of patients. The close physical proximity of nurses and patients throughout the working day, coupled with the nurses' over-riding concern with social control, facilitated the development of various strategies designed to increase the psychological distance between nurses and patients. This was achieved through two key mechanisms, firstly, through the physical division of the ward into areas which were off-limits to patients but where the nurses were implicitly expected to spend most of their time, either working or socializing, and secondly, through the development of strong group norms concerning the actions and characters of patients. These norms often contained various unexamined and derogatory assumptions about patients which strengthened the nurses' solidarity with their peers and diminished their identification with patients. The nurses on 'F' ward thus derived their main source of emotional support from their colleagues and, in practice, tended to perceive themselves as a beleaguered group trying to maintain order within a potentially hostile and chaotic environment.

In contrast to the ward nurses, the community nurses had individual responsibility for their own caseloads, worked with colleagues of similar status and were physically isolated from their colleagues during their interactions with patients. The individualized nature of their work was generally experienced by the nurses as more anxiety-provoking than the shared responsibilities of ward life and many of the norms of social interaction within the unit could be interpreted as an attempt to ameliorate the psychological pressures of the new work environment by re-creating a semblance of the collegiate responsibility found on the wards. The protected space of the community nursing office provided the venue for many of these activities and it was recognized by all the nurses that time in the office provided an important means of escaping from the demands of patients and re-establishing emotional equilibrium by socializing with colleagues. The degree of protection provided by the community nursing office was far greater than that given by the ward office as the physical proximity of patients was no longer a continuous problem. The nurses were, therefore, able to relax their guard rather more than the ward nurses whilst they were in the office, which probably helped them remain more emotionally available to patients during other parts of their day.

Much of the time which the nurses spent in the office involved a mixture of administration and socializing similar to that which occurred in the ward office. Whilst some social interaction involved topics unrelated to their work a large proportion of the nurses' conversations involved descriptions of the various problems they were experiencing with patients. Whilst these accounts were generally listened to sympathetically by colleagues they seldom volunteered advice on solving the problems and this was rarely solicited by the complainant. The implicit message of these interchanges thus seemed to be that the problems described were an inevitable result of the type of work the nurses performed and not a consequence of their handling of the case, and the main function of such encounters seemed to be that of off-setting the isolation of the nurses' work through a collective affirmation that such problems beset everyone. The final strategy which the nurses utilized to compensate for the isolated nature of their work involved developing a measure of shared responsibility for more awkward patients through the mechanism of emergency or holiday visits carried out by whoever was available. Unfortunately, this strategy sometimes had the undesired effect of escalating the patients' demands on the service and could also created a certain amount of insecurity in the nurses by rousing fears that when their colleagues gained greater insight into their handling of specific patients they might be privately critical of their work.

Whilst both the ward and community nurses valued their relationships with colleagues and derived considerable support from them, the workgroups in both settings seldom provided a constructive forum for tackling the various problems faced by the nurses, functioning instead as a mechanism for transmitting group norms concerning the practice of psychiatric nursing, and for giving and receiving the emotional support which helped the nurses cope with the psychological discomfort engendered by their work. The workgroup thus dealt thus with the nurses' experience of problems rather than the problems themselves and by doing so often helped to perpetuate the problems of the psychiatric system. Ironically, the function of the nurses' relationships with their colleagues often mirrored the function of their relationships with patients in that the nurses frequently provided patients and their families with short-term relief from emotional crises rather than tackling the underlying causes of their distress. In both cases this pattern seemed to arise because the ambiguities and contradictions of the psychiatric system were generally denied and hidden rather than consciously acknowledged and tackled. Thus, the nurses rarely acknowledged the ambivalence of their feelings about their work in public although they were willing to admit to them privately during their interviews. As a result, the insecurities and frustrations arising from the contradictory nature of the work were publically transformed into safe grievances against seemingly unresolvable problems such as the size of their workloads and the opportunity for using the workgroup to develop rational policies for tackling the stresses of the immediate environment was repeatedly neglected.

Relationships with Doctors

The nurses' relationships with the medical profession were also fraught with ambivalence and ambiguity and their tendency to simultaneously resent medical power and collude in maintaining it often mirrored their patients' attempts to avoid personal responsibility for their problems by transferring it to psychiatric professionals. Whilst the nurses clearly occupied an objectively weaker structural position within the organization the power of both the psychiatrists and G.P.s was seldom exercised overtly and was generally reinforced and maintained through the active assistance of the nurses. This strategy not only avoided overt conflict but also enabled the nurses to abnegate responsibility for many of the negative consequences of psychiatric intervention and to minimize their own insecurities concerning their lack of therapeutic competence by deferring to the putatively greater expertise of the medical profession. The behaviour of both nurses and patients seemed, in some senses, to resemble a transference reaction in which the emotional distress attached to problematic and personally significant situations is mitigated by transferring responsibility to a wiser or more powerful individual. Under these circumstances, the actual efficacy of medical expertise may be less important than its symbolic significance as a means of reducing a perceived threat. Thus, the medical ideologies and power structures which caused the nurses so many problems in their daily work were, paradoxically, supported by them to some extent because the giving of such support helped mitigate the various insecurities which the contradictions of the psychiatric system created.

The equivocation which characterized the nurses' reactions to the medical assumption of authority and expertise was often very evident on 'F' ward. The hierarchical division of labour on the ward created sharp divisions in the responsibilities of medical staff and nurses, with all key decisions concerning the admission, discharge and organic treatment of patients being taken by consultant psychiatrists whilst the daily running of the ward was left to the nurses. This division of labour meant that the nurses generally had a rather limited understanding of the reasons for the patients' admission, whilst the psychiatrists rarely had a detailed knowledge of either their patients' behaviour on the ward or the more general effects of their decisions on the overall ward environment. As a result, treatment decisions were often taken on the basis of very limited evidence and with scant regard for the patients' phenomenological states. Whilst the nurses frequently resented the psychiatrists' behaviour and could be quite disparaging about their decisions when talking amongst themselves they rarely challenged them openly. There seemed to be three main reasons for this. Firstly, the official ideology of the ward was based on the concept of a multi-disciplinary therapeutic team in which individuals from a variety of disciplines collaborated to provide comprehensive care based on an eclectic model of psychiatric dysfunction. Whilst this model was not adhered to in practice and the decision-making power remained firmly in the hands of the psychiatrists, the illusion that the ward operated on a relatively egalitarian basis conferred some professional advantages on the nurses which they were reluctant to jeopardize by openly challenging the psychiatrists' authority. Secondly, the nurses unquestioning acceptance of medical decisions enabled them to disguise the limited extent of their own knowledge about patients and obscured the fact that they often avoided close contact with patients' emotional distress because they found it painful to observe or engage with the patients' feelings when they felt powerless to help them. Thirdly, the nurses were often insecure about their own lack of therapeutic expertise and were unwilling to challenge the psychiatrists in case the latter group possessed more advanced skills. Whilst the psychiatrists rarely demonstrated advanced psychotherapeutic skills during their interactions with patients they generally acted as if their training had equipped them with privileged access to insights denied the nurses which enabled them to make reasoned decisions on the basis of very limited information. Thus, as a result of possessing high status and acting in an authoritative manner the psychiatrists become, to some extent, endowed with almost mystical expertise by many nurses.

The community nurses' relationships with the medical profession revealed a similar ambivalence. In comparison with the ward-based nurses, the community nurses had a far greater degree of autonomy and were theoretically empowered to accept, discharge and treat patients as, and when, they saw fit. This was an important source of professional status for the community nurses, and they frequently emphasised their status as independent professionals when arguing a case for professional advancement. However, in practice, the nurses' relationships with the medical profession mirrored the power relationships within the ward setting to a greater extent than either the formal structure of the unit or the nurses' self-presentations implied. The nurses rarely, if ever, challenged the doctors' reasons for referring patients and seemed to regard it as axiomatic that patients should enter treatment after being referred. This view appeared to be shared by many medical practitioners who seemed to expect their referrals to be accepted unquestioningly. The nurses were equally compliant about discharges and frequently appeared reluctant to discontinue seeing patients without receiving medical approval. The most obvious reason for this behaviour was that the nurses were dependent on the goodwill of the medical profession to ensure their supply of patients. However, the nurses' former socialization within a hierarchical and medically dominated organizational structure also seemed to influence their behaviour and make them unwilling to challenge medical authority. This tendency was probably exacerbated by feelings of insecurity which the nurses sometimes seemed to have concerning their own judgements, as such doubts may have inclined them to collude in maintaining a situation in which professional responsibility for patients remained ambiguous and difficult decisions could be transferred to the medical profession. This situation also benefited the doctors by freeing them from the everyday decision making about patients whilst enabling them to retain status differentials by claiming ultimate responsibility for patient management. The actual relationships between the community nurses and the medical profession were thus quite similar to the patterns which prevailed on 'F' ward. Once again, the transfer of responsibility often seemed to function as a mechanism through which the nurses could gain some protection from the feelings of anxiety, uncertainty and powerlessness which were aroused by recurrent exposure to their patients' distress.

In conclusion, the empirical data presented in this research suggests that the patterns found within the nurses' relationships with their patients, colleagues and the medical profession were shaped not only by the contradictions of the psychiatric system but also by the various strategies which those involved used to interpret and respond to the pressures of their situation. Such strategies were often defensive and were aimed at exploiting the ambiguities of the psychiatric system in order to try and decrease the problems and insecurities these same uncertainties created. Unfortunately, the outcome of these strategies was often to increase the paradoxes and equivocation which characterized the nurses' relationships and to increase their feelings of insecurity and powerlessness. This was often reflected in the discontinuities and contradictions between the practical knowledge which the nurses used to organize their everyday activities and the more nuanced and considered accounts which emerged in their interviews. For many nurses, their uneasy awareness of the discrepancy between their professional ideals and the way they found themselves acting in their daily work was, in itself, a further source of discomfort and anxiety. Regrettably, such knowledge rarely facilitated constructive change as it was seldom shared and remained the private burden of the individual nurse.

STRATEGIES FOR CHANGE

The analysis of occupational stress developed within this research has been critical of the individualistic models and intervention strategies promulgated within the traditional stress and burnout literatures and has advocated an alternative conceptual framework which pays greater attention to the reciprocal relationships between social conditions and human experience. Whilst this form of analysis is more likely than traditional models to focus attention on the root causes of occupational stress, it is, unfortunately, beset by problems of its own, as radical reforms are often easier to advocate than to implement. If they are truly interested in practical interventions within organizations such as the psychiatric system, social scientists must grapple with the limitations of their own power and resources, and with the various constraints within the system they are studying, and try to accommodate such restraints within their recommended change strategies. This inevitably involves compromise and an acceptance that the pursuit of practical alternatives is, of itself, an ambiguous and contradictory process which will probably involve limited gains, uneasy alliances and localized solutions to specific problems, rather than fundamental alterations to the total organizational or societal structure. Whilst this approach is, perhaps, less intellectually satisfying than more uncompromising stances it does have the advantage of allowing the search for solutions to the immediate problems facing employees to be taken seriously. These problems are often very real and can cause a great deal of distress. The root causes of such problems may well be interpretable in institutional and societal terms but, unfortunately, neither the individuals concerned nor the social scientists who study them are in a position to transform society overnight. Under these circumstances it is of limited practical value simply to say that the social system is at fault for producing untenable situations. The problems still exist and the partial and equivocal relief which applied social scientists can offer should not be dismissed out of hand. The key point of an analysis such as that presented here is not that compromised solutions should necessarily be rejected, but that their limitations and implications should be clearly recognised and the search for more fundamental changes should be maintained.

The insights generated by a clearer understanding of the interrelationships between subjective experience and social conditions can be applied at a number of levels ranging from the individual to the societal. A more structurally oriented analysis of occupational stress is thus still compatible with the lower level intervention strategies traditionally advocated within the stress and burnout literatures. A growing number of studies within these literatures recommend the use of individual psychotherapy or counselling as a mechanism for combating occupational stress (Fineman, 1985; Firth, 1985) Unfortunately, the rationale for using such techniques often reflects the inherent conservatism of the more traditional approaches to therapy and generally emphasizes adjusting the individual worker to an organizational context whose effects on the individual remain relatively unexplored. In marked contrast to this perspective several more radically oriented psychotherapists have argued that individuals must grasp the various ways in which their personal experiences are moulded by the structural and cultural contradictions of their society if they are to come to terms with, and change, their particular responses to stressful situations (Kovel, 1981;Fromm, 1984). This perspective suggests that stress researchers could facilitate reductions in stress by encouraging individuals to analyse their own experiences in a more systematic and socially aware manner and by introducing them to alternative theoretical frameworks for examining the ways in which they conceptualise and respond to the demands of their working environment.

A clear example of the practical value which a heightened understanding of the relationship between subjective experience and social conditions can have for the individual welfare worker is provided by Satyamurti's (1981) influential study of stress in social workers. Satyamurti's work demonstrates that many of the stresses experienced by social workers have their roots in firstly, the social workers contradictory mandate to care for and control underprivileged populations and secondly, the imbalance between the demands which society places on social workers and the resources that it places at their disposal. As Satyamurti shows, the chronic lack of material resources available to the social workers in her study often forced them to tackle their clients social deprivation through individually focussed strategies aimed at changing their clients behaviours or providing them with emotional support. Not surprizingly, such strategies often failed or were interpreted by clients as social control measures. Their clients rejection of them could, in turn, create feelings of professional inadequacy and dissatisfaction in many social workers and eventually lead them to withdraw from and censure their clients. Interestingly, Satyamurti found that those social workers who had a clear understanding of the structural contradictions of their work were less inclined to feel personally incompetent when their attempts to help clients failed and were therefore better equipped to cope with the vagaries of their work without withdrawing from, or blaming, their clients. An appreciation of the complex effects which the superordinate social structure has on their everyday tasks thus seems not only to enable individual social workers to cope with the stresses of their work more easily but also to improve the calibre of their services to clients by enabling them to form relationships in which the contradictions of their respective roles are more clearly spelt out and accepted by both parties.

At a slightly higher level of intervention stress researchers could encourage workgroups to develop collective analyses of, and solutions to, the problems which they face. The use of consciousness raising and problem solving groups has been widely advocated in many contexts as a key strategy for encouraging people to take greater responsibility for tackling the problems of their immediate environment. The stress and burnout literatures also prescribe the development of social support networks and groupwork, although, once again, the rationale for using them is generally conservative and emphasizes the importance of social support in helping people adjust to the pressures of their current situation, rather than the value of collective analysis of the work environment. Rather then simply using support groups as a way of cushioning employees from the stresses of their work, such groups could be used as a forum in which psychiatric professionals could begin to examine, firstly, the ways in which the structural context and ideology of psychiatry influences both their ability to help patients and their own feelings about work and, secondly, the extent to which they could take collective action to change their immediate working environment. Such action could take two main forms. Firstly, nurses could be encouraged to act collectively to challenge the more obvious abuses within the system. As Beardshaw's (1981) chilling case study of staff intimidation within British psychiatric hospitals reveals, many nurses who are deeply troubled by the events which they witness are too afraid of reprisals from their collegues and management to complain officially. Whilst such fears are often justified when nurses consider acting individually, sanctions are less likely to be employed against a united group of staff. Secondly, nurses could be encouraged to think creatively about alternative ways of working. Whilst the scope for grassroots innovation is obviously limited by structural constraints which cannot be altered by small groups of employees most situations contain enough flexibility for small-scale changes in working practices. For instance, the community nurses in this research could probably have created the conditions in which they worked collectively with groups of clients to counteract their own, and their clients, feelings of social isolation. A clear example of this type of project is provided by Elliott (1985) in her description of a community mental health project for women with postnatal depression. In contrast to the more traditional psychiatric perspective, which generally ignores the social context of motherhood and treats depressed women through chemotherapy and hospitalization, Elliott's work was guided by an explicitly feminist interpretation of this issue and involved female clinicians working collectively with groups of women to counteract their loneliness and material deprivation through the development of social support networks, shared analysis of the social contradictions and personal strains of motherhood and information on statutory benefits and local facilities. Thus, this project consciously utilized the resources of the psychiatric system to develop an alternative method of working which explicitly sought to tackle the inter-relationships between social circumstances and personal distress.

At the organizational level of intervention, social scientists are sometimes given an explicit mandate to analyse and improve organizational functioning. Menzies (1967) classic study of stress in general nursing provides one of the most famous examples of this level of intervention within the stress literature. This study was an action research project carried out at the behest of the senior management of a group of London teaching hospitals who sought to help in curtailing the high levels of turnover amongst nursing staff. The research was carried out from within a psychoanalytically oriented theoretical perspective which interpreted the hospitals presenting problems as the surface manifestation of a maladaptive and collective social defence system for coping with the personal anxieties aroused by the nurses' work. This perspective enabled Menzies to provide a sensitive analysis of the inter-relationship between the subjective experience of individuals and the contradictions of organizational life. As her research reveals, many of the problems of organizational life within the hospitals she investigated resulted from a collective denial of the various anxieties which staff experienced in their work, coupled with the development of socially structured coping mechanisms such as task-centred and depersonalized interactions with patients, avoidance of responsibility, and heavily routinized work patterns. Whilst these strategies helped the nurses to evade some of the anxiety-provoking situations they might otherwise have faced they also created deeper structural problems which hindered effective patient care and inadvertently intensified many of the dilemmas from which the nurses sought to escape. Unfortunately, as Menzies found, the personal and organizational importance of the nurses' coping strategies, coupled with the anxiety and ambivalence engendered by their equivocal outcome, militated against the successful resolution of stress through straight-forward suggestions for rational organisational change, necessitating instead an intervention strategy which was explicitly designed to accommodate the inter-relationships between the organizational structure and ideology of the hospital and the collective coping strategies and defence mechanisms of its staff.

At the highest levels of intervention stress researchers may choose to become actively involved in wider social movements designed to challenge and transform the more repressive characteristics of social institutions such as the psychiatric system. The Italian 'Psichiatria Democratica' movement, initiated by the psychiatrist Franco Basaglia, provides the clearest example of this form of action (Basaglia, 1981; Scheper-Hughes and Lovell, 1986; 1987). This movement began in the early sixties with Basaglia's attempts to reform individual mental hospitals and rapidly grew into a national movement designed to change the legal, structural and ideological framework of the Italian psychiatric services. The explicit aim of this movement was to expose the contradictions of the psychiatric system and illuminate the dehumanizing effects which the traditional psychiatric structures and ideologies have on both staff and patients. From this perspective, staff and patients were seen as reciprocally enmeshed within an institutional framework which exploited and devalued all its members. In order to overcome this the movement attempted to replace the traditional psychiatric structures with genuine community care in which positive and demedicalized frameworks were set up to meet the social, economic and housing needs of the mentally ill. This involved a variety of professional, academic and political coalitions working simultaneously on a large number of fronts and levels which ranged from individually consciousness raising to the re-organization of the legal and economic framework within which the state addressed the problem of mental illness.

The results of the 'Psichiatria Democratica' movement have been equivocal. At its best, the movement has demonstrated that staff and patients can both benefit from the environmental changes which occur where psychiatric professionals and the local community share a genuine grassroots commitment to providing truly social forms of care. At its worst, the movement has revealed that where the legal framework of deinstitutionalization is unaccompanied by a real desire to provide effective alternatives, staff may feel highly threatened by proposed changes and patients may simply be dumped on an uncaring or actively hostile society (Robb, 1986; Bollini, Reich and Muscettola, 1988). Whilst such outcomes obviously detract from the idea that decarceration is an instant panacea for the problems of psychiatry they do not invalidate the premises on which the 'Psichiatria Democratica' movement was based. The goal of this movement was to expose and redefine the ideology of psychiatry rather than to simply transfer the location of the traditional psychiatric practices from the asylum to the community. The various failures of community care which have occurred in Italy do not negate the importance of this goal, although they are indicative of both the difficulty and the importance of implementing institutional reforms at a variety of levels. Where 'Psichiatria Democratica' has failed it has often done so because the institutional level of reform has been divorced from a grassroots commitment to change. Where it has succeeded the varigated elements of social reform have coalesced into a complex and multilayered mosaic of differing change strategies, perpetrated by numerous social groups, at a variety of levels and in a range of contexts. Within a social milieu of this type social scientists who are interested in diminishing occupational stress clearly have the chance of developing innovative intervention strategies which advance beyond the traditional solutions.

Finally, we need to remember that the value of deeper analyses lie not only in their implications for immediate change but also in their capacity to stimulate critique and debate concerning the purposes and future of social institutions. Social scientists are in a privileged position to kindle such deliberations as their training and social role provides them with both the analytical tools necessary for studying organisations and a degree of detachment from the daily problems of organisational life. In the final analysis the problems of occupational stress within the various caring professions raise far deeper questions concerning the role of welfare institutions within our society. Hopefully, this book will help promote further debate concerning such issues.

APPENDICES AND REFERENCES

APPENDIX A
ACTIVITY SCHEDULE/DIARY

Instructions for Filling in Diaries

Please make sure you've got the same number each day.

Please fill in the time each activity starts and finishes with the location and activity codes for each. If you think that several activities are going on a the same time put them down together, e.g. 10 & 11 means discussing clients whilst writing casenotes.

The last three columns need only be filled in when you think that there is something especially important to say. e.g. a description of a tricky situation you had to deal with, an unexpected crisis which disorganized your plans etc.

I'll collect the sheets each evening and hand out sheets for the next day.

Jocelyn

DIARY CODES
LOCATIONS

1= CPN offices

2= Other area of the hospital

3= Clients home or normal place of residence

4= Professional establishment e.g. G.P. surgery

ACTIVITIES

5= Routine visit (including initial)

6= Emergency Visit (including initial)

7= Group Therapy

8= Telephone to/from client

9= Arranging Services for Clients e.g. day care, meals on wheels, psychiatrist's visit.

10= Contact (inc. phone) with non professionals about clients, e.g. relatives.

11= Informal discussions (inc. phone calls) with colleagues, doctors, social workers etc. concerning clients

12= Administration e.g. casenotes, referral letters

13= Clinical meetings e.g. ward meetings.

14= Other meetings e.g. staff meetings policy meetings

15= Formal teaching or preparation e.g. lecturing, marking projects

16= Travel

17= Meals, recuperation, personal etc.

18= Other

Note: If you've got a student please put S in the "Others Present" box.

Acute/Elderly	Nurse's No.	Date

time	place	code	others present	brief description	general comments sources stress, satisfaction, irritation

APPENDIX B
INTERVIEW SCHEDULE

FACE SHEET DATA

Unit

Date of Interview

Place of Interview

Duration of Interview

Name / No. of Interviewee

Sex

Age (approx)   18-20   20s   30s   40s   50s   60s

Marital Status

Qualifications   Basic
 & Dates
                        Post

No. of Years in N.H.S. (approx.)

Service Breaks

Time on Current Unit

OUTLINE OF INTERVIEW TOPICS

1 Reasons for career choice
2 Reasons for choosing community nursing
3 Basic job conditions e.g. Pay, promotion prospects
4 Value of training
5 JOB CONTENT
5.1 Workload
5.2 Patient Contact
5.3 Dealings with Non-professionals associated with patients e.g. relatives
5.4 Access to resources e.g. Day Care
5.5 Administration
5.6 Meetings
6 Relationships with Co-workers
7 Supervision
8 Relationships with other Professionals
9 Relationship with rest of hospital
10 Changes you would like on this unit
11 Effects of work on home life
12 General feelings about Psychiatric Nursing and N.H.S.

All information will be treated in confidence and individual names will not be revealed.

If you would prefer not to be taped or if there are any areas you don't want to discuss please say so.

Some topics may not cause problems for you now but may have done in the past or may affect others - please mention these if you feel it's appropriate.

Jocelyn

INTERVIEW GUIDELINE FOR COMMUNITY NURSES

1. **Reasons for Career Choice**

    Why did you decide to become a psychiatric nurse?
    When you first thought about psychiatric nursing what did you expect to like about it?
    What did you expect to dislike about it?
    Looking back, would you say that your original ideas were accurate or inaccurate?

2. **Basic Job Conditions**

    How do you feel about the level of pay you get?
    Do you think that jobs in the N.H.S. are safe?
    What do you think about promotion prospects in the N.H.S.?
    Do you want promotion?
    >   if yes - why?
    >   if no - why not?

3. **Speciality Choice**

    Why did you choose to work on the community?
    What are the things you like about the community?
    What are the things that you dislike about community work?
    How does community work compare with ward based work?
    Would you prefer to work with the over 65s or the acute team?

4. **Training**

    How well do you think that basic training prepares people to work on the community?
    How useful did you find the community nursing course?
    Are there any changes you would like to see to make training more relevant to the community?

5. **Job Content**

    5.1. **Workload**

    What do you think of the workload?

    5.2. **Referrals**

    What types of patient do you think the service should take?
    From which sources?
    Can you think of any referrals you've got/had which are

inappropriate?
What did you do?
How do you decide to discharge patients?
Do/have you ever gone on seeing patients you think you should discharge? Why?

5.3. Interactions with Patients (practical)

What sort of aims do you have when working with patients?
What do you think of the Nursing Process?
How do you plan or evaluate what you are doing with patients?
Is this ever difficult?
Quite a lot of people have said they don't really believe that any sort of psychotherapy or counselling works very well. Do you ever feel this?

5.4. Interaction with Patients (Emotional)

On your current caseload you must have some patients who you enjoy seeing more than others.
Can you describe one or two and tell me why you like seeing them?
I expect you also have some you you don't like seeing.
Can you describe one or two and tell me why?
What sorts of behaviour make you anxious when seeing patients?
Do you/ your collegues ever become over involved with patients?
Can you give me an example?
What sorts of things do you do to cope with getting too involved or upset by patients?

5.5. Interactions with Others in P's life

Do you ever find that other people in the patients life make your job stressful?
Can you give me an example?

5.6. Effects on Home Life

How do you feel at the end of a day's work?
    a)Physically
    b)Emotionally
Do you ever find that you can not "switch off" from work when you go home?
Can you think of an example in the last week?

Does working with people all day ever make you want to avoid people outside work?
Do you socialize with anybody from the unit out of work?
Some people have said that dealing with other people's problems all day can make it difficult for people in the caring professions to listen to their own family's problems.
Has this sort of thing ever happened to you?
Have your family ever said how they feel about you having this job?

5.7. Relationships with Co-workers

How do people get on together on this unit?
How much practical help/ advice do people give each other?
How much emotional support do people give each other?

5.8. Access to Resources

Is the fact that you do not have direct access to backup resources like Meals on Wheels ever a problem?

5.9. Administration

How do you feel about the paperwork?
prompts - Casenotes
    letters
    Statistical returns

5.10. Meetings

How do you feel about the meetings you go to?
    a) Clinical
    b) Staff/Admin

6. Supervision

What do you think of the supervision on this unit?
Prompts contact, clinical guidance, feedback, general running of unit
How do you feel about supervising students?

7. Interdisciplinary relationships

What other disciplines do you work with?
Prompt psychiat., G.P., S.W., other nurses, home help, etc.
How do you find relationships?(personally/as team)
What sorts of problems arise?

8. **Relations with rest of hospital**

   How would you describe the relationship between the community unit and the rest of the hospital?
   How do you feel about moving your base away from the hospital?
   What changes would you like to see on the unit/hospital generally?

9. **General feelings about psychiatric nursing and N.H.S.**

   The N.H.S. has seen a lot of changes recently.
   How do you feel about them?
   Probes cuts,
   Mental Health act
   nurse training Griffiths reorg of districts
   Do you think the changes have made any difference to the
   way people feel about their work?
   How do you think the general public regard psychiatric nursing?
   Some people have said that psychiatric hospitals do
   more harm than good. How do you feel about this?

10. **Miscellaneous**

    Are there any other points you would like to raise?

References

Albee, G. (1985). The Answer Is Prevention. *Psychology Today.* February. 60-64.

Albee, G. (1986). Towards a Just Society: Lessons from Observations on the Primary Prevention of Psychopathology. *American Psychologist.* 891-898.

Aldrich, H. (1979). *Organizations and Environments.* Englewood Cliffs, N.J.: Prentice-Hall.

Allen, H. (1986). Psychiatry and the Construction of the Feminine. In Miller, P. and Rose, N. (Eds.), *The Power of Psychiatry.* Cambridge: Polity Press.

Aries, P. (1962). *Centuries of Childhood: A Social History of Family Life.* New York: Vintage.

Ashford, S. (1988). Individual Strategies for Coping with Stress During Organizational Transitions. *Journal of Applied Behavioural Science.* **24.** 19-36.

Badinter, E. (1980). *Mother Love, Myth and Reality.* New York: Macmillan.

Baron, C. (1987). *Asylum to Anarchy.* London: Free Association Books.

Barton, R. (1959). *Institutional Neurosis.* Bristol: John Wright and Sons.

Baruch, G. and Treacher, A. (1978). *Psychiatry Observed.* London: Routledge and Kegan Paul.

Basaglia, F. (1981). Breaking the Circuit of Control. In Ingleby, D. (Ed.) *Critical Psychiatry.* Harmondsworth: Penguin.

Bean, P. (1986) .*Mental Disorder and Legal Control.* Cambridge. Cambridge University Press.

Beardshaw, V. (1981). *Conscientious Objectors at Work.* London: Social Audit.

Beehr, T. and Newman, J. (1978). Job Stress, Employee Health and Organizational Effectiveness: A Facet Analysis, Model and Literature Review. *Personnel Psychology,* **31.** 665-699.

Bhagat, R. and Chassie, M. (1980). Effects of Changes in Job Characteristics on some Theory-specific Attitudinal Outcomes: Results from a Naturally Occurring Quasi-Experiment. *Human Relations,* **33.** 297-313.

Bohart, A. and Todd, J. (1988). *Foundations of Clinical and Counseling Psychology.* London: Harper and Row.

Bollini, P., Reich, M. and Muscettoloa, G. (1988). Revision of the Italian Psychiatric Reform: North/South Differences and Future Strategies. *Social Science and Medicine.* **27.** 1327-1335.

Booker, J. and Imerschein, A. (1979). Psychiatry and Society: Professionalism and the Control of Knowledge. *Journal of Sociology and Social Welfare.* **6.** 313 - 325.

Borda, O. (1985). (Ed.) *The Challenge of Social Change* Beverly Hills, C.A.: Sage.

Bott, E. (1976). Hospital and Society. *British Journal of Medical Psychology.* **49.** 97-140.

Braude, M. (1988). (Ed.) *Women, Power and Therapy: Issues for Women.*

New York. Howarth Press.

Braverman, H. (1974). *Labour and Monopoly Capital.* London: Monthly Review Press.

Brenner, N. (1981). (Ed.) *Social Method and Social Life.* London: Academic Press.

Brief, A. and Atieh, J. (1987). Studying Job Stress. Are We Making Mountains Out of Molehills? *Journal of Occupational Behaviour* **8.** 115-126.

Brown, D. and Pedder, J. (1979). *Introduction to Psychotherapy* London: Tavistock

Brown, L. and Tandon, R. (1983). Ideology and Political Economy in Enquiry: Action Research and Participatory Research. *Journal of Applied Behavioural Science.* **19.** 277-294.

Brown, P. (1985). *The Transfer of Care.* London: Routledge and Kegan Paul.

Browne, K. (1986). An Ethological Approach to Child Abuse. *First Conference of European Clinical Psychologists.* July. University of Kent at Canterbury.

Burgess, R. (1984). *In the Field.* London: Allen and Unwin.

Burgess, R. (1985). (Ed.) *Field Methods in the Study of Education.* Lewes: Falmer Press.

Burke, R. (1987). Burnout in Police Work: An Examination of the Cherniss Model. *Group and Organization Studies.* **12.** 174-188.

Burrell, G. and Morgan, G. (1979). *Sociological Paradigms and Organizational Analysis.* London: Heinemann.

Busfield, J. (1983). Gender, Mental Illness and Psychiatry. in Evans, M. and Ungerson, C. (Eds.) *Sexual Divisions: Patterns and Processes.* London: Tavistock.

Busfield, J. (1986). *Managing Madness, Changing Ideas and Practice.* London: Hutchinson.

Buss, A. (1979). The Emerging Field of the Sociology of Psychological

Knowledge In Buss, A. (Ed.) *Psychology in Social Context*. New York: Irvington.

Cahoon, A. and Rowney, J. (1984). Managerial Burnout: A Comparison By Sex and Level of Responsibility. *Journal of Health and Human Resources Administration*. **7.** 249 - 263.

Caplan, R. (1983). Person-Environment Fit: Past, Present and Future. In Cooper, C. (Ed.) *Stress Research: Issues for the Eighties*. Chichester: Wiley.

Carr, P., Butterworth, C. and Hodges, B. (1980). *Community Psychiatric Nursing* Edinburgh: Churchill Livingstone.

Castel, R.; Castel, F. and Lovell, A. (1982). *The Psychiatric Society*. Guilford: Columbia University Press.

Cherniss, C. (1980a) *Staff Burnout : Job Stress in the Human Services* London: Sage.

Cherniss, C. (1980b) *Professional Burnout in Human Service Organizations*. New York: Praeger.

Chesler, P. (1974). *Women and Madness*. London: Allen Lane.

Clegg, S. and Dunkerley, D. (1980). *Organizations, Class and Control*. London: Routledge and Kegan Paul.

Cohen, S. (1985) *Visions of Social Control*. Cambridge: Polity.

Cohen, S. and Scull, A. (1985) (Eds.) *Social Control and the State*. Oxford: Blackwell.

Conrad, P. and Schneider, J. (1980). *Deviance and Medicalization. From Badness to Sickness*. London: C.V. Mosby.

Cooper, C. (1986) Job Distress: Recent Research and the Emerging Role of the Clinical Occupational Psychologist. *Bulletin of the British Psychological Society*. **39.** 325-331.

Cooper, C. and Kasl, S. (1987). *Stress and Health. Issues in Research Methodology*. Chichester: Wiley.

Corlett, E. and Richardson, J. (1981). *Stress, Work Design and Productivity*. Chichester: Wiley.

Cormack, D. (1983). *Psychiatric Nursing Described.* London: Churchill-Livingstone.

Cox, T. (1978). *Stress* London: Macmillan Press.

Cox, T. and Mackay, C. (1981). A Transactional Approach to Occupational Stress. In Corlett, E. and Richardson, J. (Eds). *Stress, Work Design and Productivity.* Chichester: Wiley.

Crump, J., Cooper, C. and Smith, M. (1980). Investigating Occupational Stress: A Methodological Approach. *Journal of Occupational Behaviour,* **1.** 191-204.

Denzin, N. (1978) *The Research Act: A Theoretical Introduction to Sociological Methods.* New York: McGraw-Hill.

Dewe, P. (1988). Investigating the Frequency of Nursing Stressors: A Comparison Across Wards. *Social Science and Medicine.* **26.** 375-380.

Dingwall, R. (1977) *The Social Organisation of Health Visitor Training,* London: Croom Helm.

Dizard, J. and Gadlin, H. (1984). Family Life and the Market Place: Diversity and Change in the American Family. In Gergen, K. and Gergen, M. (Eds.) *Historical Social Psychology.* London: Lawrence Erlbaum.

Donaldson, L. (1985). *In Defence of Organization Theory.* Cambridge: Cambridge University Press.

Donzelot, J. (1979). *Policing of Families.* New York: Pantheon.

Doyal, L. (1980). *The Political Economy of Health.* London: Pluto Press.

Eaton, W. (1986) *The Sociology of Mental Disorders.* New York: Praeger.

Elger, A. (1975). Industrial Organizations - a Processual Perspective. In McKinlay, J. (Ed.) *Processing People.* London: Holt, Rinehart and Winston.

Elliott, S. (1985) A Rational for Psychosocial Interventions in the Prevention of Postnatal Depression *Paper presented at Women in Psychology Conference :Cardiff*

Elms, A. (1975). The Crisis of Confidence in Social Psychology.

American Psychologist. **30.** 967-976.

Erickson, E. (1963) *Childhood and Society.* New York: Norton.

Eulberg, J., Weekley, J. and Bhagat, R. (1988) . Models of Stress in Organizational Research: A Metatheoretical Perspective. *Human Relations.* **41.** 331-350.

Farber, B. (1983). (Ed.) *Stress and Burnout in the Human Service Professions* Oxford: Pergammon Press

Fielding, N. and Fielding, J. (1986) *Linking Data.* Beverly Hills, C.A.: Sage.

Fineman, S. (1983). *White Collar Unemployment: Impact and Stress.* Chichester: Wiley.

Fineman, S. (1985). *Social Work Stress and Intervention.* Aldershot: Gower.

Fineman, S. and Payne, R. (1981). Role Stress - A Methodological Trap? *Journal of Occupational Behaviour,* **12.** 51-64.

Firth, J. (1985). Personal Meanings of Occupational Stress: Cases from the Clinic. *Journal of Occupational Psychology,* **58.** 139-148.

Firth, J. and Shapiro, D. (1986) An Evaluation of Psychotherapy for Job-related Distress. *Journal of Occupational Psychology* **59.** 111-119.

Fischer, H. (1983). A Psychoanalytic View of Burnout. In Farber, B.A. (Ed.) *Stress and Burnout in the Human Service Professions* Oxford: Pergammon Press

Flaskerud, J., Halloran, E., Janken, J., Lund, M. and Zetterlund, J. (1979). Avoidance and Distancing. A Descriptive View of Nursing. *Nursing Forum,* **18.** 158-174.

Fletcher, B., and Payne, R. (1980). Stress and Work: A Review and Theoretical Framework I. *Personnel Review,* **9.** 19-29.

Forester, J. (1983). Critical Theory and Organizational Analysis. In Morgan G. (Ed.) *Beyond Method.* London: Sage.

Fox, D. (1985). Psychology, Ideology, Utopia and the Commons. *American Psychologist.* **40.** 48-58.

Frese, M. (1985). Stress at Work and Psychosomatic Complaints. A Causal Explanation. *Journal of Applied Psychology.* **70.** 314-328.

Fromm, E. (1978). *To Have or To Be.* Cape.

Fromm, E. (1980). *Beyond the Chains of Illusion.* London: Abacus.

Fromm, E. (1984) . *The Fear of Freedom.* London: Ark.

Furby, L. (1979). Individualistic Bias in Studies of Locus of Control. In Buss, A (Ed.) *Psychology in Social Context.* New York: Irvington.

Gardell, B. (1971). Alienation and Mental Health in the Modern Industrial Environment. In Levi, L. (Ed.) *Social Stress and Disease.* London: Oxford University Press

Garfinkel, H. (1967) *Studies in Ethnomethodology* Englewood Cliffs, New Jersey: Prentice Hall.

Gauvain, M., Altman, I. and Fahim, H. (1984). Homes and Social Change: A Case Study of the Impact Resettlement. In Gergen, K. and Gergen, M. (Eds.) *Historical Social Psychology.* London: Lawrence Erlbaum.

Geertz, C. (1974). From the Native's Point of View: On the Nature of Anthropological Understanding. *Bulletin of the American Academy of Arts and Sciences.* **28.** 26-45.

Georgoudi, M. (1983). Modern Dialectics in Social Psychology. *European Journal of Social Psychology.* **13.** 77-93.

Gergen, K. (1978). Experimentation in Social Psychology. A Reappraisal. *European Journal of Social Psychology.* **8.** 507-527.

Gergen, K. (1984). An Introduction to Historical Social Psychology. In Gergen, K. and Gergen, M. (Eds.) *Historical Social Psychology.* London: Lawrence Erlbaum.

Gergen, K. (1985). The Social Constructionist Movement in Modern Psychology. *American Psychologist.* **40.** 266-275.

Gergen, K. and Davis, K. (1985). *The Social Construction of the Person.* New York: Springer.

Giddens, A. (1979) *Central Problems in Social Theory.* London:

MacMillan Press

Giddens, A. (1984) *The Constitution of Society*. Cambridge: Polity Press.

Glowinkowski, S. and Cooper, C. (1985). Current Issues in Organizational Stress Research. *Bulletin of the British Psychological Society*, **38**. 212-216.

Goffman, E. (1961). *Asylums*. Harmonworth: Penguin.

Goffman, E. (1971). *Asylums*. Harmonworth: Pelican.

Golembiewski, R. (1984). Organization and Policy Implications of a Phase Model of Burnout. In Moise, L. (Ed.) *Organizational Policy and Development*. Louisville, Kentucky: Center for Continuing Studies, University of Louisville.

Golembiewski, R., Hilles, R. and Daly, R. (1987). Some Effects of Multiple OD Interventions on Burnout and Work Site Features. *Journal of Applied Behavioural Science*. **23**. 295-313.

Golembiewski, R., Munzenrider, R. and Stevenson, R. (1986). *Stress in Organizations: Towards a Phase Model of Burnout*. New York: Praeger.

Golembiewski, R., Munzenrider, R., and Phelan-Carter, C. (1983). Phases of Progressive Burnout and Their Work Site Variants: Critical Issues in OD Research and Practise. *Journal of Applied Behavioural Science*. **19**. 461-481.

Gray, D. (1984). Job Satisfaction among Australian Nurses. *Human Relations* **37**. 1063-1077.

Greater London Council Health Panel, (1985).*Ethnic Minorities and the National Health Service in London* London.

Green, J. (1968). The Psychiatric Nurse in the Community. *International Journal of Nursing Studies*. **5**. 175-183.

Grimshaw, R. and Jefferson, T. (1987) . *Interpreting Policework*. London: Allen and Unwin.

Hall, J. and Fletcher, B. (1984). Coping with Personal Problems at Work. *Personnel Management* **February**. 30-33.

Hall, P. (1983). Individualism and Social Problems. A Critique and

Alternative. *Journal of Applied Behavioural Science.* **19.** 85-94.

Hall, R. (1982). *Organizations, Structure and Process.* Englewood Cliffs. New Jersey: Prentice-Hall.

Hammersley, M. and Atkinson, P. (1983). *Ethnography: Principles in Practice.* London: Tavistock.

Harre, R. (1972). *Philosophy of Science.* Oxford: Oxford University Press.

Harre, R. (1979). *Social Being: A Theory for Social Psychology.* Oxford: Basil Blackwell.

Harre, R. (1986). *The Social Construction of Emotions.* Oxford: Basil Blackwell.

Harre, R. and Secord, P. (1972). *The Explanation of Social Behaviour.* Oxford: Basil Blackwell.

Heath, C. (1981) The Opening Sequence in Doctor-Patient Interaction. In Atkinson, D. and Heath, C. (Eds.) *Medical Work: Realities and Routines.* Farnborough: Gower

Heelas, P. and Lock, A. (Eds.) (1981). *Indigenous Psychologies.* London: Academic Press.

Henriques, J., Holloway, W., Urwin, C., Venn, C. and Walkerdine, V. (1984). *Changing the Subject.* London: Methuen.

Heydebrand, W. (1983). Technocratic Corporatism: Towards a Theory of Occupational and Organizational Transformation. In Hall, R. and Quinn, R. (Eds.) *Organizational Theory and Public Policy.* London: Sage.

Horowitz, A. (1982). *The Social Control of Mental Illness.* London: Academic Press.

Hunter, P. (1974). Community Psychiatric Nursing in Britain: an Historical Review. *International Journal of Nursing Studies* **2.**223-233.

Illich, I. (1976). *Limits to Medicine.* London: Boyars.

Ingleby, D. (1985). Mental Health and Social Order. In Cohen, S. and Scull, A. *Social Control and the State.* Oxford: Basil Blackwell.

Ingleby, D. (1981). (Ed.) *Critical Psychiatry: The Politics of Mental Health.* Harmondsworth: Penguin.

Jackson, S. (1983a). Participation in Decision-making as a Strategy for Reducing Job Related Strain. *Journal of Applied Psychology.* **68.** 3-19.

Jackson, A. (1983b). Treatment Issues for Black Patients. *Psychotherapy Theory, Research and Practice.* **20.** 143-151.

Jahoda, G. (1986). Nature, Culture and Social Psychology. *European Journal of Social Psychology.* **16.** 17-30.

Jick, T. (1979). Mixing Qualitative and Quantitative Methods: Triangulation in action. *Administrative Science Quarterly,* **24.** 602-611.

Johnson, J. (1976). *Doing Field Research* New York: Free Press.

Kahn, R., Wolfe, D., Quinne, R., Snoek, J., and Rosenthal, R. (1964). *Organizational Stress.* New York: Wiley.

Kanas, N. (1986). Support Groups for Mental Health Staff and Trainees. *International Journal of Group Psychotherapy.* **86.** 279-297.

Kaplan, M. (1983). A Woman's View of DSM-III. *American Psychologist.* **38.** 786-792.

Karasek, R. (1979). Job Demands, Decision Lattitude and Mental Strain: Implications for Job Redesign. *Administrative Science Quarterly.* **14.** 285-308.

Kasl, S. (1978). Epidemiological Contributions to the Study of Work Stress. In Cooper, C. and Payne, R. (Eds.), *Stress at Work.* Chichester: Wiley.

Katzman, R. (1983). (Ed.) *Biological Aspects of Alzheimers' Disease.* New York: Cold Spring Harbour Laboratory.

Katzman, R; Terry, R. and Bick, K. (Eds.) (1978). *Alzheimers' Disease: Senile Dementia and Related Disorders.* New York: Raven.

Kearney, D. and Turner, K. (1987). Peer Support and Stress Management for Head Teachers. *Educational Psychology in Practice.* **3.** 20-25.

Kohn, M. and Schooner, C. (1982). Job Conditions and Personality: A Longitudinal Assesment of their Reciprocal Effects. *American Journal of Sociology.* **87.** 1257-1287.

Kovel, J. (1981). *The Age of Desire: Case Histories of a Radical*

Psychoanalyst. New York: Pantheon

Kushnick, L. (1988). Racism, the Natural Health Service and the Health of the Black People. *International Journal of Health Services.* **18.** 457-470.

Lacey, R. and Woodward, S. (1985) *That's Life: Survey on Tranquillizers.* London: British Broadcasting Corporation.

Lasch, C. (1977) *Haven in a Heartless World: The Family Besieged.* New York: Basic Books.

Lasch, C. (1979). *The Culture of Narcissism.* London: Abacus.

Lasch, C. (1984). *The Minimal Self.* London: Picador.

Leatt, P. and Schneck, R. (1985). Sources and Management of Organizational Stress in Nursing Sub-units in Canada. *Organization Studies,* **6.** 55-79.

Light, P. (1979). Surface Data and Deep Structure. Observing the Organization of Professional Training. *Administrative Science Quarterly.* **24.** 551-559.

Littlewood, R. and Lipsedge, M. (1982). *Aliens and Alienists: Ethnic Minorities and Psychiatry.* Harmondsworth: Penguin.

Llewellyn, S. and Osborne, K. (1983) Women as Clients and Therapists. In Pilgrim, D. (Ed.) *Psychology and Psychotherapy.* London: Routledge and Kegan Paul.

Llewellyn, S., Elliott, R., Shapiro, D., Hardy, G. and Firth Cozens, J. (1988). Client Perceptions of Significant Events in Prescriptive and Exploratory Periods of Individual Therapy. *British Journal of Clinical Psychology.* **27.** 105-114.

Mangen, P. (1982). *Sociology and Mental Health.* Edinburgh: Churchhill Livingstone.

Marshall, J. (1980). Stress Amongst Nurses. In Cooper, C. and Marshall, J. (Eds.), *White Collar and Professional Stress* Chichester: Wiley.

Marshall, J. and Cooper, C. (1981). The Causes of Managerial Job Stress: A Research Note on Methods and Initial Findings. In Corlett, E. and Richardson, J. (Ed.), *Stress, Work Design and Productivity.* Chichester:

Wiley.

Maslach, C. (1982) Understanding Burnout: Definitional Issues in Analysing a Complex Phenomenon. In Paine, W. (Ed.), *Job Stress and Burnout* London: Sage Publications.

Maslach, C., and Jackson, S. (1981) The Measurement of Experienced Burnout. *Journal of Occupational Behaviour* **2** 99-113.

May, A. and Moore, S. (1963). The Mental Nurse in the Community. *The Lancet.* **1**213-214.

Mayers, M. (1972). *A Systematic Approach to the Nursing Care Plan.* New York: Appleton-Century-Croft.

McGrath, J. (1970). A Conceptual Formulation for Research on Stress In McGrath, J. (Ed.), *Social and Psychological Factors in Stress.* New York: Holt, Rinehart, Winston.

McKenna, S. and Fryer, D. (1984). Perceived Health During Layoff and Early Unemployment. *Occupational Health.* **36.** 201-206.

Menzies, I. (1967) . *The Functioning of Social Systems as a Defence Against Anxiety.* London: Tavistock.

Mercer, K. (1986). Racism and Transcultural Psychiatry. In Miller, P. and Rose, N. *The Power of Psychiatry.* Cambridge: Polity Press.

Miller, P. and Rose, N. (1986). (Eds.) *The Power of Psychiatry.* Cambridge: Polity.

Milne, D. (1983). Assessing and Reducing the Stress and Strain of Psychiatric Nursing. *Nursing Times.* **87.** 59-62.

Minton, H. (1984), J.F.Browne's Social Psychology of the 1930's: A Historical Antecedent to the Contemporary Crisis in Social Psychology. *Personality and Social Psychology Bulletin.* **10.** 31-42.

Mitroff, I. (1974). *The Subjective Side of Science.* New York: Elsevier.

Mora, G. (1975). Historical and Theoretical Trends in Psychiatry. In Freedman, Kaplan, and Sudock (Eds.) *Textbook of Psychiatry.* Baltimore: Williams and Williams.

Morgan, D. (1975). Explaining Mental Illness. *Archives Europeenes de*

Sociologie. **16.** 262-280.

Moscovici, S. (1972). Society and Theory in Social Psychology. In Israel, J. and Tajfel, H. (Eds.) *The Context of Social Psychology: A Critical Assessment.* London: Academic Press.

Moscovici, S. (1984). The Phenomenon of Social Representations. In Farr, R. and Moscovici, S. (Eds.) *Social Representations.* Cambridge: Cambridge University Press.

Moscovici, S. (1988). Notes Towards a Description of Social Representations *European Journal of Social Psychology.* **18.** 211-250.

Navarro, V. (1986). *Crisis, Health and Medicine: A Second Critique.* London: Tavistock.

Newton, T. (1989) . Occupational Stress and Coping with Stress: A Critique. *Human Relations.* In Press.

Overton, P., Schneck, R. and Hazlett, C.B. (1977). An Empirical Study of the Technology of Nursing Sub-units. *Administrative Science Quarterly,* **22.** 203-219.

Parkes, K. (1982). Occupational Stress Among Student Nurses: A Natural Experiment. *Journal of Applied Psychology,* **67.** 784-796.

Parry, G., Shapiro, D. and Firth, J. (1986). The Case of the Anxious Executive: A Study from the Research Clinic. *British Journal of Medical Psychology.* **59.** 221-234.

Parsons, T. (1951). Illness and the Role of the Physician: A Sociological Perspective. *American Journal of Orthopsychiatry* **21.** 452 - 460.

Payne, R. (1978). Epistemology and the Study of Stress at Work. In Cooper, C. L. and Payne, R. (Eds.), *Stress at Work.* Chichester: Wiley.

Payne, R. (1984). Review of Paine, W. (1982) Job Stress and Burnout: Research Theory and Intervention Perspectives. Beverley Hills. Sage. *Journal of Occupational Psychology.* **57.** 175-176.

Payne, R. and Firth, J. (1987) *Stress in Health Professionals* Chichester: Wiley.

Penfold, S. and Walker, G. (1984). *Women and the Psychiatric Paradox.* Milton Keynes: Open University Press.

Pepitone, A. (1981). Lessons from the History of Social Psychology. *American Psychologist.* **36.** 972-985.

Perlman, B. and Hartman, E. (1982). Burnout: Summary and Future Research. *Human Relations* **35.** 284-305.

Pines, A. (1982). Changing Organizations: Is a Work Environment Without Burnout an Impossible Goal? In Paine, W.S. (ed.), *Job Stress and Burnout: Research, Theory and Intervention Perspectives.* London: Sage.

Pines, A. and Maslach, C. (1978). Characteristics of Staff Burnout in Mental Health Settings. *Hospital and Community Psychiatry.* **29.** 233-237.

Pope, B. (1985). Psychiatry in Transition - Implications for Psychiatric Nursing *Community Psychiatric Nursing Journal* **5** 7-13.

Quick, J., Bhagat, R., Dalton, J. and Quick, D. (1987). (Eds.) *Work Stress: Health Care Systems in the Workplace.* New York: Praeger.

Ramon, S. (1985). *Psychiatry in Britain: Meaning and Policy.* London: Croom Helm.

Rapson, M. (1982). Strategies for Coping with Role Stress, *Nurse Practitioner* **8.** 75-79.

Ravetz, J. (1971). *Scientific Knowledge and Its Social Problems.* Oxford: Oxford University Press.

Reason, P. (1988). *Human Inqury in Action.* London: Sage.

Reason, P. and Rowan, J. (1981). *Human Inquiry: A Sourcebook of New Paradigm Research.* Chichester: Wiley.

Reed, M. (1985). *Redirections in Organisational Analysis.* London: Tavistock.

Rees, C. (1981). Records and Hospital Routine. In Atkinson, P. and Heath, C. (Eds.) *Medical Work: Realities and Routines* Farnborough: Gower

Robb, J. (1986). The Italian Health Services: Slow Revolution or Premanent Crisis? *Social Science and Medicine.* **22.** 619-629.

Robbins, S. (1983). *Organizational Theory: the Structure and Design of Organizations.* Englewood Cliffs, N.J: Prentice-Hall.

Rorty, R. (1979). *Philosophy and the Mirror of Nature.* Princeton, N.J.: Princeton University Press.

Rose, R. and Veiga, J. (1984). Assessing the Sustained Stress Management Intervention On Anxiety and Locus of Control. *Academy of Management Journal.* **27.** 190-198.

Ryan, W. (1976). *Blaming the Victim.* New York: Random House.

Sallis, J., Trevorrow, T., Johnson, C., Hovell, M. and Kaplan, R. (1987). Worksite Stress Management: A Comparison of Programs. *Psychology and Health.* **1.** 237-255.

Sampson, E. (1981). Cognitive Psychology as Ideology. *American Psychologist.* **36.** 730-743.

Sampson, E. (1985). The Decentralization of Identity: Towards a Revised Concept of Personal and Social Order. *American Psychologist.* **40.** 1203-1211.

Sampson, E. (1988). The Debate on Individualism. Indigenous Psychologies of the Individual and Their Role in Personal and Societal Functioning. *American Psychologist.* **43.** 15-22.

Sarason, S. (1981). *Psychology Misdirected.* London: Macmillan.

Sarason, S. (1982). *Psychology and Social Action.* New York: Praeger.

Satyamurti, C. (1981) . *Occupational Survival.* Oxford: Blackwell.

Scheper-Hughes, N. and Lovell, A. (1986). Breaking the Circuit of Social Control: Lessons in Public Psychiatry from Italy and Franco Basaglia. *Social Science and Medicine.* **23.** 159-178.

Scheper-Hughes, N. and Lovell, A. (1987). (Eds.) *Psychiatry Inside Out: Selected Writings of Franco Basaglia.* New York: Colombia University

Schweder, R. and Bourne, E. (1982). Does the Concept of the Person Vary Cross Culturally? In Marsella, A. and White, G. (Eds.) *Cultural Concepts of Mental Health and Threapy.* Boston: Reidel.

Scott, R. and Starr, I. (1981). A 24 Hour Family Oriented Psychiatric

And Crisis Service. *Journal of Family Therapy.* **3.** 177-87.

Scott, R. (1973). The Treatment Barrier (Pts. 1 and 2). *British Journal of Medical Psychology.* **46.** 45-67.

Scott, R. (1974). Cultural Frontiers in the Mental Health Service. *Schizophrenia Bulletin.* **10.** 58-73.

Scott, R. (1980). A Family Oriented Psychiatric Service in the London Borough of Barnet *Health Trends* **3.** 65-68.

Scott, R. and Ashworth, A (1967). Closure at the First Schizophrenic Breakdown: A Family Study. *British Journal of Medical Psychology* **40.** 109-145.

Scull, A. (1977). *Decarceration: Community Treatment and the Deviant.* Englewood Cliffs N.J.: Prentice-Hall.

Scull, A. (1985). Humanitarianism or Control? Some Observations on the Historiography of Anglo-American Psychiatry. In Cohen, S. and Scull, A. (Eds.) *Social Control and the State.* Oxford: Blackwell.

Sedgewick, P. (1982) *Psychopolitics* London: Pluto Press.

Seltzer, J. and Numerof, R. (1988). Supervisory Leadership and Subordinate Burnout. *Academy of Management Journal.* **31.** 439-446.

Semin, G. (1986). The Individual, the Social and the Social Individual. *British Journal of Social Psychology.* **25.** 177-180.

Sharit, S. and Salvendy, G. (1982). Occupational Stress: Review and Reappraisal. *Human Factors* **24.** 129-162.

Shotter, J. (1974). What is it to be Human. In Armistead, N. (Ed.) *Reconstructing Social Psychology.* London: Penguin.

Shotter, J. (1980). Action, Joint Action and Internationality. In Brenner, M. (Ed.) *The Structure of Action.* Oxford: Blackwell.

Shotter, J. (1984). *Social Accountability and Selfhood.* Oxford: Blackwell.

Silverman, D. (1970). *The Theory of Organizations.* London: Heinemann.

Silverman, D. and Jones, J. (1979). *Organizational Work.* London: Macmillan.

Sladden, S. (1979) *Psychiatric Nursing in the Community.* London: Churchill Livingstone.

Spradley, J. (1980). *Participant Observation.* New York: Holt, Rinehart and Winston.

Stanley, S. and Nolan, Z. (1987). The Role of Culture and Cultural Techniques In Psychotherapy: A Critique and Reformulation. *American Psychologist.* **42.** 37-45.

Strauss, A. (1978). *Negotiations.* San Francisco: Jossey Bass.

Strauss, A., Schatzman, L., Ehrlich, D., Bucher, R., and Sabshin, M. (1964). *Psychiatric Ideologies and Institutions.* New York: Free Press of Glencoe.

Towell, D. (1975). *Understanding Psychiatric Nursing.* London: Royal College of Nursing.

Turner, B. (1987). *Medical Power and Social Knowledge.* London: Sage.

Turner, J. and Oakes, P. (1986). The Influence of the Social Identity Concept for Social Psychology with Reference to Individualism, Interactionism and Social Influence. *British Journal of Social Psychology.* **25.** 237-252.

Van Harrison, V., (1978). Person-Environment Fit and Job Stress. In Cooper, C. and Payne, R. (eds.), *Stress at Work.* Chichester: Wiley.

Verhave, T. and Van Hoorn, W. (1984). The Temporalization of the Self. In Gergen, K. and Gergen, M. (Eds.) *Historical Social Psychology.* London: Lawrence Erlbaum.

Wallis, D. and de Wolff, C. (1988). (Eds.) *Stress and Organizational Problems in Hospitals.* London: Croom Helm.

Willmott, H. (1986) Unconscious Sources of Motivation in the Theory of the Subject: An Exploration and Critique of Giddens' Dualistic Models of Action and Personality. *Journal for the Theory of Social Behaviour* **16.** 105-121.

Wexler, P. (1983). *Critical Social Psychology.* London: Routledge.

Whyte, W. (1988). *Learning from the Field.* London: Sage.

Wilden, A. (1980). *System and Structure: Essays in Communication*

Exchange. London: Tavistock.

Willis, P. (1977). *Learning to Labour*. Farnborough: Saxon house.

Willmott, H. (1986) Unconscious Sources of Motivation in the Theory of the Subject: An Exploration and Critique of Giddens' Dualistic Models of Action and Personality. *Journal for the Theory of Social Behaviour* **16**. 105-121.

Wing, J. and Brown, G. (1970). *Institutionalism and Schizophrenia*. Cambridge: Cambridge University Press.

Yalom, I. (1975). *The Theory and Practice of Psychotherapy*. New York: Basic Books.